Weather Watch

A West Kerry Book of Days

Trish Howley
Sandra Landers

Utter Press

Utter Press
Ballymore, Ventry, Tralee, Co. Kerry, Ireland

www.utterpress.com
info@utterpress.com

First published 2007
2nd edition 2008

Printed and bound by
CPI Antony Rowe,
Chippenam, Wiltshire

ISBN: 978-0-9557255-1-7

Set in Bembo
Photographs by S. Landers
Cover photograph by Chris May

To friends and the weather.
Held by both.
Buíochas.

Introduction

Weather Watch takes place at the edge of County Kerry in the southwest of Ireland, where the weather looms large. Enormous storms come raging in across the North Atlantic, sweeping over the land. The skies are huge, often dense with clouds, the cliffs a dramatic edge meeting the sea. Yet the mountains curve gently, one ridge slipping behind the other. The calligraphy of stone walls outlining fields speaks of agriculture, and sheep mark white dots amidst the green. The early primroses and violets are followed by rafts of yellow iris. In summer, fuchsias line the roadsides, dropping their blood red blossoms as the intense orange montbretia bloom along the lanes.

It is a place of extremes and contrasts. Days of lambent sun when bumblebees burrow into foxgloves can be followed by days of winds that send the rain horizontal. The wise resident almost always has a sweater to hand, even at the height of summer. A certain twoness exists here. Two languages – Irish and English – mark two cultures that meld at the edges but keep their separate parts. Two landscapes – ocean and mountain – exist side by side. Two perspectives – ancient and modern – inform each other. And in *Weather Watch*, two friends – Trish Howley, who is Irish, and Sandra Landers, an American – speak to each other of their days, of their experiences with and in the weather.

Their conversation takes place in the distinctive landscape of the Dingle Peninsula, one of the fingers of land stretching into the sea from the southwestern tip of Ireland. A narrow peninsula, it is situated just north of the Iveragh Peninsula visible across the waters of Dingle Bay. Both women live west of the town of Dingle, an area that can be circumnavigated by a good walker in not too many days. That circumnavigation would follow along the sides of mountains overlooking both sea and bays, descend to fine sand beaches and secluded coves. It could veer to ascend one of the three highest mountains, passing cupped lakes, and pools formed by tumbling waters. The mountains here are not high as mountains go – the highest, Mt Brandon, measures just under three thousand feet – but they are powerful, stretching to their full height from sea level as they do, and more complicated in the ascent than they seem from the base.

Some of the mountains are holy mountains, held as such by humans long before the arrival of Christianity. Holy wells, the ruins of round stone dwellings called *clocháns*, megalithic tombs, ring forts, stone forts, Norman towers, all are scattered over the land. It is not unusual to find, in the middle of a field, a boulder carved with a circled Christian cross and perhaps some of the older Ogham writing inscribed along its edge. The long history of humans with this landscape underlies every journey. As in any journey, it is good to know the names, and here the twoness comes most prominently into play. Almost everything has two names, one

Irish and one English. The three highest mountains, called in Irish Cnoc Bréanainn, Sliabh an Iolair and Cruach Mhárthain, carry the English names of Mt Brandon, Mt Eagle and Marhin.

In *Weather Watch* the names of places appear sometimes in Irish, sometimes in English. Trish lives in Baile Móir, Ballymore. Sandra first in Dún Chaoin, Dunquin, and then Baile an tSléibhe, Ballintlea. Trish, being Irish, has the language from her childhood, though only from school. Sandra, being what is called here a blow-in, is learning it. Their interchange of the languages in naming is characteristic. To both women, the true names are the Irish ones. This has become the legal state as well, as they live in the Gaeltacht, an area where Irish is the common language, and where, by recent current law, the road signs give place names only in Irish. Thus Dingle has become An Daingean, and Ballyferriter has become the much more difficult to pronounce Baile an Fheirtéaraigh.

Even the Irish seasons hold a twoness, as they are marked by the celebrations of ancient feast days rather than the turning of the sun. *Weather Watch* is divided by the older system. Samhain on November 1st begins winter, while Imbolc on February 1st starts spring. Summer arrives at Bealtaine on May 1st, and Lughnasa on August 1st brings autumn. These precise dates are modern demarcations, but set the observations now. Bonfires are not unusual on the eves of the feasts, keeping ancient ways.

Weather Watch began in mid-November, 2004, well into the West

Kerry winter, as Trish and Sandra sat one night by the fire talking about writing, about dailiness and practice. They decided that to encourage each other, they would daily exchange a short piece of writing by email. That night an obvious subject raged outside the house, the wind splattering rain against the windows. They would write about the weather.

At the start, they set only the loosest of timetables − to the end of the year. Yet as the days passed, they found the writings a pleasure. The challenge of each day, the variability of the weather as a spur, the story that was unfolding, all contributed to a growing sense that they wished to go on. In spring they were still writing. In May they mounted an exhibit in Dingle, their entries side by side on pages in books that unfolded to hang against the wall. They read at the launch of the exhibit, giving voice to the days, sharing them outside themselves. They decided to go on for the whole year, to complete the cycle and arrive where they began. Yet even as they would reach the same date the next November, they could have no idea where each of their journeys might take them. This is no story with a preconceived plot, but one that unfolded − often to their amazement − over time.

When the story began, Trish was living in a caravan in Ballymore just west of Dingle, and Sandra in a rented house in Dunquin at the end of the Dingle Peninsula, still with a home in Oregon, where she had lived for over thirty years. Trish was working with Beehive Theatre Company in Dingle and Sandra as a book artist. They shared the magnificent West Kerry landscape and a number of friends. The friends are not identified beyond name in the entries where they appear, as companions on walks or visitors to dinner, but their comings and goings give a sense of their place in the story. In the course of the year, both women fell in love, one with a man, the other with a house. Enormous transitions, largely unanticipated, moved through the days' entries.

Weather Watch is the record of their year. Trish's entries appear first each day, while Sandra's follow in italics. Occasionally, due to travel or illness or just general busyness, they missed a day. These days are noted in bold type by *No Weather Report Today*. On two occasions in January, 2004, marked NOLLAIG na mBAN and WIND, they agreed to make no entries. Most days though, whatever the events of their lives, their calm or turmoil, each woman managed to record a moment of weather watching. Sandra's entry on October 3rd in 2005, as they approached the second November, speaks of their journey:

> *I stay home…to work on the manuscript of* Weather Watch. *It's grown mightily since it was begun last November. I work to edit for consistency amidst all the variant spellings of this place, and then print it out for the first time. Trish is coming up tomorrow for a final edit before she leaves for Senegal later in the week. As it prints, I watch the pages scroll out, seeing the titles and the paragraphs flash by, remembering the days they record. They are full of dailiness, these pages,*

v

laundry and walks, birds and tides, but they also record a story of changes we had no way of knowing when we began. I bought the orange house in Baile an tSléibhe, moved from my Portland house to here. Changed home and country, and even name, returning to my birth name of Landers. Trish has decided to move to Senegal for the better part of next year, to see what the shape of a life there might bring, leaving her home here — and Sooki the cat — in the care of friends. Large steps for both of us, but steps unfolded day by day. When it is printed, the manuscript — with still six weeks to go — is 333 pages. I look with wonder at the stack as it sits on my desk, amazed at what can be done one day at a time.

SL
Baile an tSléibhe, Ceann Trá, Co Chiarraí
Ballintlea, Ventry, Co Kerry
April, 2007

Samhain
Winter

November

20 Amaryllis

The white amaryllis leans toward the fading light, drawing into itself the muted muffled glow of a late November Sunday on the Atlantic seaboard. A scarlet flower would flame magnificently in these brain-numbing, choked-up drizzly days yet the incandescent creamy-white bell, so delicate for all its bulk, seems to vibrate from the windowsill into our conversation, stealing my attention. Amaryllis. The thought of a beautiful, strongly made and graceful man with fair, gently curling hair...well, I can imagine whatever I want, to hell with the ancient Greeks and their pastoral shepherdesses! In the spring, I think I shall plant one in a pot for my own window. Then wait to see who shows up.

Moon

The blue winter dusk forms outside the window as the misted day slides into night. I look past the amaryllis, accustomed now to its white curl, drawn to the blue, to the fading curve of land's edge above the sea. Tigh Mhéiní down in Baile Ícín, and Eibhlín's house beside it are still visible, faint bright rectangles in the oncoming night. When I go outside later, I see the moon amidst a wash of clouds. I think of the amaryllis in the window in conversation with the moon, calling it out, incandescent white to incandescent white. The moon's responded, come out from the clouds. Now I wonder what else might appear.

21 Dusk

Dusk to dusk. Closing in rapidly. Mist creeping in over Fenton's Point soon blanks out Baile Móir. Until darkness is complete, I sit with tea and chocolate for the final fading of the light. Willows, thinly pencilled lines, crisscrossing, reaching into indigo. Muffled sound of homeward-going traffic. The ocean, at a lower register, pounding cliffs and coves below. When all is dark on land, the overhanging mist seems opalescent, a chromatic tone stretching something that might otherwise give itself up to slumber at this much too early hour of 6 p.m. The pulsing glow from the resting computer recalls the amaryllis incandescent in Sandra's window at Dún Chaoin. I wonder if complete absolute darkness ever happens, outside of black holes?

Darkness

On the way into Dingle today, even though the surface of the bay is a matt molten sheen, I see a wave reach high for the headland at Baile Móir, yearning in every curve of it. Out my door now, in the opalescent moonlight, I too can hear the surge of the sea. Once, on a drive north from San Francisco along the coast, I saw how endangered the dark had become, lights linking town after town, leaving no space in the sky for stars. Here in Baile na Rátha, the computer's pulsing eye is gently covered at night. Darkness reigns.

22 Castlemaine Harbour

Hardly a ripple on Castlemaine Harbour this morning. The distant Macgillicuddy's Reeks darkly towering in a sky painted with

18

clouds of all kinds, immobile. A pale lemon sunburst shines through, highlighting dinghies and small trawlers moored in still, black water. Herons survey, one-legged sentinels. Outside Keel National School, a small traffic jam provides me with an opportunity to watch the sky for a few minutes. A dense thermal streams straight up to the heavens from deep in the mountains. Dragon's breath skirts the range from the southwest. As I shift the car into gear, I look left to see the pale winter morning light illuminate a hill rising sharply behind the little school. Although the summit remains darkly veiled in dense fog, the slopes show off their wild attire, richly textured robes of coppery fern and crimson-berried branches, the hillside randomly dotted with white woolly sheep and an eternity of boulders. A different world of weather on either side of a country road on a November morning in 2004.

Blood Orange

Mags visited today, and as we talked and the afternoon moved into evening, I kept being distracted by the sky. Over the Great Blasket the sun was breaking through the clouds, filling the house with slanting light and the air with gold. At one moment, an incandescent cloud rested on the island. In the next, bars of grey and amber crossed the sky. Even after Mags left and the windows filled with an ethereal deep blue, I watched a single band of colour, blood orange, still glowing in the night. It stayed a while, faded to coral, then peach, and finally disappeared. Now, the wind murmurs and growls, rolls along the house. This morning I looked out the back window to see a primrose in bloom on the green bank nearby. I hardly know what season it is.

23 Tunnels of Gold

I overnighted with Pleun who lives on a wooded hillside in the country behind Macroom. To get there, you travel along tree-covered roads, tunnels of gold this unusually mild November. Her house looks out over wooded valleys and pasture, all purple, gold and molten orange over morning coffee. 'What's the weather like?', we ask each other, acknowledging that emotional life is just like weather: it changes all the time and should never be isolated as a singular event. I tell Pleun that her home is a chic modern gallery but that the real artwork is outside. She smiles in her wry kind of way and notes that here land is utilitarian, for working, for farming, not for a city person's sentimental pastoral notions. A year from now, that hill across the river from where we sit might be a housing development, or the trees might be wrenched out for tillage or extended pasture. Who knows? If it gets dug up, Pleun will undoubtedly experience a heavy weather front inside for however long it takes. The huge plaster-cast image of the Buddha that rests in the alcove of the glass-walled house will continue to gaze in an attitude of compassionate joy, whatever the weather.

Wind

Today's weather in Dunquin is all about the wind, wind to snatch the clothes from the line if they aren't securely anchored with at least three pins apiece. Midday, I really become aware of the steady pull of the wind on the house, and think to hang the laundry out instead of cycling it through the dryer. The day is grey, but bright, the high clouds leaving space for light beneath them. It seems as if it won't rain. I gather damp clothes - a blue load - and clothespins, and head for the back yard to contemplate the maze of lines there. This is my first laundry in this house, and I see I have a choice of direction, lines crossing at right angles to each other, some apparently sheltered by a large bush. It turns out that strategy is hopeless, as the wind blows fiercely in what seems to be all directions. The most use I can make of the shelter of the bush, which is leafless and stopping nothing, is to hang my tights and underwear behind it so as not to display them to the neighbours and make a scandal in the parish. When everything is anchored to the lines, I still go out from time to time, imagining my favourite skirt blown halfway across to Gleann Mór, or my blue towel back on An Cheathrú. Dusk arrives. I wrestle the clothes off the line and into the basket, find several of the pins clinging to the clothes, but no longer to the line. When I drive out in the evening, my headlights briefly illuminate the side yard of the blue farmhouse at the end of the lane. There, I see clothes streaming horizontal from the line. I cannot tell if they yearn to hold on or yearn to escape, these frantic banners in the night.

24 Sci-Fi Weather

Weird things began to happen in the bronchial atmosphere in the mid-afternoon. As I drove down the high road out of town, I realized that Dingle and its environs seemed to be ringed by a low-lying, grey-black dense fog bank, weighted down by layers of off-white clouds, reminiscent of a smoker's nicotine-stained fingers. The lower fog bank looked like a nuclear accident. I had the sensation of being in the eye of a storm. Over Milltown Bridge and on up the rise past the graveyard, heading towards Cluas, I can see a wall up ahead, probably at Ceann Trá, a thick woolly cloud wearing a necklace of shining silver. I drive into Ballymore, looking very sorry for itself indeed, and head for the loo-with-a-view out in the front field. The ocean is steaming, the tide coming in vigorously now, shifting coastal fog threatening to vanish the world in an instant. In a second, the cloud bank out at Parkmore Point has turned indigo, the steaming water is now a bright metallic blue and the upper atmosphere is the blue of forget-me-nots miles above the humidity. Five minutes later, it's back to bronchitis.

Misery

It's a misery of a day I see outside my window when I wake this morning, fog so dense the islands are hidden, rain streaking the window. It is Thanksgiving in America, but not here, and I wander about remembering all the gatherings in the past, the meals eaten, the stories shared. All I want to do today is sleep, and after a brief interval of facing the day, I take a nap, the Bach cello suites playing as I drift in and out of wakefulness. Dimly, I register the rain falling hard on the roof above me. When I wake at five in the evening, the islands have re-appeared in a perfect blue winter dusk. I make phone calls to friends in the States, into their mornings full of preparations for the feasts to come. Near seven, I answer a knock on the door, Trish with a Thanksgiving bottle of wine. We make a feast of the evening, and I pass my first Thanksgiving in Dunquin.

25 Night Colour

The full moon of November comes and goes behind veils of dense cloud high in the atmosphere. All the features of Ballymore are visibly distinct but in sepia tones, not the silvery pale of a clear full moon. I wonder about night colour. Navy, indigo and black aren't quite themselves under moonlight. The tops of the caravans and the house below in the cuaisín are clearly white but everything else has a bruised quality. The black ocean isn't quite black, more like dubbing. Indigo is on my mind searching for a description of the lower sky but the blueness just isn't blue enough to merit the term and yet, it isn't a grey shade either. Pondering this problem, I notice that the smoke coming out of the caravan chimneys doesn't rise straight up (as it would in a dense, windless fog) but is travelling flat over the roof tops, proving that there is a breeze after all on this seemingly dead still night. The only sound is the sea eternally rumbling into the cuaisín. Valentia lighthouse winks unerringly from twelve sea miles distant. Everything out there under the pale moon is made of the exact same stuff as I am, the same stuff as everything else in the universe. Technically colourless, night and day.

Stillness

Sometime in the hours between sleep and dawn, I come fully awake. The night is inhabited by an enormous stillness. Not a thing seems to stir, no breath of wind, not even the usual faint murmur from the sea. Out the window in the bright night, I catch the silver gleam of a nearby roof, and when I rise to look, see the moon riding high in the sky, each house in the fields around me clear. All the houses I can see are old, their shapes satisfyingly simple. Glowing white rectangles, they seem utterly at home in the landscape. Not a light in sight but the moon.

26 Weather and Society

The morning was golden. I sat in the wicker chair wrapped up in the blue shawl for a quiet hour warmed by winter sunlight. By the time I was ready for the outdoors, the weather decided to have a change of mood, so I headed for town instead of the beach and then society took over. The weather gets a lot of flak here. When it's good, people like me don't want to be stuck inside, missing it when there are beaches and hills to be walked, when bicycles long to be cycled. When it's lousy, we want it to be good because we get cabin fever. A no-win scenario. But occasionally, the weather forces people like me into society. Arriving in town, I met Shelley who suggested coffee in the Goat Street Café. I like the café a lot in its newest incarnation. It's very brightly lit and painted white with pale timber panelling. The coffee is good, the soup too. Very suitable for grey winter days. We talked about life, the universe and Bina, whose life is running out quickly. I consider going to visit her today, but don't. Getting ready to leave, I meet Steve, fresh from his new life in sunny Hawaii but thoroughly enjoying being wet and back in his old haunts, a respite from post-election America. So I stay for another while and then agree to do a postering job which took me two hours because I was having conversations with people as I went along. I admired Pauline's cat in MacCarthaigh's, discovered I could get an instant, seven euro haircut from the hairdresser across the road from Ashe's and then discovered a spectacular diamanté spider in Simple Pleasures. As a rule, I don't like clutter and Christmas commerce generally makes me nauseous but I was bewitched by the glitter, the silver tableware, the silks, the shining diamanté jewellery and then the bejewelled yellow spider, only nine euro, only plastic jewels but exceedingly flirtatious in a spidery kind of way. Turning to go, I noticed the ceramic frog in a glass case. Determined to be admired, it lured me over and discreetly communicated the secret of its hidden chamber, a perfect hidey-hole for an illicit pleasure, a lump of dope, say, or a forbidden, calorie-laden chocolate, or the telephone number of a person you shouldn't be calling. Then I went to the music shop down on the pier and got the lowdown on bands worth hearing from Kevin with the nice Brummie accent. Is the weather hinting that perhaps I'm not quite as antisocial as I think?

Curtains Drawn

At nightfall, I draw all the curtains in the house, making a ritual of it, but not until true dark night. If a wash of even indigo still shows, the curtains stay open, and I stay visible to the world outside, reading, eating sticky buns for tea, or a pear. Once they're shut, I have to hear the weather to know what it might be. Rain on the roof, the wind picking up. I'm surprised at how I notice, even when engrossed in something else. Only music playing – especially the opera on Saturday night – cuts me off from this. Today, when the sun suddenly warmed the room, I was inside with Dominique who had come to see my work, to get acquainted. Even as I yearned to be suddenly outside, the conversation held me in. After she'd gone, the sun soon was too, and by the time I went to Ventry for the Irish Times, *mist had turned to drenching rain. A man came into the store saying that when he'd left for town a short while ago, there'd been a mountain, and now it was gone. He thought we should take better care of our mountains. I returned home and lit the fire, left the curtains open admiring the blue dusk which arrived even in the rain. Before bed each night, I go outside, and often am amazed. I will have been hearing rain, and a bit of wind, and then be dazzled by stars. Tonight, I anticipate the moonlight, the Dunquin hills so bright it's almost possible to see colour. It's been quiet a while outside though, so there may be surprises. I'm going out to see.*

27 Tiaracht

Once upon a time, on a languid Saturday afternoon some July past, I reclined under the taut sails of a Frenchman's elegant yacht as it forged ahead for the Blaskets. In the warm, golden afternoon, I sipped fine wine offered by the skipper, a finely wrought man with long grey hair and a red bandanna, and watched as he and his three beautiful crewmen played the sails and spinnakers, hung out of the rigging and urged the yacht towards and around Tiaracht, that elusive, most mysterious rock beyond the Blaskets. Rounding the rock, the yacht caught the wind and raced home like Oisín's white stallion returning from Tír na nÓg. I, then, was Niamh, all golden and eternally young, riding pillion.

Persimmon

There, tonight, just as I had been speaking earlier about my search for the name for this elusive colour at sunset, a band of persimmon sky steady above Tiaracht.

28 Confusion

On a Sunday afternoon stroll around Baile an tSléibhe, we

saw in bloom a single montbretia as well as many fuchsia buds, and in one curious garden a primrose and a pansy and – even stranger given the season – a bumblebee clinging to a pink snapdragon flower, desperately seeking a final honeyed sustenance before death. A last supper. A last rite. Something is confused here. Is it me, the bumblebee or nature itself? The peninsular weather systems on the southwestern Atlantic seaboard account for milder, wetter weather in wintertime, so winter roses, Kaffir lilies and the odd primula in cultivated gardens, as well as year-round flowering hebe, are no big surprise down here. Wind is the killer factor in gardens, hillsides and hedgerows yet the Baile an tSléibhe side of the mountain seems to be wind-starved this November. On the other hand, the profusion of boreens, the well-tended stone walls and the careful landscaping that went into this mountainside garden probably account for the unseasonal flowering here. Anyway, I don't suppose nature succumbs to confused states except in her human manifestation. That accounts for her and me. The bumblebee, though, had gone over its sell-by date: it clung to a closed petal all the while I was in the garden.

Phases

After Irish class tonight, I drive home trying to catch glimpses of the moon visible behind a thin scrim of clouds. It seems the November full moon was just a moment ago, and now a sizeable slice has gone to dark. I have a sense of time flying by. I saw the last full moon from An Cheathrú, and now I am moved in to Baile na Rátha, thinking about a home in Baile an tSléibhe. All the while, the moon steady in her course. I stand outside a moment, admiring, then walk into the house thinking moon thoughts, close the door on the bright night, and by the time I step into the living room, the wind is howling outside flinging rain against my windows. Where did this come from? How did the damp moonlit calm I walked through only a moment ago turn to this fierceness? I stand amazed, wondering at this agile climate, then strike a match and bend to light the fire.

29 Cock Crow

It was a bright night – *oíche geal* – and I made my usual forays outside for night pees in the small hours. As I squatted, the Ballymore cock began to crow although there was no sign of the dawn which probably wouldn't show for at least another three hours. Perhaps nobody has explained Daylight Saving Time to the fussy fellow, a stickler for tight schedules, scornful of human newfangledness. Or else he's a lunatic like me, under the influence of strong moons and tides in this coastal wonderland. As I put my foot in the door, rain fell like a burst of gunfire. Half a minute later, the only sound cutting the gentle ocean rumble was his lordship pouring forth again up in the henhouse.

Sapphire

I took the wrong way to Farranfore this morning. A changed schedule left me still thinking of Castlegregory and Tralee, well on that route before I realized I really just wanted to go straight to Farranfore. Yet as I went over Connor Pass, I was given the gift of the lake on Mt Brandon, the one we all climbed to on a summer's day, glowing a pure blue reflection of the sky, a deep sapphire blue. Only for a bit, at the right angle, at the right time, then it shifted to bronze. Compensation enough though for the wrong route, and for a good walking day gone to commitments made days before. In the blue moment, the I Ching *trigram* The Joyous, Lake, *came to mind, and I thought surely it was over there across the valley from me. Then in late afternoon, the sky turned a mass of persimmon-tinged waves. I was still in Tralee, the sunset blocked by the mountains, and I could only imagine the light flooding Dunquin. Driving west, I watched the colours change, trying on flamingo for a name, remembering that their colour comes from the shrimp they eat, then trying various versions of rose, until the sky was little more than grey clouds tinged shell pink above a deep sapphire sky.*

30 No Weather Report Today

Roil

I look out on this nearly windless sun-filled day and see the sea a blue roil. I remember coming home last night, being startled by its roar far down at the cliff edge, there every time I opened the door to check, with me through the open window as I slept. This morning – daytime sounds, perhaps some difference in density between sun and moon lit air – I do not hear it, but what I see is the same as what I heard last night, the same thing known through two senses. I wonder if my skin can feel the commotion, or my heart.

December

1 Robins

Waiting for the coffee to bubble through the percolator, I glance out the window into the willow garden and a pair of robins are doing their dance on the bare branches, limbering up on this frosty morning. The willows shine in lemon winter morning light, budding already although it's only the beginning of December. The Purple Sprouting plants are crystalline, like the silvered grass and I'm glad now that I didn't root them all out of their bed after caterpillars stripped the lot one August day. They won't fruit but never mind: they look so pretty this morning! Standing up to retrieve the coffee, I smile at the pencil-thin silver line that marks the border between the ocean and the coast of the Iveragh Peninsula, twelve sea miles yonder. I hope the robins know that Sooki is on the prowl. But they tend towards the higher branches and since she is a lousy climber – being a rather curious cat with only half a tail – there's no fear of them.

Robin

Since I moved to Baile na Rátha, I've been putting out a crumbled fruit scone and birdseed each morning. I've little hope of the sweet Ceathrú birds I'd come to know so well discovering it, but have hoped to interest the birds of this neighbourhood. The Crow Boys, of course, found it right away, and after them, the magpies and the wagtails. From a distance, black and white, no colour, although splendid blacks and splendid whites, a magpie on the wall across the way yesterday dazzling. I cannot actually see the food once it's scattered, but I can hear the crows, and have surprised the others as I come out the door. Leaving for Tralee on Tuesday, I saw a robin on the hedge beside the car. Rust breast! Colour! Inquisitive eye. The first of the small hedge birds to appear. We looked at each other a while, I inviting him to eat as Trish suggested I do, and he seemed interested. In Tralee, I got a feeder to hang from the spare clothesline that I can see from the back window. It seemed a small bird fled as I went out with the wash today, so perhaps that will be discovered too. It's turned cold, and I worry about the Ceathrú birds. I still miss their flutterings and company, their companionship in the morning, and throughout the day. I wish I could explain my leaving, even as I tried.

2 Smoke Rising Straight Up

Smoke rose straight up from chimneys today indicating a virtually windless atmosphere. It is very cold. I woke to a wondrously coloured dawn, rosy pink, crimson red, purples and mauves. The sea shone metallic blue with a hazy veil of mist above, a silver line glistening, pencil thin, where the ocean meets the Iveragh, the next peninsula to the south. In the west, ominously bruised and red rumpled cirrus clouds loitered above Sliabh an Iolair, delinquents waiting for a fight. But the fight never materialised as the day progressed. Dawn psychedelia gave way to a thinly overcast cold day with highly reflective properties in all this watery world. A green and purple painted trawler bobbed double in and over the water as did the various piers and jetties, while Burnham Wood admired its own image on the far side of the harbour. I overheard someone say that the temperature today in Chicago was slightly warmer than here but I really don't believe that!

No Smoke Rising

When I look out my front windows in Baile na Rátha, what I see is mostly older homes, settled into the landscape. Even the holiday home twins – Barr na hAille and Dún Binne – above the pier seem from this distance as if they've been here a long time. Often the shapes of these older Irish houses are to me as simple and satisfying as a child's drawing. The landscape curves, masking parts of houses, one curve after another crossing my eye until the final rise of Dún Mór, then the sea and the islands with their own curves beyond. It is cold today, as cold as it's been this winter, yet no smoke rises from any chimney in sight. This includes my own, as the night heaters are giving out warmth, and although the peat fire is laid, I do not light it until evening. The once necessary fire in the hearth has become, it seems, an evening luxury, for comfort as much as warmth. Perhaps the smokeless chimneys belong to homes of people who now are gone for the day, leaving the house empty. Perhaps I am looking at houses that have become vacation homes, closed for the winter, such houses now making up almost seventy per cent of Dunquin. Perhaps central heating has permeated Dunquin, and others are kept warm as I am in the day by electricity or oil. It seems a sadness though. A friend recently told me that in some system of analysis, smoke curling out of a chimney in a drawing is a sign of happiness in the home of the one who draws it. In my mind's eye, I imagine a curling line of smoke rising from each chimney I see, wishing happiness on the parish.

3 Cloud Cocktail

Early on Friday afternoon, the sky seems enormous above Ventry Beach. At mountain level, the tops of Sliabh an Iolair behind me and the Macgillicuddy's Reeks, far ahead in the Iveragh, are cloaked in dense, rain-laden clouds, but directly to the southwest, the lower sky is striped apricot and lavender and a paler mauve that I don't have a name for, trailing off past Valentia Island and into the great yonder, somewhere out of sight now behind the low green pasture of Parkmore Point. The insistent breeze has a sharp edge to it and I'm wondering what's happening out there in the ocean. Is stormy weather brewing? Why are there so many varieties of cloud in the southwesterly sky? Rising damp feeds the bruised, heavy clouds on all the hillsides. I am feeling cold and don't have enough time for a beach walk – I have to be in town for a three o'clock reading. But the beach dogs are irrepressibly jolly, longing to be escorts, while a pink-coated blond child is intent on her sandcastle job. A cormorant plays hide-and-seek as I walk along – now you see me, now you don't – black beak and head bobbing on the long neck, brightly looking up and, quick as lightning, vanishing underneath. There are very few birds in sight, just odd ones bobbing around, early arrivals to nature's afternoon show. Sundown. A bit on the early side. I hope their friends show up to join them. The cormorant is a smart alec show-off the other birds clearly disdain. Driving uphill from the village, I pass Parkmore and can now see the two lavender-coloured Scelligs poised immutably, weightlessly, in the distant ocean.

Tír na nÓg

Coming across the Clasach this afternoon, I see lavender cloud banks far out to sea to the south. In this light, with this colouring, they do look like a distant mountain range, not a great journey away. I know they are clouds, know a bit of the meteorology of why they come and go, appear some days on the horizon and on other days cannot be seen, just as the mountains of the Iveragh Peninsula to the south sometimes seem to vanish. Or the Blaskets to disappear. But what if I didn't know about cloud banks on the horizon? Or had not made the twelve mile crossing to the Iveragh and come back to tell that mountains were truly there? Mightn't there be some confusion as to what was reachable and what was not? And, having journeyed to the Iveragh, mightn't one set out for the clouds?

4 Sound

I wake to a colourful array of sound this Saturday morning in early December. A determined southwesterly is gearing up for a bigger blow later on and it sounds like there's already quite a swell challenging the cliffs down below. Busy clucking tones outside alert me to the hens having a good old scratch in the corner of the garden where I planted a dozen snowdrop bulbs...The morning is full of muted light despite the overcast which is painted in a grey-blue wash giving the green of continuing new growth a somewhat psychedelic hue. White horses ride the steel grey ocean, the Iveragh a delicate line drawing under a pale cotton wool sky, at least for these few minutes!

Grey

Grey. Still and grey. Anonymous weather. I watch all day for some variation, but the overall feel is grey. In Dingle, the power has gone out in the town. It's that kind of day. People, on errands, wanting to shop for Christmas, wander past the darkened stores, peer in through the open doors. Fire alarms triggered by the outage are beeping, whining, the shopkeepers trying to endure a sound designed to make one flee. As the light fades, stores give up and close, leaving notes taped to the windows. Going home to Dunquin over the Clasach, I hope for a blue December dusk, that vibrant blue full of the promise of a few snowflakes, but it stays grey. Later, as I'm drawing the curtains, I see the window is soaked. Silent rain. And when I go outside before sleep, I find a fog has descended, a fog so deep I can't see Maria's light that always burns through the night on the Ceathrú. Grey night too.

5 2 p.m. Sunday

Sky grey, ocean black.
Blue-white tide
On purple rock.

Silver line, charcoal peak.
Apricot ribbon
Horizon line.

Wind blows, hair flies.
Green silk book
The image holds.

Pathetic Fallacy

Did Trish and I inhabit the same yesterday? I send off a paragraph full of grey and stillness and receive back from her one full of sound and subtle colour. We live not too many miles distant, share parts of the sky, and yet yesterday we lived in different worlds.

6 Zen

Stillness in Ventry Harbour this afternoon: the tide receding, gently massaging the beach. No wind. Between the headlands of Parkmore Point and Ballymore, only sea and sky. No Iveragh. No silver line. Just the palest outline of Sliabh an Iolair, Cruach Mhárthain and the rest, veiled in a soft, thin shower at this hour of mid-afternoon. In front of me, shining water, undulating, hypnotic, stretches away into the cloud cupola. Dream stuff. No substance. Not far from shore, the water is muted pale green, reflected light, which at the harbour mouth turns to palest mauve, seeping skyward. Amazing! how light is concealed in shades of grey. At the half-way point, a single bird. It shows two sides as it ducks and dives, one side fluorescent white in this light. I meet Simon who tells me it is a Great Northern Diver, also called a loon.

The Solace of the Colour of Water

A day so rich, so all ahoo. A day of driving, to Tralee, to Farranfore, to Killorglin, to Killarney, to Tralee. Through sideways drenching mist, through luminous fog, through grey descending, through clear dark night, human lights but no stars visible. A day of phone calls, at home, in the car, the mobile on, always with me. Waiting for word of a mortgage approved.

Stretched thin with questions. Yet. Coming into Ventry in the early part of a day already whirling, I look sideways and see the ruffled bay a pale grey green, a sustaining colour sending the pleasure of it deep inside. Calming. All the rest of the day, the trína chéile *day, amidst the upset, I look for water.*

7 Hey Presto

I crawl out of bed this dark, damp morning and get the fire started in the stove straight after setting the percolator to brew. Another very late night and a late morning start. It's after nine already. Strong coffee is required to kick-start the day. Such a dull, grubby day it is that I even switch on the little reading lamp to provide some cosiness. Not a sign of a soul up and about in Ballymore. After half an hour, after the black brew, I head up to the loo-with-a-view. Not much of a view today. But just as I walk back, hey presto! the sun shows up and it's another little world altogether. Now people are meeting and greeting in the field, a bit bleary-eyed still but cheerful that the weather has done its magic show once more, delighting us all this December morning. Now everything is glistening, those willows look fit to burst and Tinka, who has just arrived with Britta, is doing a waggy-dog dance around Sooki, who isn't impressed. Wade greets us in passing: he's going fishing this lovely morning and is looking cheerful.

The Brightness of a Morning without Visible Sun

I look out the front windows at my green, house-dotted view, more than half of which is occupied by sky. This December midday the sky is white, not a colour, but a light, with a cap of stormy grey feathering down into it from above. This light, somehow brighter than sunlight, reveals every detail. In the field across the way, the tangle of bushes beyond the mossed and lichened stone wall shows lavender and burgundy, silver, and more greys than I can name. Beyond that, the edges of the roof of the huge new building behind Mags' house gleam rigid and bold above the bushes. In my window well, the water in the glass pitcher holding a bouquet of white tulips, their leaves a tender yellow-green almost chartreuse, reflects the white sky. When I look out, I squint at the brightness. Once, years ago on a midsummer afternoon, I stood on a beach in Hawaii. Although I was under a parasol, I found the light searing, intense all around me. I thought this must be what it is to be in the eye of God. Yet as my eyes narrow against today's piercing light, I wonder if it is not closer to the nature of God. It is more merciless and serene than Hawaii's yellow light. As I write, shadow blooms across my page, and sunlight appears, warming the room. Some detail fades. Shadows give relief, and I am brought from a moment of pure clarity into the blurred everyday.

8 Hey Ho, the Wind and the Rain

At nine o'clock this December evening, I suddenly realize that I've missed the weather because I worked in the theatre office all day, a modern concrete colossus impervious to weather of any kind. How dull! When I work at home here in the caravan at Ballymore, the weather is constantly in my senses, the 'van breathes with me, waxing and warping in a weather dance; trips to the loo-with-a-view enhance weather watching opportunities and I can look out these big caravan windows and see what nature is up to all around me. I woke to driving wind and rain and general overcast and came home to the same weather in the dark. It's funny, though, how one's emotional mood colours the weather. Today, my head was completely involved with a list of items to do relating to the March theatre festival. My eagerness to get cracking on the organizational business has made me impervious to the lousy weather. Hmm. I don't think I'd be quite so focused if this were summertime and I were stuck inside the concrete box all day. Out on the Blasket, under the full moon of September, Britta and I agreed that camping on the island in fair weather was the ultimate cultural highlight of our lives. Well then, we must be the ultimate Philistines!

Drum

Yesterday the wind came up, and it has been buffeting this Baile na Rátha house ever since. Some combination of bank and wall causes this wind to turn the house into a drum. No steadiness to it, but random gusts that pummel, reverberating. I remember when I stayed in Claire's small Ceathrú house, my bedroom wall was the gable wall which faced the prevailing winds, as gables tend to do here. During the fierce winter storms, wind would punch the house, a sensation I could feel. Especially the first year, I tried to reassure myself that the house had stood for two hundred years, and would likely stand for more. This was before I knew that the second floor, where the bedroom was, had been added in very recent times. Although I feel the wind drumming in this house, it is more a sensation of sound, deep vibrating boom. Last night, when I opened the curtains in my bedroom before sleep, it was to utter dark night. The wind pushed against the window when I went to open it, then burst into the room and roamed around.

9 Wind from Below

Sun replaces rain in this morning's weather cocktail. I'm warmed by it as I sit in the wicker chair with coffee and cat. Dust motes hang in the air. Sooki's dusky coat glistens in the sunlight. She crows, rather than purrs, a slightly trilling vibration. Outside looks pretty wild but strangely, I don't hear the wind. It seems to be blowing a direct westerly so it doesn't hammer the side of the caravan, which faces the southwest. The wind sounds far away, as if it were coming from somewhere below. Shining willows dance wildly. Out the back, crows wheel in slow motion above the whitewashed house in the intense blue. The dead ash tree shines quicksilver and nasturtiums, vermilion and orange, flame on livid green tendrils. Everything is so obviously in motion: air, light, energy. How amazing to know that I, too, am in motion in the same energetic system.

Rocked

I finally returned home to Baile na Rátha at dusk tonight. Too tired to move, I just sat there resting my head against the back of the seat while the wind gently rocked the car. This odd wind that all day has been coming from one direction, then another, roiling up the sea, but leaving the meadow almost still. Ventry Bay a churn of green. A ring of light around Inishtooskert. Apricot glowing morning. I stayed in the car until blue dusk turned to night and the neighbour's light slanted across the yard. Rocked, gently rocked, by the wind.

10 Rising Mist

At about 5 pm., the sky was crimson in the west, the harbour metallic blue, the town lights already reflecting in the utterly still water. Smoke rose straight up. No breeze. As I crossed Milltown Bridge, an eerie mist was rising waist high over the river behind the timber mill, like thick bonfire smoke. The sun-filled day had warmed the ground tremendously but after sundown the temperature dropped sharply and the ground heat, now dissipating in the cooling air, hung spectral and eerie over the river.

Gift

A tender gift of a day. No descriptions necessary. Just gratitude.

11 Grey Day

A grey day with no sparkle. I went to Ventry intending to walk on the beach, but didn't. Then I went on to Burnham Wood, hoping to walk in a more sheltered spot, but got back in the car after five minutes. In town, I bought mince pies, intending to visit Bina, who is ill, but, although I went and parked outside her house, I didn't knock on her door but just drove away after a while. Looks like it's really an internal weather low.

Clarity

I love this winter light in Dunquin. Even on the darkest days, it holds a remarkable clarity. If I look out toward the islands, I see haze, but nearby, each curve, each house is distinct. The stone wall across the lane is etched in detail, every stone a colour faintly different from the one next to it, the spaces between them a true black. The field is vivid green. I can almost see each twig of each bush there. The far hedge is a brown calligraphy against the bright fields rising beyond. On land, only the curve of Dún Mór is hazed, a flat grey-brown. Yet today would be called a grey day, dull, by most. I raise my camera to the scene to see if its internal meter will tell me not enough light. But, no. It agrees. A good day for detail.

12 Blue-Grey World

Blue-grey ocean, blue-grey islands under a blue-grey sky. Sepia tint. But the wash in the small cove is aquamarine, the colour, Sandra tells me, of the glacial current in the McKenzie River in Oregon. We pause to listen to the shuck-shhhh of the wash in the pebbled cove below. I can't find a colour for the sound.

Intense

When I go out this morning to feed the birds their seeds and scone, I find intense bands of clouds above An Ghráig. Although it is a grey day, overcast, these clouds are an intense colour, a deep purple plum, made brighter by the silver spaces between them. Stretching from behind the rocks that rise there, rocks I know to be the home of ravens, they form straight lines reaching far out over the sea. So bright I must squint when I look at them, they fascinate me in the midst of an otherwise featureless sky. Are these clouds some manifestation of the ravens' dark feathers? Or something happening on An Cheathrú? I stand with the bag of seeds tucked under my arm and drink in the colour. Small birds in the hedges wait for me to be gone so they can come and eat.

13 Stormlet

There's a baby storm, a stormlet, blowing. The weather knows it is December but this year it's in a comic mood and just can't get serious about storms and stuff. So it's just playing. Or else it's teasing, waiting to get us later.

Windows and Weather

I live in an old cottage with deep window wells. Each night before I go to bed, I draw aside the curtains and open the window to let in the night air. This morning, I lie in bed watching the curtains shift, admiring the design of the window. The well itself is about two feet deep, the wooden frame inset about a quarter of the way in from the front of the house. Hinged at the top, the upper half of the window opens out from the bottom, held in position by two metal arms perforated with holes that fit onto pegs in the lower frame. Today the window is fully open, and I can see that, although a good deal of fresh air is coming into the room, no part of the window extends beyond the outer edge of the well which shields the openings on the sides. What this means, I realize, is that the window is perfectly designed for a climate of rain and wind. The way this window is set, rain would have to be falling upwards at a forty-five degree angle to come in. While in this climate of capricious winds this is not impossible, it is highly unlikely. This window pleases me deeply, shaped as it must have been over time from the interaction of humans and wind and rain.

14 Bonsai Waves

The tide has created a wide shallow basin at the far end of Ventry Beach. By the time I arrived there this afternoon, the misty drizzle had abated and the wind was gathering momentum again. All the birds seem to be hanging out on this end of the beach. The pickings must be good there. I stopped awhile, wanting to still myself, and my attention was caught by the miniature waves rolling into the shallows. Everything was wave perfect: the roll, the spray flying up, the break, followed by the next one and the next, on and on. All in miniature. Bonsai waves.

Every Which Way
The wind today seems to blow in every direction at once, playfully testing my theory about windows. I cannot say a moment occurred when the rain was falling upward at a forty-five degree angle, but if ever there was such a moment, it might have been today. A curious day really, a day so pale as to not even be called grey, yet full of movement, and with a dark parenthesis at each end. Last night when I opened the curtains before bed, it was to utter dark, no moon, no starshine, no human light. Tonight, when I go outside after an evening of listening to the rain lashing the roof, dashing against the windows, the door is soaked, but the sky is bright with stars. They are the first stars in days, and I rejoice to see them.

15 Cúl Iarthaigh
Glorious wandering in the great gouged bowl of Cúl Iarthaigh above Baile an tSléibhe on the side of Sliabh an Iolair. The bowl was already partially in shadow an hour before noon but there was no cold in it on this pet day so close to the winter solstice. I didn't even bring a sweater and donned the fleece but briefly. Very quickly one achieves the sensation of being quite high up above

the district and today, the wonderful world of mountains and ocean spread out before my gaze is mirror-like in its absolute stillness. Every detail of both Ventry and Cuan Pier is perfectly doubled in the water. Even at this distance and height from the ocean, its eternal roar underlies all other aural perception: the trickling down of streams from the mountaintop, dripping water off black rocks, occasional bursts of birdsong. Crossing the side of the bowl, I'm back in warm, lemon winter sunlight. Not a breath of wind.

Sun

Sun makes everything possible.

16 Etiquette

Today, etiquette prevailed. The weather stopped its silly sweet nonsense at about 4 p.m. and remembered that, it being mid-December, what is supposed to happen is strong wind and lots of rain and everyone having an excuse to rush into cosy hostelries to whinge about how awful the weather is and how they've got nothing done for Christmas.

Squalls

The rain beats on the roof, the wind at the moment quiet. The temperature has dropped, and winter finally come, chimneys all around me sending up smoke from early in the day. No one waits for night to fall, or even afternoon tea, to light the fire. All day alternating weather, sun flooding the room one moment followed by wind-driven squalls of hard rain. As I go in and out the door to tend the laundry in the shed, the wind pushes me along, gusting at my back. I see the branches from the hedge at the Ceathru house, carefully tended these weeks as starts I hope to root, gone from their jar of water. No sign of them at all, blown utterly away by the wind.

17 First Quarter

The moon in its first quarter graced the early evening, a delicate pale lantern in outer darkness nodding towards the golden glow of candles inside. There's a chill in the dampness but it won't turn hard cold, there's too much cloud cover. I have a feeling there's more wind and rain on the way.

Wild Sea and Slanted Winter Light.

For the past two days, with the wind up, the seas offshore from Dunquin have been wild, whitecaps racing across the sound, waves breaking high in slow-motion exuberance on the offshore rocks. The meeting of water and rock, the white explosion, releases something in me that turns to laughter. Delight? Such wildness. Such spray. Such grace. All of this lit by the slanting December sunlight, sun nearly as low as it will go on its path, catching the brilliant water, revealing the contours on the sides of the mountains. In their winter coats, the mountains look today even more like huge animals at rest, muscles defined by shadow and light. All the world is alive today. Sea dancing. Mountains sleeping beasts. Sun bowing low.

18 Downtown Tralee

Downtown Tralee a week before Christmas. Six o'clock, all the shops closing, dazzling lights everywhere, awful music blaring out. It's pouring. I'm dressed incognito, in black, hair plastered down, glasses useless in the rain but I'm on walkabout now that business is over and I can move through the streets unassailed by commerce. It occurs to me that I have too much aversion to our material culture.

Jade

Another misery of a day, drenching rain falling through sepia light, the last Saturday for shopping before Christmas. While I stand talking with a friend near the entrance to Garvey's, people come in dripping, heads lowered, shoulders hunched against the rain. Then on the way back to Dunquin, I look to the left as I pass Ventry Bay. There it sits, glowing a pure milky jade, an exquisite colour made moreso by the surrounding grey. I go on refreshed, return home to read the Irish Times *and light the fire. When I pull the curtains at dusk, I see a line of pure pale lemon in the midst of the clouds to the south, and a patch of blue to the west.*

19 Loo Light

The cold of the past twenty-four hours is gone, the sky is clouding over and the moon, now close to the halfway stage, has a yellow and red halo forecasting a storm. I sit on the loo-with-a-view, door wide open to the moonlight and the ocean roar, amused by the aesthetics of the situation.

Silver Lake Far at Sea

I come across the Clasach late at night, the moon appearing and disappearing amidst the gathering clouds. Just as I crest the hill, my eyes are drawn to a silver oval far out at sea. The moon is shining there, making a lake in the ocean. No one is behind me on the road. I stop and turn out the headlights, allowing dark to surround me. The clouds have settled in over the land. The dark is dense and complete. No light but that silver shining. Later, when rain pelts the roof, and I think I even hear thunder, the calm of that light stays with me.

20 Under a Sistine Sky

In the hour before dark on the day before the winter solstice, the cold, low sky occasionally opens in glorious cameos of eggshell blue, pale pink and lemon yellow with a faint, gilded edge. Admiring the sky and the limpid stillness, I wonder if this is what the ceiling of the Sistine Chapel looks like. The temperature is definitely dropping.

Sound and Fury

As I read last night I was aware of the rain pelting down onto the roof, lashing the windows. Occasional intervals of silence would be followed by another furious squall, loud enough to draw my attention from my book. With the curtains drawn against the night, I couldn't see the sky, but I imagined only darkness, a veil of clouds drawn across the moon. Before bed, I drew back the curtains to open the window and was astonished to see a sky bright with stars, utterly free of clouds. Not wanting to be doused with rain, I'd not opened the door as I usually do to see the night, to breathe it in before sleep. Then, not a stitch on, I went to the front door and opened it. All the sky I could see was clear, the stars vivid. I stood elated, looking. Then raced back to my warmed bed and sleep.

21 Solstice

In thrall to an inner storm, I didn't connect with the weather.

Sky Like a Painting

The first time I was in Venice, I had only eight hours there, but they were packed with event. It was a clear April day. I took the wrong water taxi, and ended up being dispersed with all of the other passengers onto the platform at the remote cemetery island. As I spoke no Italian, I understood little of what was going on, but was assured it was merely a strike, and another taxi would be by shortly to pick us up once the point had been made. One did soon come, and I re-boarded in the midst of a group of nuns in their black habits. None taller than my shoulder, they clustered around me, pressed in by the crowd, and seemed to have no bones. A strolling cat was full of a vaguely sinister significance. When I was finally back in the city and off the taxi, I followed sign after sign through narrow and twisting streets to St Mark's Square. As I turned and turned, I began to imagine the signs leading only one way, and none would lead me back to the train station and the train to Paris that I was to take later in the day. Then the square opened up before me, stunning after the tangle of streets. I wandered its edges, looked across its expanse, sat on the edge of a fountain eating a gelato, heard a nearby piano play 'Summertime', and watched a beautiful young man walk past me whistling 'As Time Goes By'. I did not, as I was tempted to do, rise and follow him, but instead sat looking at the sky, a delicate blue-green filled with piles of creamy clouds. I was looking at the exact sky I had seen in so many Italian paintings, distinguished and otherwise. For the first time, I realized how true art was to life, and then wondered if, over the centuries, the sky may not also have shaped itself in some way to the representations of it, as a stone is shaped by water.

22 Solstice, Part Two

At half past four on this second day of the winter solstice, the sun is a gigantic disc riding low over Parkmore Point opposite my seat on Ballymore rocks. Above the bright yellow orb, thick banks of storm clouds race in from the southwest. Ventry has vanished. The sky to the south turns a delicate smoky pink behind a lavender veil as the sun bows out behind the cloud banks. The milky jade ocean below is tinted with pink overtones. Gulls wheel and screech, storm riders all. I watch the solstice sundown, and walk back over the field in gathering darkness, lighter inside as the outside light slips away.

Exuberance

A wind day, strong and blowing. I open the door this morning to the sound of a churned sea. Up in Baile an tSléibhe, I feel the full force of the wind for the first time, hear it whistling in the vents. I am with the young woman who will do the bank evaluation for the house I wish to buy. She has appeared in city clothes, a pin-striped pants suit and what Trish would gleefully call 'witchy shoes', black high heels with very pointed toes. Having been in the garden before, I am wearing wellingtons, jeans, and a yellow slicker. The woman measures the house with a small hand-held laser then valiantly braves the wind and the mud to walk to the lower edge of the field. I cannot, however, interest her in a full tour of the delights of the place. Later, I walk on Ventry Beach, drawn by yet another astonishing green.

Watered silk. Blown sideways and forward and back, hair all ahoo even in its clip, I find a storm beach, thick collars of seaweed, the bog exposed, shells delicate and bold. The sky toward the Clasach holds a pelter of rain, but out over the water, the sky is blue, sun streaking down, flaring up. Even later, out at night, these darkest solstice nights, I can still see the white foam of the water below me as I come around Clogher Head. All the day is exuberance, the sea, the wind, the light.

23 Dark

Today felt like the darkest day. A grey day somehow featureless and flat. I hung up the fairy lights and lit candles at midday. But come the evening, the dull grey gave way to a blue-white, moonlit night and lights burning in all the windows hereabout. My cave animal has no real interest in the revelry of the Christmas season; if I didn't prong it with the pitchfork of sociability, it would slumber indifferently until a whiff of spring tweaked its snoring nostrils.

Ventry Green

I have a friend who is not a painter of pictures, although I suspect he could be. He is a painter of houses, outside and in, and occasionally a reference to his past gives light to a sophistication about art that leads me to wonder if he did once paint pictures, and to wonder further why he might have stopped. I know he loves paintings, the colour and the stroke of them. He has just sent me an essay he wrote, an interview with a woman who paints. In the midst of the facts, he describes her palette, the colours she uses: '… alizarin crimson, burnt and raw sienna, terra and quinacridone rose, mixed greenish umber, transparent gold and yellow ochre. Hansa and phthalo and Naples yellow'. He notes that her finished work is often 'brushed with amber shellac'. I can feel how he loves to record the colours' names, and how distinctly he can see each one. I think of his essay as I round the curve into Ventry this afternoon, to see that the bay is yet another breathtaking green, darker than the milky jade of a few days ago, more blue than yesterday's clear and windblown green. These greens appear in the midst of days of uniform greyness, vivid with a source of their own. I imagine a colour, Ventry Green, added to a painter's palette. A tube of it would produce a different water green each time it was used, but only ones that might occur in Ventry Bay in the days around the winter solstice.

24 Hail

A hail flurry hit like bazooka fire just as I rounded the corner after the river at Ventry Beach. All of a sudden, the sky was absolutely grey, closing in fast, the harbour turned milky green and the sand was encrusted with icy pearls of hail, as if an army of pale sea maidens had embroidered the beach in the twinkling of an eye. When the sky closes in and strong wind flurries whirl up the sand, I sometimes think I'm back in the desert.

Forecast

It is late on Christmas Eve, the moon-blue night bright outside. After listening all day to predictions of snow (Snow!) for Christmas, I drove out earlier onto dry roads, even as I had spent some of the afternoon walking on Béal Bán watching rainbows, seeing the dark grey veil of rain across the hillsides, encountering downpours as I drove. Then, coming back from the gathering at Trish's, warm with food and friendship, there on the Clasach was snow (Snow!). Not sleet, not hail, but real snow coming fast and bright into my headlights. None of it was sticking to the ground, although I could see the tracks of a car that had passed ahead of me on the road. I climbed and descended carefully into candlelit Dunquin where the sky was suddenly clear, moon and stars floating in it serene. All the rest of the night, as the candles burned lower and madrigals played on the radio, I could think with pleasure of the snow, and how the mountains might look in the morning, snow-capped for Christmas.

25 White Christmas

The Met Office promised a white Christmas for Ireland. Here in Corca Dhuibhne, it was certainly a stormy one with great hail showers, huge ocean swells and howling winds. As I drove down the Clasach, I was enthralled by the height of waves and spray breaking against the Blaskets and the headlands round about. It occurred to me that landforms only exist as a playground for ocean swells to bounce around on. Later, driving back to Ballymore, the grey overcast parted briefly to the south revealing a mysterious snowy peak: my Kanjiroba. No sign of the snow leopard yet.

Hail Cocktail

I wake this Christmas morning with my back turned to the window, facing the mirror. What I see when I open my eyes is the Great Blasket, its familiar haunch curve, but higher, floating, stretched almost to the scale of a Chinese mountain. It takes me a moment to realize I am looking at the reflection of a cloud in the mirror. As I lie in bed not wanting to leave the warmth of the flannel sheets and the feather duvet, several weathers pass through. The day begins with clouds of palest amber tinged with rose. The wind drums random against my open window, and suddenly the sky darkens and a tattoo of hail smatters across the roof. Sun again. Wind sound. If I rise onto an elbow to look out, I see the water, white-capped, seething in the wind, racing across the Sound. Later still, I do get up, pull on skirt and sweater over my nightgown and go out to feed the birds. I do this barefoot, even in winter, a grounding for the day. When I turn to go back into the house, I see a small pile of hailstones-almost-snow nestled into the corner beside the door. I reach down, as I did as a child, and scoop up a small piece to eat. Hail cocktail.

26 World Weather

The Feast of Stephen falls under the last full moon of the year. The hail flurries of Christmas Day have melted to a glorious sunny morning with no cold left. I turn on the radio at midday to check road conditions countrywide – Seán, Julie and Eoin are due to travel down from Dublin – and I hear about a thousand-mile band of tidal waves north of Sumatra wrecking coastal communities around Sri Lanka, southern India and the islands off Thailand. I immediately think of Arunthete who has gone home to Colombo to visit her ailing father, leaving Nigel and the boys to Christmas alone in Swansea…

The Dubliners arrive before nightfall, welcomed by Sandra's amazing chocolate brownies and a good bottle of wine, and later on Nigel calls to tell me that Arun and family in Colombo are okay. We also talk about Darfur, western Sudan, where Nigel has recently done an emergency relief assessment. The habitually tough weather conditions there seem kind compared to the cruel violence being meted out on the local population by government-armed militias.

Putting the phone down, I notice how bright the night sky is. All is still. Lights are reflected in Ventry Harbour and the Valentia lighthouse flashes its signal clearly over a mirror calm ocean. Weather, a Jekyll and Hyde phenomenon.

Freesias Against a Changing Sky

This St Stephen's Day is bright with light, no rain to wet the Wren. As I sit drinking coffee, I watch the white freesias on the windowsill across the room. The sun comes and goes, making them translucent, then opaque. In one particular glowing moment I reach for the camera only to find it has no film. By the time I load a roll, the light has changed. I wanted to record the white flower, the delicate yellow stamens in its throat illuminated, against a dark grey sky. What I find is the creamy flower against a now white sky, something not as exciting to me. I take one photograph anyway, as a mnemonic to the lit moment just passed.

27 Wet Wren

The Wren, the Wren, the King of All Birds is still parading around Dingle streets despite a howling gale and flogging rain. Straws flying everywhere, the big drum going boom, boom, very peculiarly-robed folk lurking around the town and blue, chapped fingers stuck to whistles belting out 'Sweet Marie' for another year: this is the highlight of the Dingle Christmas. You have to be a hard-core weather watcher to play in the wren band as it's a six or seven hour shift and, no matter how salubrious the hostelry of the moment, you must drink up and move on until the day's end in Rowan's (the John Street Wren), Flaherty's (the Green and Gold) or MacCarthaigh's (the Goat Street Wren), regardless of how wet or cold it might be. I'm just a Wren renegade: after two hours of being soaked, it's off to Ashe's for hot port and proper grub with the Dublin mob. Young Eoin thought it was great craic to be marching with the Sráid Eoin Wren but, no more than his aunt or his dad, he was happy to decamp to cosy Ashe's too. We'll have to learn the whistle tunes for next year's Wren. A resolution easily made and quickly forgotten, alas!

Auditory Hallucination

At near midnight, the candles in the windowsills have burned low, and I move to blow them out and draw the curtains. As I lean over, I see Orion glowing high in a near-blue sky. I go to the door, open it, and find the moon floating above me, the sky inhabited by white clouds, the night bright. I step beyond the dark shadow of the house and into the moonlight, spinning in its light. Later, as I read by the fire, I hear the wind come up, rain spattering across the roof. Before bed, I open the door again, astonished to find the night serene, the same high moon, white clouds, bright stars. Was the rain there at all? Where did it come from and where did it go?

28 Power

Awed by news of the tsunami, I need to go out west and witness the ocean's vast energy for myself. I call on Sandra and we walk down to the little cove near Baile na Rátha before darkness falls. The force of the ocean rolling in over the Blasket Sound is mind-blowing: pure energy packaged in complex physical matter, water.

Axis

Trish has come to visit. We pull the chairs up to the window and talk about the recent tidal waves that have swept across a part of the earth. As we talk, our eyes watch the surge of waves crossing the sound, watch the white reef of breakers out beyond Beginish, watch the sun move molten in and out of dark clouds as it sets. I suggest we walk down to the cuaisín, to see the true height of the waves. Pulling on jackets and scarves, hats and gloves, we set out in the early dusk. I am elated by the energy of the waves, move toward the edges to look over, to look out. I notice Trish stays back, and remember her looking at me as she explains how she feels part of all this, of the quake, of the wave. We reach the cuaisín only to find the waves more subdued than might have been expected. Still, I am drawn to the edge of the sea, look to the north to the water breaking over the headland there. I turn to say something and see Trish far back in the cove, her hands in her pockets, looking out, still. I leave the edge, and we return to the house in the falling dusk. Later, on the phone, a friend tells me that the quake and the wave have been so powerful, the earth has been knocked a bit off its axis. I think of my elation, my bold dance along the cliffs, and then of Trish's quiet distance, and see her suddenly holding the centre for a world askew.

29 Inward

Has anyone spoken yet about inward weather? Weather turning in on itself, dropping a silver veil between you and the outside world, forcing you inward? That was today's weather.

57

Fog

The fog settled in today, obscuring the islands, but not the sound of the sea. Grey everywhere, lifting occasionally, then lowering again, a fine spray of moisture hung in the air. Day slipped away in grey.

30 Mud

Walking up to the loo-with-a-view, I hear myself cursing the mud. It's a quagmire underfoot and I've given up wearing regular boots to come and go. Wellies are the only footwear worth using. Even as I curse the mud, I withdraw the curse, thinking of the thousands of miles of quagmires, waterborne diseases and zero sanitation across the Indian Ocean rim. Mud is my only tangible connection to the plight of some millions of people swamped in agony following the tsunami…but my mind can't handle the concept and tries to screen it out.

Night Walking

When I close the curtains at dark, the rain is falling diagonally and the wind moaning around the house. I want to walk to and from the sean-nós singing at Kruger's, but am not willing to get drenched to do it. At 9.30 when it is time to go, I open the door to a quiet night, a bit misty, warm. I hardly need my winter jacket, or the wool scarf I've wrapped round my neck. I grab the small torch and set out, quickly there. As usual, I'm told that things were different, better, in the past, and I know this is so because I happened one night upon a session at Tigh Uí Chatháin in Ballyferriter where the musicians wandered in and played or didn't play on a schedule entirely their own, and occasionally someone would sing from wherever it was they were. Tonight, Kruger's is crowded. Mícheál de Mordha is the Fear an Tí, a microphone is set up for the singers, and a circle is cleared around them as they sing. The only thing left of the old way seems to be the joining in, on some of the choruses, and at the very end of the song, as if the lifted voices are helping the singer to the end of the journey and bringing him or her back into the crowd. Tonight is not a competition, although I'm told two men from Connemara have come down to sing. I've been here long enough that I know some people and they me, and almost everyone looks familiar. After a while when I turn to the bar I'm told the serving is over, and suddenly so is the night. It's 11.45. No winner. No more drinks, and everyone drifts away quickly, all of us passing through the smokers outside the door. I turn on my torch for protection against passing cars, although the larger-than-quarter moon is visible through a thin veil of clouds. I need no other light to walk by. I can see easily, even past the glare of outside lights. No one passes me on the way home. The night glows around me. The sea, after days of turmoil, has finally become a murmur again, underlying the night.

31 Last Light

On the last day of the calendar year 2004, I walk towards the huge golden orb of the sun, brilliant over Ventry in mid-afternoon, surprising after the earlier grey soak. In the fen land at the Cuan side, I cross the bridges over black water, almost blinded by the low golden light. Then I am standing in a silver-webbed world, the fen land held in a silken tension of illuminated droplets of moisture clinging to golden rushes, incandescent. I watch until the satiated sun drops behind Sliabh an Iolair and turn toward the beach, mutating each second in shades of purple and mauve, the waters of the harbour now a brilliant lunar metallic blue. The water seems so far away: one of the lowest tides of the year, perhaps. The Brent geese bob near the foreshore. I doubt if they know that they are formally classified as fish in the Episcopal Diocese of Emlach but since Christmas is over, and it's not a Friday, they're safe enough until next year's visit.

By the time I get back to Ventry, darkness is gathering and I head over the hill to greet Sandra out the west. At the top of the Clasach, I'm astonished to see bands of sunset still radiant over the islands. I bang on Sandra's door, encouraging her to come out for a stroll in the last light of the year. Eagerly, we head down the steep way to the pier and discover that the west is still filled with pale bluish light way past Tiaracht. We lean on the wall, being spattered with spray, marvelling at the light, admiring the growing starlight of the Milky Way and the many candles in the windows of the parish. We are pulsing with cosmic light and energy as the calendar year ends, inevitably and completely part of it all.

Revision

The last day of the year seems to offer all weathers, all seasons. I wake to a clearing sky, almost a patch of blue. Within minutes, rain dots the windows and the sky becomes a uniform grey. Putting a sweater on to go to town, I have to remove it because the day has grown too warm. In town, I walk through drenching rain with the hood up on my yellow slicker. By the time I return across the Clasach to Dunquin, I am blinded by the sun. At home, after running to answer the phone, I sit talking in the living room with warm sun streaming in, then unload the car watching a spectacular long sunset carmine the sky. When Trish comes by, I've lit the fire, but not the candles, and she lures me out to a twilight walk. At the Dunquin pier, we watch the light on the water and the stars appear in the sky. I find myself dizzy with motion as we walk home in the dark-that-is-not-dark. As I write, the candles have burnt out, the year passed into another, and the moon rides above Mt Eagle. I can hear a faint lift to the wind. Did I say the first green tips of montbretia have appeared, incandescent shafts of light, reminding us of spring?

January

1 **Stormy Weather**
I sit in the wicker chair watching this first day of the New Year 2005, happy not to go out for a change. Sun, hail, light, dark, all are subservient to wind, today. It batters the 'van quite violently at times but I'm an old hand and it would take a very big bang indeed to alarm me. Now it's lashing rain and the delicate pastel sky of a moment ago is no more. Quickly, the shower has passed on and the setting sun now gilds the delicate cupola of the sky. Crazily dancing willows shine jet black before a golden sky. The two young sheepdogs from the farm below me gambol and snuffle, full of young life, exuberant doggy energy in the wild windy afternoon. I feel my face crease with silent laughter at their antics and recall the Buddhist 'inner smile' and all the unexpectedly easy and pleasant ways to practice this. Much later, putting these notes on email, I am glad to have spent all this day content at home, watching the weather, resting in a friendly silence with Sooki.

Azure

I look out the window and see the windsock at Farranfore stretched out stiff and full beside us, and the plane takes off into gale force winds. We rise above the clouds and suddenly are in an azure sky. When I was a girl, I loved the books of Walter Farley whose subject was always horses. Among the books, my favourite was one called Island Stallion *in which a boy, Alec, and a horse, Flame, are marooned together on an island. I loved this book with an almost erotic love, and the island in it was called Azure Island for the colour of the sea around it. Tonight, I recognize azure in the sky. A pure, tender blue, it holds just a hint of green. As we fly east, I watch it at the edge of the clouds, and see the band of colour change into a blue rainbow, azure fading into indigo fading into violet, three strips of colour above the tops of the clouds which are not quite white or quite blue, but faintly brushed with a colour slightly deeper than fresh cream, with the merest hint of rose. Inside the plane, laminated cards with photographs of food for sale are being distributed, and then the food. The man at the end of my row orders a cappuccino. The flight attendant announces a lottery for charity. Estée Lauder cosmetics and discount train tickets from Stansted into London can be purchased. None of this is as real to me as the sky outside the window, a sky I cannot touch or feel, but which I drink in, more nourishment than any food from carts passing through the aisles inside the plane.*

2 Energy

There's a certain kind of chiaroscuro which, when combined with moving water, makes it easy to see energy in motion rather than separate forms of juxtaposed matter. Today's weather had this quality. Three hours on Ventry Beach was a kaleidoscopic experience wherein a perceptual difference between sun, sky, wind, water and sand was no longer a sure thing. Everything was in motion, flowing, timeless. An expert wind-surfer rode the waves all those hours like a magnificent black water bird, showing the wind in his every twist and turn of the single sail. Later on I met Glen, who excitedly brandished a weather map describing a massive low pressure system

63

south of Iceland, veering towards Donegal – that means big surf in Sligo. 'Forty-three foot waves!' he told me gleefully as if he hadn't heard anything about the tsunami throughout the week. Then I told him how Sandra had seen whales riding the surf down in Baja California. He got a kick out of that.

No Weather

After the storm and wave of Dunquin, weather in London seems hardly to exist. The days are bright, crisp. Occasionally the light lowers or rises, evidence of a cloud passing across the sun somewhere I cannot see it. Life is all internal, the weather registered through windows, of houses, of taxis, of buses. When we are outside, the weather is unobtrusive. Moving through the canyons of the city, I have no access to the wide sky. I remember a comment in a book of Margaret Atwood's, that it seems as if the air of England has been breathed in and out for centuries.

3 Blowing Hard

Everything is shaking and rattling since morning. Things go thud on the roof of the 'van every so often but nothing has fallen off so far. In the afternoon, I sat in Ashe's with Esther looking at photographs of her last year's journey deep into Niger and I was reminded again of my life in Sudan, twenty years ago. Now, feeling and listening to a ferocious southwesterly, I try to recall the sound of wind in the desert, but can't.

Bled

The blue turned to grey then bled into rain today. Soft rain, barely felt,

barely registered, but drenching. Even wet, I find the weather distant, the
sky so far away.

4 Inside Looking Out

Today I only saw the weather from inside, looking out.
Alternating sun, showers and lots of wind gathering force in the
afternoon. I was tricked by the computer: it lured me into its jaws
and the task of doing email PR for the dance book project, so that
I forgot everything else until suddenly I noticed it was pitch dark.
I ended up with a fine headache, the penalty for having ignored
myself and the environment.

Dome

The day is grey, colder than yesterday. It does seem as if there is no weather
in London, that the city exists beneath some glass dome with an artificially
produced sky like those strange places in Las Vegas where light on a ceiling
is programmed to go from dawn to dusk several times a day. Where is the
wind? Where is the touch of the weather?

5 Still Storming

It's still storming and more of the same is predicted for
tomorrow. The tide at Ballymore is deafening and the beautiful
green breaking wave that rises majestically just outside the cove
in heavy weather at a regular interval is, these days, a constant
presence.

No Weather Report Today

6 NOLLAIG na mBAN

7 Wind

I went to bed last night, The Women's Christmas, to the sound of a howling, violent wind, woke up to it again mid-morning and now, near the day's end, it is howling with even greater intensity out there, like an animal caught in a trap or a woman scorned. I laugh at my own similes! In fact, there's nothing at all like the sheer power of weather, no emotion or physical feeling that can describe the awesome force it can display. This week, US Secretary of State Colin Powell described the Southeast Asian tsunami as the most devastating force he had witnessed in his life; that's a considerable and considered statement from the ex-army general involved in Operation Desert Storm in the Gulf War some years ago.

Back

Late last night after Trish left, I went outside to feel the air. The rain had stopped for the moment, the front door was sheltered from the wind. I walked out past the edge of the house and stepped into the wind, turned to face it, let it wash over me, my hair streaming loose behind me. Closed my eyes. Stood there. Home.

8 Desire

In the late afternoon I called in to say hello to Bina, near now to the end of her life. In the past month her illness has accelerated rapidly, visibly. She told me she misses the fresh air. So I hugged her gently and promised to bring wind and fresh air to visit her soon again.

Spring Sills

Outside the storm rages, wind punches the house, rain clatters against the windows. Inside on my windowsills I have spring. Last year's bulbs have come back on their own. One faint yellow daffodil and the grape hyacinths bloom in the kitchen. In the back bedroom, I open the curtains to a single blue iris, iris reticulata. I was once sent a gift of three hundred bulbs of these delicate flowers, and I planted them in descending pools down the slope beyond the river house and into the field below. This year's snowdrops are coming on in the bedroom too, and in the living room, paperwhite narcissus raise tightly packed buds to the light. It seems colder than it has been so far this winter, but these flowers hold reminders of longer days and warmth to come. And outside my door, the primroses continue to bloom, as they have been since I moved here in November.

9 Frayed

I can't remember how many days of non-stop wind – gale or storm force – have been battering my tin can home side-on to the southwesterly. My nervous system, as well as the tin can, is getting a bit frayed. Even Sooki was pretty spooked last night! I walked around Burnham Wood in the warm blowing gale this afternoon, glad of a certain quietness inside the wood and the luxurious smell of leaf mold.

Captive

It is late night, and I have just been outside. The night is immensely dark, with stars fleetingly visible between the passing clouds. The wind continues, slightly muted from its earlier force. Although I've been back from London three days, I've not yet been for a walk. I scuttle from car to house, or front door to shed, grasping whatever thing has caused me to be outside – the basket of laundry, the bag of birdseed, the stack of peat. Each of these nights, before I sleep, I think 'tomorrow I will finally go for a walk, a long walk', but the unpredictable pelting rain has kept me inside. I build a good fire, I read, I write and make notes, I dream deeply, but I am yeaning for movement. No matter what, tomorrow I go out.

10 Apprehension

Today dawned sunny and silent. I walked on Ventry Beach, thrilled to feel warm sunlight on my face again, relieved to be out and about in relative calm. My bubble burst in the afternoon when I heard the extreme weather alert for tonight. Time to pull the plug on the computer.

Walking

I finally got outside today for more than a few minutes. A day so bright and full of wind that I hung sheets flapping madly on the line then headed off for Clogher Beach. A fortuitous stop that turned into tea with Claire saved me from one squall, and the only moisture after that was spray from the waves breaking over the cliffs. I stood to watch the waves roll in, banks of huge walls of water curling over the tops of the headlands, followed by swells – a respite – then more giants. I could not help but contemplate their size and think of tsunamis, but even this failed to dampen the exhilaration their explosions always cause in me. Though I walked through the late afternoon, sunset turning into dusk, bars of light radiating from the sun before it settled behind the Great Blasket and the offshore banks of clouds, I saw so little. Turned inward, thoughts whirling, conversations racing through my head, occasionally I would remind myself to look, to notice, and then fall back inside again. Only the waves were big enough to call me out of myself, and it was for that calling, that contact, that I was yearning. Some grounding here was lost to London. I know patience will find it again, but in the meantime, whirling, whirling.

11 WIND

12 Return

Having abandoned ship as Tuesday's storm gathered to a southwesterly Force 10 by midday, I returned twenty-four hours later to a sunny calm, no damage and Derrick, my insouciant neighbour, who grinned and said he had read for half an hour and then slept peacefully for a further nine, untouched and untroubled by wind or weather. Taking advantage of a fine, breezy day and the fact that I had evacuated most of my gear, I set to and thoroughly spring-cleaned the 'van. It's an ill wind that blows no good, so they say.

Rose

What wakes me this morning is the silence, the absence of wind. After yesterday's fierceness, wind to knock one over, wind to punch the house to shaking, wind to howl incessantly, the silence is almost loud. The day passes in and out of sun. Rain patters against the windows. The usual January wind comes in, strong but almost mild in comparison to yesterday. I do not manage to get outside, but at sunset I look out and see the sun glowing beyond the Great Blasket, with a thin band of pure rose undercoating the dark clouds stretching to the south. It is a beautiful colour. I watch it for a long time.

13 Drop

Sometime in the night the temperature dropped so sharply that I got up, donned fleece, long-johns and woolly socks before getting back into bed like the Michelin Man. Guess what I couldn't find after the big spring-clean? The cap for the hot-water bottle! And then, right on cue, the electricity quit so that I couldn't resort to either the electric blanket or the plug-in radiator. At least the sun was shining by morning but it was still bloody cold.

Jade Again

Lured outside by the morning's sun, I walked to Claire's house to give her my notes on her thesis. The day was cold, the wind brisk. When I rounded the corner of the house, I saw the Sound streaked with sunlight to a rich and tropical pale jade green, so strange a colour in the cold. Yet as the day turned dark and even colder, the sea held the green, more milky without the sunlight. Even into dusk tonight, there was green.

14 Torrential Rain

The rain started around noon and poured down torrentially all day. Now the wind is rising towards gale force again. I think of my promise to Bina, who died early today, that I would bring the wind with me next time I visited.

Pelting

The window I leave open for the mail has been banging erratically all night, nudged and jostled by the wind, the wind that has come up again, howling and punching at the house. Outside, it swirls around even my protected entrance, lifting my hair, sucking at the door when I open it. Earlier today, the rain suddenly fell pelting in diagonal sheets, and then continued to fall. It's falling still. I've latched the window. No mail again till Monday.

15 Pause

The day was full of pause: moments, here and there, when people were unsure, needed to gather themselves, to weep, to console one another, to go blank, take a break from tension, emotion, other people. There was a pause in the current weather pattern too: wind dropped, sun shone, rain backed off for the day, for the graveyard. Later, walking the beach towards the huge orb of the afternoon sun, very low, still, in the January sky, I wondered what it will be like to dissolve, at the end, into unspecified energy. That thought reminded me of my friend Laurie: his Aquarian mind, his closeness to weather, his manliness, his poems, his liking of a dangerous edge, his two great hounds sprawled in front of his stove, piles of books erupting all over the incredibly messy caravan, marine delights left in my bucket when he came in from fishing, the two big boxes of mackerel we salted for the coming winter, forgetting how erratic the power could be in Ballymore. Laurie died and I didn't find out until half a year later, hadn't even known where he was. He had left Ballymore without a word and hadn't announced where he was heading for. Typical Laurie Boyd. I reckon I spent more hours of my life with him than anyone else except my father. I still spend time with him, just in a different way. There was a pause in our relationship until I understood this.

Dunquin Tsunami

A friend calls midday asking for newspapers as her neighbour's house has flooded. I gather them up and go over to find a most puzzling set of conditions. Water is running down her boreen, both from the house uphill and from the road that goes up the Ceathrú. But across her field is flattened grass and the edge of a tongue of debris. Some thick wall of water passed here, then ended. Consultations with the neighbours reveal that water passed on to Máire Treasa's and even down to Molly's. As Colm and Carmel are at Bina's funeral, we cannot check to see what happened to them. Theories abound. Did a blockage form in the drainage ditch, gather water behind it, and then burst, spewing water below? Did last night's fierce wind drive the pelting rain through the stone walls of the house? Did the disconnected drainspout concentrate water onto the stones and into the house? I bail water from the road and suggest sandbags to re-route it. Things are moved out of the house into the sun, and then back in when rainshowers arrive. The dryer goes full out. One time, returning to my house in the lower down but dry Baile na Rátha, I look back to the Ceathrú and see a rainbow arched over it. Glory made from moisture.

16 Reflection

I walk across the field before the sun climbs over Fenton's Point. Across the big front window of Paddy's caravan, the crimson strip behind gilded rain-filled clouds is perfectly reflected. Far off on the horizon, the silver line glistens below purple hills. Far above rain clouds, a cold sapphire sky.

Clear Mornings and Afternoon Rain

Just after I declare to a friend I am going out for a walk on this grey but dry day, the rain begins to fall. I look out to the sea where moments ago I saw the islands, and now see nothing but a wall of rain, no blue beyond it, or any sort of lightening to the sky. I should by now have absorbed the winter wisdom of morning sun, afternoon rain, but it seems I have not. I still move slowly into the day, drinking coffee, laying the evening's fire, sitting to the slow reading of the morning book. Often, I look out to a bright day, sun streaming down. Then I think how nice it would be to be outside walking, and plan to go later in the afternoon, sunset and dusk my favourite time. This despite six winters here, day after day of clear mornings and afternoon rain.

17 Listening to the Wind

I sit, eyes closed, in the wicker chair, wrapped in the blue shawl, listening to the wind. It gusts and rolls, then dies down awhile only to pounce suddenly again, like a child playing hide and seek or a cat playing with string. Today the wind is coursing over the tops of the caravans, at the level of the dancing willows. This morning, all sound below wind level is sharply defined: a bird chortles in the willows, it's spring, it's spring; a hen clucks busily under the caravan; the cockerel crows every few minutes in the back yard but it sounds far away. I am warmed by the sun streaming in on my left side, the stove on my right and Sooki curled up in my blue-clad lap. Listening to the wind.

Sun Stretches

The wind churns the sea to whitecaps and spume, then the sun stretches out to touch them. White, bright white, on winter green dances across the Sound all day. Waves break voluptuously, splaying over rocks in the slow-motion of distance, fanning out to catch the light.

18 Bluster

Today was the day for busting out, breaking the cabin fever, offering oneself to the wind. Wendy came and we walked the beach, sand-blasted, laughing, both of us glad to be out in sun and wind, in motion. At one point, at the first bridge, the wind blew so hard that it held us up when we let ourselves fall back into it. I say to Wendy that it is like the Harmattan, except it's biting cold, not searing hot. Spray is flying up high all along the shore. We meet John who is thrilled with a shell he has found, like the fingernail of a newborn child, translucent, tiny, he himself like a child in the telling, the showing, the wonder at this natural world we are part of. Then we lunched with Mike, Camilla and Boris, big bowls of meaty Spanish soup, watching the bluster below rushing into the long beach at An Mhuiríoch. Then I walked back home over Mám na Gaoithe in wind and sunlight, glad to be out in the day, away from the cabin.

Tonnta Móra agus Sneachta

I look out this morning early and gasp at the waves coming huge and white-capped across the Sound. I am filled, as I always am, with exhilaration at the sight, wanting to race down to the headland, to be closer, to participate in the energy. On this day though, I must be in town for Irish class, and leave the waves behind, but not the wind and the weather that helps make them. In town, a rainbow. Later, crossing Connor Pass, snow and then fierce hail along Brandon Bay. As I pass back through Ventry, perfect veils of spray skeining back from perfect curves of waves, an ominous warship anchored offshore. Home, I don't even change from my city skirt, but pull on socks, wellingtons, hat and gloves, racing out the door for the cliffs. At Faill Cliath, the entire cove is churned to white, and as a wave breaks, scatters of spray are sent whirling into the air as if some giant child below were at play with bubbles. I twirl and twirl again in the wind, laughing as it nearly knocks me over. I stand a while watching out to sea, anticipating the rise and break of the largest waves when they meet the offshore rocks. As the light falls and I turn to go, I'm left with the image of wave after wave meeting Carraig Salach, fanning high and white across the storm green sea, higher than the highest cliff, across the dusk grey sky.

19 Turnabout

The temperature shot up overnight. There was no need to light a morning fire, or even to plug in the radiator to erase the usual morning damp feeling. Now, late in the evening, the wind is gathering force again and it's blowing a damp, misty wind.

A White Accumulation

I look out today at fog, through windows caked with salt from the recent storms. Although I know it is not snowing, the streaking on the windows and the mist in the air combine to make it seem so. Even the bushes dotted with moisture across the way look frosted. I grew up with snowstorms, and know the look of them. As the day passes, I am amazed to see the fields still green, and the roofs without a white accumulation.

20 No Weather Report Today

Trína Chéile

The day starts with me fumbling through the curtained living room to answer the phone, and does not seem to change in character as it unfolds. Like the wind that's blowing from all different directions, the day seems to go the same way: static on the phone; a line that won't connect to the internet; a Mr addressed as a Ms; a distant friend needing her messages checked; a sick and panicked friend nearby; the eircom robot. When I finally make it to Trish's, she calms me with good strong coffee and conversation that has to do with work. I leave her house at peace, but soon am whirling again. Dingle lunchtime presents me with one 'Be back at...' sign after another, and I wander the streets with tasks undone. Another steadying with a bowl of seafood chowder at Goat Street Café, but then more whirling as I must bare my soul and finances to the bank so I can open an account and allow them to use my money for their profit. All this time of moving my life from one country to another has been rife with what seems one invasion after another. Questions from strangers half my age about finances. The demand to see papers from a time of utter turmoil in my life. Dreams that have me back in my home of almost thirty years, leaving me disoriented upon waking, and gnawing the inside of my cheek. It is late night now, with not a hint of wind outside. I can only hope to absorb some of the calm.

21 Silence

Angelika walks the beach with me in the morning. As we talk and laugh together, I realize that for the first day in ages there's no wind, only silence except for our voices and the swish and wash of the tide. Ange is going to be a dive master by the year's end. She lauds the value of learning the skill in cold Irish waters where one must focus completely on safety and technical knowledge. We look at the water longingly, almost ready to throw off our clothes and run in. But we don't. Not today. Maybe tomorrow.

Breathe

As the weather stills, so do I, able to move through the day with a quiet heart, a relief after yesterday's turmoil. I wake to silence and milky haze. The afternoon produces brief bars of sunlight in the front room, although the top of Mt Eagle remains in deep mist. High clouds move overhead at a stately pace. I breathe again.

22 Blue Green Scene

Out at Coumeenoole, the ocean is milky green. We walk up the headland, muddy and bejewelled with lichens and mosses in vibrant greens and reds, tiny, easily unnoticed as we concentrate on solid footfall to round the narrow, crumbling path over the hilltop. A single gannet scans close to shore, gleaming white over green water, its black wingtips like sentinels. On the other side, the water is blue and the sky is streaked an amazing sapphire. A black cormorant flies a hair's breadth over the ocean. The weather may be clearing from the southwest, the sun is threatening to come out. We walk around the headland and down to the beach. There, the water is mercurial, glass-like, full of shining light and, where the surf breaks, it dreams a tropical turquoise. The sun declines to show its face, content to tantalize occasionally from behind its veil of cloud.

Reading

I am reading Bruce Chatwin, and I come across a description of rain that, in its aptness and precision, makes me smile: '…and raindrops pecked against the leaded panes'.

23 Sun Day

Sun Day! Shining, brilliant, in a brisk high-pressure airflow, it's a day to be out and about, *ag bothántaíocht*, visiting in the district. I leave my own district and head to the western world of Dún Chaoin where I meander with Shelley, gazing out over the big blue, the islands, the coves. We are thrilled with ourselves, with the sun, the cold, the brilliance of the day, life itself. At half past four, the moon rises behind us over Sliabh an Iolair, close to fullness, a filigree silver disc ascending the blue. I meet Peadar just before the sun falls into the ocean behind the islands. Then the world turns orange, red, rose, like a filter. Behind us, under the moon, the sky is shimmering lilac. Bathed in light and cold air, we stand silent

and still on this green-blue planet, spinning dizzily in the galaxy
between flaming sun and silver moon.

Moonrise to Glowing

*Today feels almost too blue, deep blue cloudless sky, deep blue ocean, clear air.
As I walk on Béal Bán, I watch the moon rise near full above Mt Brandon,
lighting, it almost seems, the faint dusting of snow there to moonlight too. It
is later though, that the true glory begins, as the moon catches light and the
sun sets casting rose gold across Dunquin. I am walking from the Ceathrú
down to the cuaisín and across the cliffs to home in Baile na Rátha as the
sun sinks into the clearly defined dark line of the horizon. Being too low at
that moment, I do not actually see it go, but watch a small gilded cloud that
Trish later tells me hovered just over Tiaracht, echoing its tip. It is when I
turn toward the east that I am stopped in my tracks, seeing the now fully lit
moon above the curve of the Clasach as it glides into Mt Eagle, resting in
a sky of rose mauve underlit with a blue to pierce the heart. As I watch, the
colours do not so much change as intensify, become complex, approach some
sort of essence of the colour they are. If I turn to the west, I see a flaming
sky, oranges and ambers and reds, the black silhouettes of rocks. But to the
east all is silver and calm. Utter intensifying peace.*

24 Beams, Cross-Fades and Full-On Spotlights

I wake to a tortoiseshell sky, mottled and dappled by layers
of cloud forms, gigantic filters carefully choreographed throughout
the day by some wild lighting designer in the sky. Beams, cross-
fades and full-on spotlights. Wow! That aerial technician must have
a really sophisticated console. We go to the west before Ange leaves,

to complete our ritual. Up again over Dún Mór, marvelling at immense bands of jade, turquoise, blue and indigo water, the huge tortoiseshell sky, the Scellig Rocks sharply wrought under beams of mercurial light. I think of Oisín on his white steed disappearing with Niamh past the Scelligs, away to the Other World. Today, the birds are really having fun riding the thermals: a chough executes rolls and half-rolls, laughing haw-haw high above us as we enjoy the display. We arrive back at base as glittering sunshine breaks through the cloud cover over Coumeenoole. Grinning like mad things, we rush down to the cove, pulling off our clothes, baring our skin to the warm spring sunshine, out of the wind now between high cliffs, and run into the silver green waves, yelling, laughing, capering around. This is IT! We did it! Hurray! We've done the ritual!

Baile an tSléibhe

In the afternoon, I am walking in the place I hope soon to be my home. I listen to tales of salt and wind and plants that do not survive. Yet I look out to the far mountains and watch coins of light gild them, watch their silhouettes emerge from the haze, think of the names of blues and blue-greys and purples. The lawn is scattered with patches of daffodils rising even into this cold winter day. Across, on the lower flanks of Cruach Mhárthain, a rainbow glows. As I leave, the sky is a mass of clouds tinted bruised peach and apricot. I anticipate the moonrise and a sky of bright patches filled with stars.

25 Skiving

When the sun fills the 'van it feels delicious, so I don't

bother making a fire, yet there's a dampness when it clouds over that makes me shiver. Two daffodils are budding and, as the song says, 'there's such an air of spring about it'. I have plans to work in the afternoon but feel disjointed, *trína chéile* and, as if to underline this, Wendy shows up begging a beach walk and we end up skiving off for the whole afternoon out on the road from Dunbeg to Slea Head and back, in sweet spring air, in that endless panorama of ocean, sky and islands, so vibrant in texture, colour and movement that we're a bit high, capricious and skitting like youngsters together. There are no cars on the road, a great trait of this early hour of the year but we meet Wendy's old neighbour who greets her most cordially indeed. She reflects how kind and friendly the people out here were when she lived at Fahan. The Lighting-Techie-in-the-Sky is doing a different show today. He dropped the tortoiseshell effect and has gone instead for a sort of pearly grey tempera underlay, through which he points his spotlights brilliantly into a silvered milky-green ocean below. Peach, apricot and lavender filters are muted, paled somehow by the underlay, although technically, shouldn't the tempera underline the light, bring it into sharper relief? Maybe it has something to do with today's full moon, or, more likely, a high humidity factor at sea is thinning the atmospheric texture somehow. I know there won't be a dramatic sundown today, so much as a paling-awayness of light until no distinction remains between material objects. Later, when the full moon has set in evening darkness, I'm sure it will have clouded over, masking her face, if my technical guess above is correct!

Moonlight Laundry

It is the night of the full moon, and I've left the laundry outside on the line. I've never done this before, left clothes out all night. I was late hanging them today, and when I went to check at dusk, they were not dry, and the moon was rising huge through the clouds over the curve of the Clasach. I thought what it might be to leave the clothes out to absorb the light of the moon. My nightdress and some pillowcases. What dreams might I have? This night is mostly still, yet every once in a while a rogue wind appears. At first a soft sound in the distance, it moves suddenly closer, like a fast train passing through, brushing the house and rattling the windows, then is gone. I almost feel I should race out and take things in. But I don't.

26 So Much Moon

Couldn't sleep, so much moon. Slumbering and shifting under its pull, like the very world itself, I finally got up and padded around for a while, admiring the great silver disc in an indigo sky hanging somewhere over Ventry way. The 'van was suffused with a slightly neon glow, an almost blue tint to the muffled whiteness of the moonlight, muffled, that is, compared to the sharpness of tone and texture of the orb itself. Engaged by indigo, I returned to bed and was surprised to register the hour as 07.29. My God! Morning already. Not yet, I decided. But half an hour later, the silver and indigo world was gone, fled away, despite my declaration.

Fire Light

What is it about the moon that makes us crazy? Where did loony begin? Although the day holds fine weather, I am dithering about, twirling from one thing to another. I wake half an hour before my alarm is set to go off, wondering why. I raise my head and see the Sound an unfamiliar blue. A smoky blue, I think, and it proves prophetic. All day the phone rings with arcane demands, and unexpected people drop by. Between, I dash in and out with laundry, carefully hanging my moonlight nightdress behind the bedroom door. I don't brush my teeth until four in the afternoon, or take a shower till then either. I've had clothes on over my other nightgown, and hope no one suspects. Sometime in all this, I burn the toast, causing the fire alarm to screech. I press its red button, but it will not stop. I stand underneath it with my hands over my ears, then race around the house opening windows to let the smoke out. The wind catches a tiny pot with a bouquet of feathers, flinging it out the window. Barefoot, I go out to the lawn, find the pot with its lip broken, and the feathers in disarray. I gather them up, and wonder about this day. I cancel an afternoon appointment in Tralee.

After the fire is laid, the house vacuumed, and I'm showered, I begin to think calm might be restored. I eat yogurt and borrow a scone from the birds' supply. I finish an email begun sometime in the morning. I call my mother who isn't home, and then take a nap. I put vegetables in to roast for dinner, and just as they come out, go to fetch the few things I've put in the dryer. When I go out, I look up to the Ceathru where I see what seems an immense fire burning, flames leaping up from a contained sphere, and smoke pouring down to the west. A wind is coming up, and I am uncertain what to do, whom I might call.

I drop the laundry basket and go inside. Somehow the emergency number seems extreme. I try Anna's thinking someone will be home, but the line is busy after several tries. I ring a friend on the Ceathru, but he is not *answering. I go outside to look again, and the fire seems larger, glowing in the night. I try Mags and am told by the eircom robot that I have not left a message, because either I am speaking too softly or the line is too bad. This is the same eircom robot who insists he cannot understand me when I phone to report static on my line. I finally ring the Dingle Garda Station to say there's a fire. When asked, I say I'm not sure whether houses are involved, as I am in Baile na Rátha, and cannot tell from here.*

Then I finally do what I should have done in the first place, which is get in my car and go up to see. It is a gorse fire on Graig, enormous, perhaps even involving the bales of silage stored up there or the trash that's been dumped, but it threatens no houses. I've of course forgotten my mobile, and as I turn around quickly to return home to phone Dingle, I see flashing blue lights coming down the Clasach, two cars at least. I meet the first of them at Kruger's corner, but do not think they would respond to my flagging them down to say Never Mind. At home I ring and get no answer. Has the entire Dingle Garda responded? What crimes might go untended while they watch the gorse blaze? I do reach a garda eventually, and apologize. He reassures me I did the right thing, but I can feel my face now ablaze, and I feel like a fool.

I ring Trish, who cannot keep from laughing, and she laughs me out of my chagrin. Still. It's a good thing I'm leaving the parish shortly, and moving over the mountain. Is this moon madness? I know the gorse is burnt this time of year. I've been here. How did I not, in my innings and outings manage to notice a fire that had been burning all the afternoon? Even Trish in far off Ballymore knew about it. Ah, news of the parish today, me outside it and in it, under the light of the moon and the glow of the fire.

27 Immanence

Half past five in the evening and such an extraordinary sky! It's becoming rather cold in a light, almost imperceptible airstream. Although the upper sky is still bright and clear, immense, dense cloud formations are extending in different directions across the lower sky as if a great dragon were lurking behind the Connor Pass, blowing smoke towards the west and southwestern world. Brandon looks like a low hill under the great dragon's breath. Above the massive grey-white cloud is a well of powder-blue and overall, a lavender hue. The smoky spume covers Dingle Harbour all the way out past the Blaskets, masses of steel-grey and purple-grey condensation racing away to the southwest and, in the distance, Iveragh and the Reeks look rather small, squashed even, the Valentia lighthouse winking away in the indigo. Above the mountains, a long thin strip of tangerine sunset. Above the Scellig Rocks, way out on the middle of the horizon line, there's another skylight, the colour of ripe pineapple and, overall, in the immense upper reaches, that powder-blue turning mauve. The only sound is the gentle swish of the tide and cars going west after the day in Dingle or Tralee. A dog barks, a tractor descends the hill above Ballymore townland, colours deepen and darken. Six o'clock. Time to light the fire.

Weather Eye

I wake slowly this morning, lying for a long while dozing with my eyes closed, trying to recapture just-past-full-moon dreams. From time to time I watch the colour on my eyelids changing from a deep, almost black, indigo through shades to a bright red as the sun breathes in and out, pulsing dark

85

and bright. From this I know it's a clear day, with clouds passing smoothly across the sun. I think of John Berger and a book of his with one of my favourite titles: I Send You This Cadmium Red. *Cadmium red, he observes in it, is the colour you see on your closed eyelids when the sun is full out.*

28 Rosy Glow

Dingle Harbour, bathed in a rosy glow, looks still, seems windless, but the breeze whispers silver atop rosy rippling water. A cold, monotonal sunset today. Sometime around nine in the evening, a pale yellow moon is suddenly revealed between masses of indigo cloud. I'm aware of intense light, day and night, night and day, since last week's full moon, although the sky holds masses of low-lying dense cloud.

Ruffled

Wind returns, water ruffled.

29 Strange Sky

The ocean is shining this morning. Not just the silver line but great orbs of light permeating black water under a cumulus-laden sky. Is it particularly cold today or am I febrile? I shiver and my nose is hot and dry like a sickly dog. In the afternoon, the sky still thickens like a ripening bruise but above all that swish and swirl, a cupola of eggshell blue delicately crossed with rose-pink lines suggests a cold weather story at odds with the deepening bruise clouds below. What a strange sky. Why doesn't it rain? These clouds have been visibly accumulating for days yet it feels damn cold, looks cold too. Or is it just me?

Glow

After the fierce winds of the past few weeks, I'm finding the silence almost eerie. Today I wake to butter yellow light stretched across the green fields, touching Eibhlín's house in Baile Ícín, a house where I spent six ambrosial summer weeks wrapped in a strange elation. In the late afternoon, I go across the Clasach to Ventry to sample the light there. Walking on Ventry Beach, I look up at the house that will soon, I hope, be mine, thinking this will be my beach now. People speak of missing the sunsets on this side of the mountain, but tonight's sky leaves little to be desired. Random sunlight marks the hills, and in the midst of clouds, the sky repeats the azure I saw when I flew to London, complete with bands of lavender and rose above. As I walk, I stop frequently. The tide is low and the bog revealed. The water is hardly a murmur. I pick up a scallop shell marked with runic tracks, and then a large spiral shell faintly coloured green. Other small shells go into my pockets, and three feathers I imagine might be from the Brent geese floating offshore. Then one rectangular flat green stone. I walk slowly, turning to look up at the house, looking across the landscape. Looking. A mist has settled on Cruach Mhárthain, and I drive into it coming toward Slea Head on the way back home. The end of the bay and the sea are shining, a metallic beaten pewter. Long luminescent ovals glow on the water from no light source I can discover. The mist breathes across the islands, obscuring them. For a moment, the entire scene becomes a watercolour of breathless delicacy. Around Slea Head it lifts, and I am looking at the familiar curve of Dún Mór, and the cliffs of Dún Chaoin, and the sea.

30 Flat

I thought this Sunday was dead flat: flat grey sky, no wind, not much colour anywhere. Then I thought, better check that out properly before I write such a flat report. So I did and just as well, because I saw a sky banded in pale blues and greys, reaching up out of a calm ocean, a trawler heading west in seeming slow-motion, so sharply defined it resembled a detail in a dream. Everything is wet this morning as if a heavy mist came and went overnight. That sky is still moisture-laden but no sign of proper rainfall. But it's not really the weather that's flat: it's me. I'm energetically flat and it is manifested physically, as usual. No inspiration. I know this kind of weather and I don't like it much.

Anticyclone

I wake this morning to a featureless sky, white, no definition in the clouds. Indoors for much of the day, I see little of the weather, but rather feel it, pressing against me, against the windows and walls of the buildings that shelter me. Two days ago I read about an anticyclone stationary offshore. A huge mass of still air rare in winter, it diverts the storms that would be rolling in this time of year, sending them north or south, or maybe even above, but not here. If I look out to sea, I don't see, as I usually do, the next hour's weather coming fast. Nothing is moving under this blanket of sky except tiny windlets, as if the air is trying to remember how to dance.

31 Prelude

It feels like spring this morning, a soft day, no cold there, daffodils bursting out in pale sunshine, the budding willows now soft and grey. It must be a prelude to tomorrow's performance, for tomorrow is Lá 'le Bríde, the Feast of Brigid, the first day of spring.

Primrose

It is the day before Imbolc and I have gone to cut reeds for the Brigid's Cross. Too late in the day and too tired, I do not climb to the rocks of Cruach Mhárthain, but go over to a local boreen. There I find fine reeds, tall and round, ones I know will be good for folding and making the cross. Although the morning sky was a clear blue with white clouds floating, the sky blanket has moved in again, making the afternoon dull. I bend and cut, finding pleasure in the slip of my fingers to the base of the stalk and the feel of the growing bundle of reeds in my hand. Far gold hovers on the horizon, and all around me water drops left by last night's mist-that-drenches-everything-but-is-not-rain hang suspended on the plants. As I turn for home, I pass a patch of primroses blooming, heralding tomorrow's first day of spring.

Imbolc
Spring

February

1 Lá 'le Bríde

It's Lá 'le Bríde, the first day of spring, February 1st. Actually, this is technically incorrect, because the first day of spring was known by the Celtic people as Imbolc and it was the day of the new moon, so it won't be spring until February 8th, sorry to disappoint! *'Anois teacht an Éarraigh, beidh na lae ag dul chun síneadh, is tar éis na Féile Bríde ardóigh mé mo sheol/*With the advent of spring, the days are increasing and after the Feast of Brigid I will set my course'. The old poem describes it perfectly: the days are on the increase now, it's still light well after 6 p.m. and everyone is shaking off winter sloth and hibernation and winter skin. This pretender to the first day of spring is mild, windless, tending later on towards a light drizzle. Driving back from Annascaul at lunchtime, I saw not the silver line but the whole medallion of the inlet glistening and silver between a gap in the hills, so bright I nearly ran the car into the curving ditch! Sometimes driving is a tricky business here: there're so many interesting land and seascapes, never mind weather watches, that it can be hard sometimes to watch the road!

Silhouette and Silver

Coming across the Clasach on this first of spring mornings, I pass through mist heavy enough to need the windshield wipers full on. Through the softness of the day, I see a band of light under the covering clouds, and in that band of light, the silhouette of the mountains of the Iveragh Peninsula.

93

The Macgillicuddy's Reeks are obscured, but the end toward Valentia is clear. In this light, no depth or detail is visible but the pure flow of the line of the highest ridges. I don't think I've ever seen this before, and I must keep pulling my attention back to the narrow Clasach road, reminding myself that traffic does come along here, and sheep. By the time I reach Dingle, the mist is behind me, the sun almost out. Later in the day, back in Baile na Rátha, I work at the computer, looking up finally when the light has grown dim. Out the window is a monochrome in charcoal blue, cloud, islands, fields, with the ocean silver amidst them. It is a silver so clear, the water seems almost not to exist, to be no more dense than air, the islands having taken flight in celebration, perhaps, of spring's return.

2 Glass

That anticyclone still prevails, the sky is laden yet still no rain, just light drizzle. Everything is so utterly still, the ocean like glass, the Scellig Rocks hovering on the horizon line like desert mirages. The memory of purple buttes hanging over red earth in New Mexico shimmers in my mind's eye, briefly...but the picture on this Atlantic shore is imbued with a northern coldness, despite it's being a spring day hereabouts. It is damp and I light a morning fire. Later, I picnic on Ventry Beach with Wendy, in full sunshine, for an hour. We are jolly, delighted with the day, happy with our work, happy to be here on this beach in spring sunshine.

A Day of Wonders and Galapagos Flamingo Sky
A town day. I was up in time to see the last of the rosy dawn. Staring sleepily at it, teasing my brain for what was familiar about the colour, I

94

remembered a day in the Galapagos Islands when, from the deck of a small ship, I watched a flock of pink flamingos standing against a black sand beach. I had been told their colour came from the pink of the shrimp they ate. An interesting fact, until I began to think that all the raw shrimp I'd ever seen were more blue than pink. But perhaps whatever it is that makes them pink when cooked transmutes itself to the feathers. This morning's dawn had that colour, even to its feather lightness as it rested on the horizon.

When I crossed the Clasach not much later, all of the water was a stippled sheen aglow with random shining patches of light. A dream image, though I was awake. The bay in Dingle was smooth as a lake, and floating on it was a tubby green and yellow boat that looked for all the world like Noah's Ark. I expected to see the necks of a pair of giraffes rising from it. Or flamingos at least. Then on Connor Pass, the lake nestled into a cup on the side of Mt Brandon was a shining mirror, still, holding a perfect reflection of the slopes around it.

I pulled over opposite the turn for Loch an Dúin, to write this down. The wonders were piling into the day one after another, and I feared forgetting. I realized, with some amazement, it was not yet 10 a.m. In Tralee, a friend had returned safely from months and half the world away, another wonder. Then the day bogged down in bureaucracy and the world narrowed. But I walked in my front door holding a massive bouquet of bright yellow daffodils, and some white tulips.

3 Rose Pink Cheer

I spent this damp – though dry – day inside in the theatre office, unable to warm my feet. The cold is inside me and only raw sunshine can warm me up properly. At dusk, under the cloud-laden indigo sky, a beautiful strip of deep rose pink was the addendum to a cold day.

Dull

I could not tell you what the weather was today. I spent the day on the phone talking to people in offices, probably without windows. Often I was not even talking to a person, but a mechanized voice that assured me my call was important. If I raised my eyes from my notes, even if it was to the window, I did not focus outside. I think it was a dull day, but perhaps the sun shone at some point. I do remember that last night the stars were brilliant enough to take my breath away. Today though passed in a blur. At some point it was wet. I can hear now the wind, and the sound of fine rain hitting the window. I realize that most people live like this, not much noticing the weather except as it influences whatever plans they might have. Most of their lives in offices without windows, or with windows that do not open. A dull day. More, a day that I was dull.

4 Wet Day

Wet, cold and frustrating: that was Friday, 4th February. No point in trying to dress it up. A bad hair day sort of day. Thank God it's Friday.

Cloud Cover

It is rare not to see at least the faint outline of the Great Blasket three miles offshore. Its familiar sleeping-beast shape seems integral to this place. I cannot even imagine the strangeness of looking out and finding only open sea, yet this morning the island is gone. A curtain of white lies offshore today, with just the faintest tip of Beginish visible to indicate the possible presence of land. When this happens, I often imagine the island to have gone walkabout, roaming the sea, visiting other shores, perhaps no more than stretching out of sight of human eyes. The island, instead of inhabiting geological time, its modifications infinitely slow, might shift to another, shiver and dance and shed, trusting the cloud to cover.

5 Relief

What a relief to wake to gorgeous spring sunshine after yesterday's miserable pall which I thought would continue through the weekend. Overnight, the cold front came in and that strange anticyclone is now over. However beautiful those skies of the past fortnight, they have been disturbingly odd, something vaguely not right for this environment. Sandra thinks this is why we've been feeling disjointed, because the pressure has been so unnatural for the time of year. So, today, we celebrated by strolling the district from Baile na Rátha to Clogher and back, with Tinka at heel. I never used to go for walks in that district unless I went with my brother Peadar, not knowing anyone else there. Going solo, I'd never think of walking around a district like that; I'd go uphill or along the beaches. So it is a friendly thing for me to walk around a neighbourhood with a resident friend, meeting neighbours and the odd fellow stuck in a rut in a Suzuki van up a boreen like old Pat Sullivan today. When Sandra comes to live in her future home in Baile an tSléibhe, it will be lovely to stroll around the trails and villages there too, something I haven't done much since Peadar moved from nearby Cill Uru. Having felt so out of joint, so disconnected with the society last Thursday night at the Blue Zone, it is a second relief to notice in myself such ease and relaxedness on a strolling Saturday out the west. This is my nature, my real environment, a country woman with a penchant for amateur drama, which I can't quite transfer to the ever-so-subtly charged ambience of a blues bar, run by a Frenchman, in a small port town in the southwest of Ireland, full of small and middle-sized fish in what would quickly become a rather stagnant pond were it not for the blessing of frequently violent weather. Oh là là! the relief of it all.

Sun with Clouds

I've been thinking about the little symbols in the newspaper, the ones that are a graphic for the coming weather. In all the years I've been in Ireland, I've only once seen just the sun. The sun does often appear, but with a variety of clouds hovering nearby. Sometimes the sun is nearly obscured by them. At other times, they're scattered about more loosely. It's a bold weather predictor that wouldn't put at least a tiny cloud lurking somewhere, just in case. Today's weather was typical in the west. Clear blue sky with bright small clouds was succeeded by ferocious squalls, the rain – almost hail – falling straight, falling slanted, falling up in certain places. Sometimes the sun stayed out for these, glinting the rain. The sky would be blue out to sea, but a glance back at the mountains might show dark clouds looming. In the midst of this, Trish and I managed to walk from Baile na Rátha to Clogher Beach, getting wet only once, and that briefly. A good weather day. Sun with clouds.

6 Dawn

I woke to a rosy gilded dawn this calm, cold Sunday and, half an hour later, when the sun made it over the hill above the cuaisín, the red cover on my bed was streaked with bars of golden light.

Above

> Above the Clasach:
> a silver cloud against the
> rose lavender sky.

7 Early to Rise

Early to rise is a good policy these days. I witnessed another coloured dawn today, welcome after such an intensely cold, but sparkling, starry night. By half past nine, the colour parade was all over and a wet, squally day ensued. February.

Weather and Words

> Tell me
> language does not come
> from landscape,
> and I will answer you
> that it does,
> will call your attention
> to the clouds
> that soften the hillcurves,
> and say to you séimhiú.

Then I will take you
to a mountaintop to watch
coins of sunlight speed across the land
changing fields below from dark to light,
and mention urú.
Will you turn to me then
and say 's ea?

8 Fair Day

If the dawn didn't serve up a palette of spectacular colours for breakfast today, it was, nonetheless, a lovely spring day with gentle sunshine coyly peeping through cloud, glittering on raindrops clinging to the yellow gas cylinders outside my door, slanting low and pale into the 'van. The warbling and twittering of busy birds so audioscaped that hour that I caught myself holding my breath, listening, coffee cup in hand while Sooki sat on the doorstep, twitching, smacking her lips.

Gaofar

This morning it seemed yesterday's edge of cold had receded, but by late afternoon the light turned dark grey and mist settled in. By the time I returned to Dunquin from town, the sky was overcast entirely and the wind was biting. Last night in Irish class, we discussed the weather as we always do. News of rain in Dingle was a surprise to Úna who had spent her day elsewhere and in the sun. When I mention 'gaofar', everyone looked puzzled until I added, 'i nDún Chaoin.' This caused a laugh and the comment that it was always 'gaofar i nDún Chaoin.' And it is. Tonight I

100

can hear the wind rustling about outside. My house faces roughly southwest, built so that a wall extends to shelter the front door from the prevailing winds. When I walk past the corner, I am usually buffeted sideways. My hair, that I thought securely clipped, goes flying, and I readjust my estimate about the warmth of the day. I'd hardly have it any other way, though, as I love the wind, become a bit uncomfortable if it disappears for a few days. The new house I hope to move to is said to be very windy – ana-ghaofar, the word itself a wind – but I suspect it will just feel familiar, wind wrapping round me as I walk out the door.

9 Burning

The internal weather is feverish, burning. Spring fever, I suppose. The external weather is lashing on windowpanes, caterwauling from the southwest, but I'm too panned out to bother much about its antics. It is the Chinese New Year today, the year of the Rooster, cock-a-doodle-doo. Wonder how that sounds in Mandarin? Wonder what the Chinese in Ireland make of the Irish weather?

Finbarr Had This Story

Finbarr had this story:
A man and his wife were out in their garden one misty day when a couple came walking by. The walkers asked how far it was to the next village.
'Sure, it's five miles to there,' said the man.
'Oh, no,' said the woman. 'Sure it's no more than two.'
The walkers thanked them and went on their way. When they'd gone out of sight, the man turned to his wife and said, 'What were you saying? You

know it's five miles to the village.'
'Of course I do,' said the woman. 'Ah, but they looked so tired.'
What has this to do with the weather? Well, it was a misty day.

10 Yarns to Soothe a Bronchial Day

A damp, still morning turned into a wet afternoon with mist hanging on hilltops and no apparent movement of air. After a night of feverish unrest, daytime came as a relief (sinus head colds are always worse at night) and my day was spent inside the theatre office, ignoring the bronchial weather outside. Afterwards, I repaired to Ashe's for a snack with Mike and this turned into a two-hour liquid sojourn of yarns and hilarity with Bernie Goggin, keeper of the town lore and erudite scholar of the natural world of Corca Dhuibhne. Clare and Heiko showed up and we laughed our heads off at Bernie's yarns and anecdotes, a great way to stave off a lousy late afternoon. Everyone went home in good cheer, not minding the awful dampness quite as much.

White Sound

A mist is down, sound muffled, the islands obscured. A still day. Yet when I take the ashes out back and turn again toward the house, I am astonished to see white spray from a breaking wave rise high above the headland below the Blasket Centre. This means that huge waves must be crossing the Sound. I stop a moment to listen, and realize that inhabiting the stillness is the roar of the sea. It is somehow the colour and density of the thick mist, a strong white sound.

11 Dampness as Memory

All day listening to rain and wind, I lie in bed, panned out, exhausted, dull. No desire but to lie down, to exit into sleep, to escape the feeling that something has smashed my face and is threatening to choke me. Weather, my link to the world, to awareness. Weather, extreme dampness, a probable agent in my body drama. This is such a childhood illness, a body memory so familiar I could be seven years old again, lying alone upstairs, away from the business of my mother's kitchen, the heart of the house. Then, as now, I would lie there, feverish, listening to the weather, cat curled up beside me on the bed, waiting, waiting, waiting for this timeless state to change.

Weather and Lorca

Yesterday I had a conversation with a friend who had seen the Abbey production of The House of Bernarda Alba *last year, as I had. We were speaking of language, and I remarked how odd I had found it to hear this tale of merciless heat and passion in an Irish lilt, an accent that is for me full of mist and coolness; but that then I had come to realize that for most of the Dublin audience, there was no lilt at all, merely a way of speaking. They would notice the West Kerry accent of the maid, or Bernarda Alba's faintly anglicized speech, yet essentially everyone would be speaking of these common human passions as life is spoken of here.*

I tried to imagine what barriers an American production of Lorca here might give rise to. Would the flat American voices invoke cities? Would their loudness speak of too much space? In Ireland, people remark, often with some surprise, that I do not sound like an American. I have come to

103

understand this is due not so much to the shape of my sounds or the cadence
of my speech, but because I speak softly. It is my volume. It is by their
loudness that Americans are identified, and, indeed, I've been in restaurants
where American voices stride over the conversation, voices that would not
register as loud in America, but that rise above the murmur here.

To this day, I must concentrate to hear a Virginia accent, as my father was
a Virginian, his voice to me just words as they should be spoken. My own
slightly mid-Atlantic vowels were lost long ago in various speech classes, and
through living in different parts if the US, and the world. Is somewhere in
my voice the singing nasal of the Chinese and Japanese greetings I learned?
I know the French purr is, and the faint Russian guttural. Africa is not in
my voice, as I've never been there, but perhaps an Inuit click exists from a
friend's travels in the Arctic. I know Irish is woven all through it now, the
trilled r, the broad t, the guttural ch. Níl sé tirim inniu, tá sé fliuch.

12 Weather and Dreaming

The Sheep-Shearer-in-the-Sky worked hard this
afternoon. Hundreds of fluffy light fleeces, spread out on a cold
blue sky, moved lightly as if still attached to ovine bodies. Maybe
I'll try counting them when I go to bed…they'll be mixed up in
my dreams with wellies and umbrellas and PVC weather bulletins
attached to thousands of sky-coloured silks, and memories of my
father in the peach house in spring, training the lateral branches
with thousands of raffia ties while he listened to the racing on his
old blue transistor.

2 a.m.

Two in the morning, wind punching the house, felt even inside these thick stone walls. Weather all over the place today, yet not a thought in my head about it. Clotted cream clouds on the way to Ventry. Cat-napping sun on the living room chair. Wind against the front door, catching the car door, lifting my skirt. An unfulfilled promise of spectacular sunset. Driving rain on the way to Baile Eaglaise. Star-filled bright night sky on the way home. Coladh sámh.

13 The Weather Channel

A heavy depression inside is characterized by sudden feverish outbursts, continuing nasal drizzle and profound inertia. At the same time, this spring Sunday is full of bright bluster and bursting outness. I get myself to the rocks for day's end: the great golden disk, at bursting point under bruised purple clouds, glistens in a direct line over metallic-blue water to my perch on Ballymore rocks. In time, bursting sun slips away, still intact. Me too. Intact, despite turmoil. Able, nowadays, to switch to the outer weather channel despite breaking storms inside. There is a season for everything and a weather system too.

Weather Wash

This morning the sun is out and the wind huge, a perfect day for laundry on the line. It is a Sunday, and I wonder if at some past time, or even now, it would be considered wrong to be involved in washing on the Sabbath, but suspect, given the weather here, that opportunity might override scruple formed in a distant dry place.

As I struggle with the wind to get the sheets on the line, I think of the blue house at the end of the lane. I do not know who lives there. I've seen a man, various dogs, perhaps a boy, but never a woman. Almost always, laundry hangs out on the line, sometimes a great many things, sometimes only a few. Frequently it is left out all night, often in all weathers. It has become almost a set feature of the house for me, this laundry, always there like the small tree in the middle of the lawn the line is strung across, or Inishtooskert in the distance. Today, a pair of black pants and a white towel flap frantically in the wind. From their position on the line, the pants might be the same ones I saw late one night last week dancing in a high wind in a downpour. I used to make it a point to bring laundry in at night, even if it was still damp, so as not to give scandal to the parish with my slovenly housekeeping. It is true that wash does seldom stay out overnight here, although it can often be seen hanging in the rain, as rain can come fast, and be over quickly. If the clothes are not caught in time, it's often just as well to leave them. This blue house down the lane though, with its all-weather laundry, fascinates me. Although the things on the line do change, I've never ever seen anyone putting them up. Or taking them down.

14 The Vanishing Trick

Light drizzle was falling this morning as I slouched up the field to the loo-with-a-view. But the view was short-lived and had vanished completely when I emerged, so that I was now looking out on a dense yet insubstantial nothingness where once there was ocean. Muffled sounds of cars passing punctuated the swish and wash of the tide, omnipresent in all weathers. Birdsong, by contrast, sounds greatly amplified on such a day.

Aspect

Yesterday's bright salt wind has gone, leaving a descending fog. As I drive home through the sepia mist, I think of my friend Darcy arriving from the States tomorrow. The landscape is in its dreariest manifestation when I would wish it to dazzle. I am leaving country and community for this place, and I would like it to be obvious why, as it so manifestly would be were we to drive down from Shannon in good weather, along Tralee and Brandon bays, across Connor Pass, through Dingle and over the Clasach to find Dunquin and the islands spread in their grace below. I would feel I'd need say no more, explain nothing. This afternoon's passage from Dingle, however, is through dripping mist without the least hint of even the sometimes present luminous light. The fuchsia hedges are brown and bare, nothing visible beyond. The gorse is sodden. Even I, loving this place as I do, am finding it hard to imagine the hillcurves, the molten ocean, the islands offshore. I feel like someone bringing a friend home to meet the family, hoping the family will behave, struggling to accept them as they are, hoping I would have the strength not to make excuses, no matter what happens.

I just hope the fog lifts by tomorrow.

15 Blue Blue Mountains

There was no sundown today, just blue blue mountains over a colourless still ocean, corridors of dense white fog slicing through hilltops, peaks, across valleys, becoming bluer white as evening deepened, as the mountains turned cobalt and the silent, shiny waters harboured a shade of palest rose. The cormorant floated darkly near the shore. Utter stillness.

Absolute calm. I long for such weather in my own turbulent microcosm.

Luminous

I set out for Shannon in predawn light, in the midst of the birds' morning chorus. From the Clasach, I see an oval of luminous light out on Dingle Bay, a glowing in the midst of grey. Scanning the clouded sky for a possible opening for light to enter, I find a distant patch of blue though which an airplane is scrolling a contrail lit bright orange by the sun. Because of the angle, it seems the plane is descending straight toward land, and for a moment the explosion of spacecraft enters my mind, the memory of an image of a tiny burst of light followed by the slow exhalation of debris, the elegant calligraphy of an enormous sudden loss, of life, of hope, of effort. This morning, it is only a commercial jet in high, scheduled flight, but as the line crosses the blue oval, a slight outcurve develops. I am certain it is little more than the result of an intersecting air current, but I image too a possible sudden swerve as cause, the jolt and panic in the tiny world above me. Strange thoughts to be having on what appears to be a bright morning on the way to meet a friend at the airport. I am not yet to Dingle before the contrail fades, I meet the first cars on the road, and the light shifts to full day. Later, I will pass through fields where a mist rises from each hedgerow, calligraphy of a different sort, and by evening walk with my friend out through Dunquin in a huge silence utterly devoid of wind, the sea a pale grey green, luminous and calm.

16 Ménagerie à Trois

Running a ménagerie à trois in a caravan in damp and

misty peninsular weather requires a major policy decision: not to be demented by muddy paws, constant in-ing and out-ing, cat and dog disagreements about who must sit or lie where and, of course, the morning demands to be fed even before I can brew my own morning poison. One is accompanied everywhere: up the greasy, muddy field to the damp-seated loo (today's view is of white mist); up to the back yard with the bucket of ashes (chase the hens); to the office and theatre spaces (lots of attention from everyone). Add muddy paws to grubby, damp car. The up side, however, is that it's not raining cats and dogs.

Mist

A day woven through with mist, mist moving, me moving, sometimes intersecting, damp, sometimes separate, as we wandered the west peninsula. Out at sea, the islands obscured, then visible. The slopes of Eagle and Marhin visible and obscured. On Béal Bán, everything hinted of rainbows, but none appeared. From Gallarus Oratory, only white where the Three Sisters should be. Everywhere grass studded with water drops. On Ventry Strand, the quarter moon high above a pastel shifting sunset with a dash of flamingo pink. Fingers of thick fog crept over Mt Eagle, holding the ridge. Not once in an entire day of wandering was Mt Brandon visible. Darcy, visiting, has begun to question its existence. We drove back to Baile na Rátha through the dense fog on the Clasach. In Dunquin, we dropped below it to find the islands still faintly visible, the Great Blasket a known dark shape floating in a transparent sea.

17 Blessed Moments

There's not much weather in my life right now. We're two weeks away from show time, so it's head down, total focus on production from here on in. But as I drove up to the theatre building this morning, a small white launch puttered gently in to port, the thin white line of turbulence bobbling in its wake, and at the moment I noticed it, the overcast parted a fraction and poured forth a light so brilliant into the pale blue harbour that I forgot everything for a few blessed moments.

Colours of the Wind

I have given my visiting friend Flann O'Brien's The Third Policeman *to read, and she reminds me of this passage starting on page thirty-three:*

> *...There are four winds and eight sub-winds, each with its own colour. The wind from the east is a deep purple, from the south a fine shining silver. The north wind is a hard black and the west is amber. People in the old days had the power of perceiving these colours and could spend a day sitting quietly on a hillside watching the beauty of the winds, their fall and rise and changing hues, the magic of neighbouring winds when they are inter-weaved like ribbons at a wedding. It was a better occupation than gazing at newspapers. The sub-winds had colours of indescribable delicacy, a reddish-yellow halfway between silver and purple, a greyish-green that was related equally to black and brown. What could be more exquisite than a countryside swept by cool rain reddened by the south-west breeze!'*
> *'Can you see these colours?' I asked.*
> *'No.'*

18 Dog and Dark

Another long day's work journeyed into night before I noticed the weather so, Tinka and I both needing an outing, I swung by Ventry in the dark to walk on the beach. An indigo evening, it wasn't really dark at all, the half moon veiled by cloud, but bright, nonetheless. Tinka fetched and I threw the stick until I couldn't stand the cold breeze any longer. The temperature is dropping after those mild, damp days. By the time of writing this Weather Watch, it is fresh outside, the indigo illuminated by the moon and some bright stars, but congregating dense bluish clouds suggest that it won't get very much colder.

Intervals of Almost Everything

Travelling the peninsula. From Dunquin around Slea Head to Dingle. A stroll along the harbour and into the town. From Dingle to Inch Beach. A stroll there, and into the dunes. Across by Caherconree into Camp to the beach near Carrigharoe Point, the one with the carved stones and iridescent oyster shells. Out to the tip of the Maharees, then across Connor Pass into Dingle again. Dinner there, and home in the dark over the Clasach. During the day, metallic calm water, the beginnings of wind. Greygreen sea with a navy blue band, with a shining silver streak. Skies blue and squall-threatening grey. Bands of brightness raying down. White dune light and a rose-infused mist at sunset. No rain, cold wind, warm sun, grey. A moonbright night with stars. Intervals of almost everything.

19 Hard Spring Day

In this peninsular climate, a hard spring day is nothing

111

like a hard spring day up the country, where one could expect a frosted-over garden that mightn't thaw much during the day. But here, it means a cold day with a sharp wind, rather than a damp one, and the ground isn't greasy mud underfoot. A heavily overcast sky ensured a wonderful green in the harbour at Ventry. Tinka didn't care about cold or wind, she just plunged into the shallows utterly focused on her stick, over and over again. Tonight the moon prevails, despite deep cloud, although not a single star is visible, at least here in the hollow of Ballymore. It's another indigo night.

Faint Rose

As with most recent days, the morning begins in sunshine then slides into grey. A day of motion, it ends with a walk across the clifftops to the pier. We go north to County Clare tomorrow on a roundabout way to Shannon and Darcy's early Tuesday flight, so this is her last sunset in Dunquin. Each day of her visit we have managed to be elsewhere at the end of day, but tonight we are outside looking westward to the horizon. The sky seems an unbroken grey, and I say I fear no evidence of sunset will appear. Yet as we come up from the pier and face the Clasach, a faint rose rests above the curve. Pale peach begins to tinge a few of the clouds that then part to reveal a tender blue sky. The colours deepen. The rose moves gradually from the east to the western sky. I recall one evening last year when I looked out to bands of descending sunlight colouring the entire sky gold, rims of flamingo around the indigo clouds, Beginish gilded, molten. 'Looks like the Second Coming,' Mags said when I passed her door. And indeed it almost seemed possible to hear trumpets in the midst of all the glory. Tonight though, sunset is muted. It requires attention, and as we walk we stop from time to time to look, to look back, to look up, to see the fattening moon overhead. The right music tonight would be the flute, delicate and piercing the heart.

20 At Day's End

At day's end on this cold February Sunday, all is still. I sit in the wicker chair gazing out at the last light and the growing darkness. Three apricot-coloured strips punctuate the heavily clouded indigo sky and fade to zero, leaving the orange glow from Ursula's window as the solo illumination for the evening while the waxing moon, ominously circled by a stormy, reddish-green aura, remains muffled by cloud. The birds have gone to bed and the cow in the farmyard below me has stopped bawling. I wonder if she was calving on this cold evening?

No Weather Report Today

21 Baby, It's Cold Outside!

Baby, it's cold outside! Those massing clouds of the past few days opened their bulwarks around two in the morning and pissed down like a tropical rainstorm for half an hour. I was too wired to sleep. It was so bright, and my head was so full of the forthcoming theatre gig plus the notion of going on a journey to Senegal when the show comes down, that I heard every drop as it hammered on the roof of the caravan until eventually I fell into a stupor. I woke to a damp cold, chill wind, the kind of day that would numb your body quickly although the weather wasn't visibly ferocious. Sooki reluctantly left my bed and, even more reluctantly, was booted out the door when I went to the theatre. I don't know if I'm cold because I'm physically low with this damn bug, or if it's actually cold temperature-wise. Which or whether, baby, it's cold outside!

No Notice

I have travelled today from the dark of the morning in Newcastle-on-Fergus through the midday rain in Tralee, then on to the warm afternoon sun of Dunquin. It is now a moonlit night bright enough to walk easily in, bright enough to see colour clearly. I can say almost nothing about the weather. It is astonishing to me that I managed to glean even the above facts. I can add that it is cold, and getting colder. Sometime while I was away there must have been a wind because I found the daffodils potless near the front door, no pot in sight. Otherwise, I took no notice, absorbed and exhausted, just passing through.

22 Cold Snap. Brr!

It really is a cold snap! The Met Office crowd say it will last through the week with sharp frosts and snow on high ground. Poor spring lambs! So weak and skinny, so vulnerable, such hard weather to be born in, blasted by a fierce northeasterly that would tear the nose off your face. But the sharp dryness, the pristine skies, the swelling-to-fullness February moon casting her impassive gaze on a cold landscape, a shining harbour, the same harbour glistening, earlier, in cold bright sunshine, our faces red-raw from the wind, thrilled to walk the length of Ventry Beach after days inside focused on work, weatherless. Last summer, I met a young musician from Houston, Texas. We stood chatting on a summer night outside the church of St James in Dingle during the concert interval. He was fascinated by the experience of spending the summer more or less out of doors because in Houston it's too hot to go out, so people get from A to B via air-conditioned malls, insulated from sun and air and dust. How bizarre!

Eyelid Weather

I wake to a clear blue day and a headcold turned vicious. Once I've staggered to the living room in an attempt to feel I've entered the day, most of it is spent on the couch with my eyes closed, the colour on them, when I notice it, the only record of a splendid day. Cadmium red is full sun, indigo when clouds pass over. Sometimes a greyish green appears, veiled clouds maybe, wisps. Occasionally swells of indigo cross and merge, but I think that's internal. I'm beginning to wonder what the colour of moonlight will be, but fear I won't have the strength to go outside tonight and see.

23 No Weather Report Today

Moonlight Eyelid
Violet indigo.

24 Dense Cloud Under Cold Sky

It's so cold out there under the full moon, so bright, so still. This morning, there was still rime on the field despite bright sunshine at nine o'clock, and when I stuck my hands under the cold water tap they nearly fell off! Sooki wouldn't budge from the bed and I got back into it myself for the morning coffee, the caravan was so chilly. But the hard northeasterly had left, at least for today, so being outside was a pleasure. Clouds are doing strange things again, massed on the horizon like mushroom clouds, dense blue-white thermals rising into a cold, clear sky. How can it be so cold when there is so much precipitation rising? What is keeping all that cloud sitting on the horizon line? It's as if cold air in the stratosphere is sealing off the upper sky so that warm moisture cannot rise. The effect is of a Dali painting. You see the sky and think 'that's impossible' but it ain't, at least not in West Kerry.

Blue Serenity

I wake to a blue serenity from a dream of aching loss of my river house, home for so many years. Sleepy birdsong laces the air. The night's full moon has set. A single star floats high to the south. I rise from my warm bed, go to the door, open it and greet the dawn.

25 Hot Dinners Required

Hot Dinners Required. No lukewarm replies. Drop-offs to Beehive Theatre Company, Cúilín, An Daingean anytime of the day or night for the foreseeable future. In case nobody hears from us during the weekend, please break into the theatre space to check we haven't frozen solid. Baby, it's cold inside as well.

Apricot Dawn

This morning I wake from a dream more tranquil than yesterday's, to find an apricot dawn. Lazy birdsong curls up through the early light. I wonder why I am awake. Once again I rise and go to the door, open it to a slight and fresh breeze, the sight of sleepy Dunquin, the Ceathru above me. No car stirs yet, or any human that I can see. After standing a minute, I go to the living room where I pull back the curtain. It is from above Mt Eagle that the apricot clouds stream across the sky, passing just over the place where I know my new home sits on the mountainside. I wonder if the mountain, with all this morning brightness, is putting me in practice for living on its dawn side.

26 Scellig Rocks Indicator

This morning's ramble to the loo-with-a-view revealed an interesting clue about gauging low temperature in the atmosphere: the Scellig Rocks – which often loom large and purple foreboding a low weather system, or else vanish in an instant in a southwesterly squall – this morning were blue pinpricks, finely wrought on a faraway horizon...

No Weather Report Today

27 Holy Smoke!

Holy Smoke! The peninsula's on fire! Well, not quite on fire – smoldering, more like. Funny word that, smoldering; moldering, but more so. Hmm. I'll have to think about that...but getting back to weather, there's a change coming in. It's clouding up again, becoming overcast. The big Scellig is looming large and purple on the horizon, the Iveragh is getting closer and Mt Eagle threatens ominously behind me. To the north, the hummock of Brandon's rounded peak, Masatiompan, still wears its mantle of sugar snow frosting, peeping up behind Cathair Ard above Ventry Beach where I walk on this cold, bright afternoon, relieved to get a lung-full of fresh air and a ruddy, wind-burned face after round the clock capers in the theatre. Walking downwind, I thought it wasn't so cold after all. Walking back, the sharp breeze slashes my face and I pull the hat down over my ears and reconsider my weather forecast.

Ramble

Today starts almost warm after yesterday's chill, but by midday the clouds thicken and the temperature drops. Even so, it's a day for a ramble across Mt Eagle, walking the territory from my old home to my new. The trail up from the Clasach switches back and forth, giving shifting views of Dunquin. The sea is flat, the day still with almost no wind. The path turns, revealing Smerwick and Mt Brandon in the distance. Ovals and strips of sunlight dapple the mountain, but none warm Mt Eagle on either side. Suddenly the lake appears below, and I look out to Ventry Harbour and down to the orange houseen. My new territory. And all the rest of the afternoon is spent crisscrossing the slopes above it, dropping down, climbing up, traversing. The summit doesn't figure in the day, but the way down is along toward Binn an Choma and into Coumeenoole. Fires smoking on Brandon and the Iveragh suddenly glow as dusk falls, become long molten streaks across the hillsides. The sunset is sulky, a bit of colour showing through the bruised clouds. The flask of tea left in the car hours ago is welcome. A walking day, a grey day, a day of shifting perspectives, my body learning new terrain, the terrain of home.

28 El Greco Sky

Driving home at half past midnight after feasting with Sandra, there's an El Greco sky over Ventry Harbour: folds of thick indigo cloud illuminated by a veiled moon, the folds and edges all silvered and here and there, the odd twinkling star. I am in Toledo again, fascinated by the huge, eerie canvases hanging in the church where El Greco worked. West Kerry under an El Greco sky.

Repeating Epiphanies

Part of today's weather — sun a moment ago, a dash of hard rain now — is the reading of Weather Watch. *I am struck by how often I note I am astonished at the weather, how often I return home at night under stars and close the door only to hear sudden rain, how often behind the closed curtains I hear rain and wind, only to open the door to calm stars. This morning, I have experienced the daylight version. Outside not ten minutes ago, I stood in a bright day admiring a slant of sun resting on the Great Blasket, now I look out to the island through a grey veil. This is, it would seem, commonplace here, yet I remark again and again at how it surprises me. I find some humour in these repeating epiphanies, as if I've forgotten the last time it happened, and experience the amazement all over again.*

March

1 Theatre Weather

High pressure prevailing in theatre atmosphere/General forecast for high energy, warmth and goodwill/Flurries in atmospheric pressure likely as show time draws nearer/Hopeful about getting the heating fixed for the dressing rooms before Thursday night's opening.

Dazzle

Driving home over the Clasach yesterday after learning that the money to conclude the transaction for the new house in Ballintlea had finally reached the solicitor's office, I came into sight of Dunquin all a-shimmer. The entire sea was a dazzle of light, the afternoon sun lying mellow and golden across fields of deep velvet green. Each house glowed. Each stone fence cast a distinct shadow. I remembered an evening in one of my first years here when I'd stopped the car up on the hill and looked down over Dunquin, comparing my feeling for its detail to that one might have for a lover. Now on this day when I knew I was to be leaving, even if only across the mountain, Dunquin shone at its best. Today the sun still shines, the wind is up, the sea a bright blue roil. Dunquin is dancing, joining me in my happiness, generous always with its gifts.

2 We Are Stardust

Starlight guides my way home at quarter to midnight. The firmament is dazzling, still cold, although the sky to the north over

Brandon is sporting a few thin-looking clouds. 'We are stardust/ billion year old carbon/We are golden/caught in the Devil's bargain/And we've got to get ourselves back to the Garden'... Joni Mitchell's 'Woodstock', running through my tired brain.

Tiaracht in a Copper Sea

> *Morning sunlight*
> *etches*
> *every detail*
> *of Tiaracht*
> *floating*
> *in a copper sea.*

3 No Weather Report Today

Snow on Mountains

Yesterday coming across the Clasach, I found snow-covered Carrauntoohil in sun, all its shape a brilliant sculpture of light and dark. It took my breath away. Today, all the way to Cork I drove beneath snow-capped peaks, thinking how my friends arriving from the States would find them as fine as I did. Their plane was late, however, and we missed the light. I was reduced to waving my hands toward the mountains' vague silhouettes, describing the snow. These friends are westerners, used to ten thousand foot peaks. They scoffed a bit, calling the mountains hills. 'Oh, no,' I said. 'These are truly mountains.' But how do I describe what it is like to be on them, to understand how they unfold with walking, become larger than they seem at the beginning? How to say these are older mountains than the showier peaks, that they are mountains shaped by time into wisdom? How to describe the tenderness of the faintest dusting of snow just beneath the tips of the Paps? I only said, 'Oh, no. I've walked them.'

4 No Weather Report Today

All Weather Day

Sheets of soft rain, Brandon clouded, laundry two days on the line. Far dappled sun, near wind. Béal Bán studded with stones turning suddenly to shells smaller than fingernails. No visible snow, but felt in the wind. In the afternoon, a visit to Baile an tSléibhe, grey, then sudden sunlight slanting into the room. Peace. In the evening, a taste of the theatre weather, gathering crowds, precipitations of mirth, hails of applause. Elation.

5 No Weather Report Today

Custom

A fine weather day. My visiting friends cannot get over the fact that, as we wander the streets and shops tourist-style, everyone comments on its brilliance. They postulate that clear days must be rare, to cause such notice. I return that it's just the custom of the place, that after the greeting and the how are you, the next step is the weather. I run through it for them in Irish:

Dia dhuit./Dia 's Muire dhuit.

Conas tánn tú?/Ana-mhaith.

Tá sé fuar inniu./Tá sé ana-fhuar, ach tá sé tirim, buíochas le Dia.

I tell them there'd be just as much comment whatever the weather, run through 'go hálainn', 'go holc', 'te', and 'fliuch'. Their eyes glaze over. Clearly they come from a place where the weather causes no excitement, where weather is just the backdrop and not a player on the stage.

6 Starry Starry Night

Sunday night/Monday morning, the early hours when I arrive home after the last night's show of the 5x2 Festival of Theatre Shorts. As I left town, the windscreen had frosted over. Back in Ballymore, in rural darkness, the firmament is brilliant, every star and planet of the northern hemisphere glittering above me as I run up the field to the loo-with-a-view, so I leave the door open, don't want to miss a single twinkle, and then, back in the caravan, Sooki and I curl up for the dream time, blessed by the living starlight. Yum!

Guests

Weather? Weather? Who can have weather with guests?

7 Exhaustion

No weather.

Driving

Driving, all day driving. From Dunquin to Dingle, from Dingle to Muckross, from Muckross to Kenmare, then back again through Moll's Gap down to Killarney, along through Milltown and Castlemaine and Inch and Lispole, into Dingle and across the Clasach to home. A glance only for the orange gable of my new house. The weather? At some point the sun disappeared beneath a thick grey blanket of clouds. The splash of water under the tires somewhere indicated an earlier rain. But mostly it was eyes on the road. Driving.

8 Post-Show Clean-Up

The weather in the office is pretty good despite having to do the awful clean-up and tally the books. The festival has been a real success. Now I can't wait to get out of here and hit the trail for sunny Senegal. The weather here is pale and wan but not wet.

Still, So Still

At dusk in Baile an tSléibhe I stand outside seeing for the first time the lights come on below me. Far off on the Iveragh Peninsula, a shimmering. Here on the mountainside, a rich stillness filled with birdsong, a summer sound in the mild night.

9 Last Minute

Nothing ever runs to plan. Too much to do at work and nothing in the bloody rucksack yet. Grey weather all day.

Flat Grey

Although all day we travelled through extravagant country – the rocky mountainsides of Ballaghbeama Gap and the soft green curves of Cork – the sky remained a flat grey. No fields bursting into emerald. No sea changing from green to blue. No wind to froth whitecaps or whip branches about. A delicate peach tinge faintly at sunset. That's all.

10 Setting Out

It's bitingly cold on the platform at Mallow, waiting for the Cork-Dublin mainline train to show up. There's an easterly wind howling down the line and everyone looks a bit blue. I look at my rucksack and decide to toss half of the contents when I get to Seán's house; I'm not carrying all that stuff to Senegal. There was no time to think about packing, it was all rather ad hoc, a miracle to be actually getting out of here. It'll probably be freezing in Milan tomorrow.

A Sunset the Colour of My House

As I am leaving Cork, I see the horizon glowing a deep throbbing orange. I think immediately of my new house. Tactful friends have called it apricot and nasturtium. It might be fashioned melon. But it is in fact orange. Although I'm likely to change the colour, in these days before I can move in, when the most I can do is locate it on the mountainside as I pass over the Clasach, I'm glad for the orange. Most days, I spot it immediately, a beacon glowing off in the distance. Tonight outside of Cork, I see the orange sky, and head for home.

11 Tale of Two Cities

The roof of Milan's Duomo is a wonderful discovery. Myriad sculptures glisten in the light, each one uniquely crafted, gazing out over the city on this sunny spring morning. The air is luminous, cold and dry. Before I leave, I go down into the cathedral and ask an old priest for a blessing for a safe journey. He smiles warmly when I tell him I'm from Ireland and asks me to give my love to it when I return. In the afternoon, I am thrilled by the shining, craggy Alps below us as we clear Milanese airspace, snow glistening under the pristine blue. I hadn't factored this into my journey to a hot country at all. How odd, flying from one climate to another in a few hours. The long, bumpy taxi ride from Dakar airport downtown seemed to happen in a dust storm. I'd forgotten about things like zero city lights and virtual streets, easily erased by sand. It was just like a night-time arrival in Khartoum, Sudan's capital city, where I lived twenty years ago. But after half an hour or so, we turned into a small side street and came to a halt outside the Hôtel St Louis Sun. Made it.

Time and the Weather

It is three in the afternoon and I stand at the window eating a bowl of pasta, looking out. I suddenly realize that this is the first time today I have registered the view, which is of the sea and the Great Blasket Island. Racing from here to there, packing, sorting, making phone calls, I have taken no time to notice the weather at all. I stop. It is a flat grey day, cold. A slight breeze is rising. The entire cover of clouds is moving slowly but steadily east. I am certainly not jaded with either place or light. It is the speeding, the filling of time with tasks that has caused me to not notice. One of the pleasures for me here has been time, the time to notice, to see. Ireland has always been a refuge for me. Now that my entire life is moving here, I wonder what will happen. I long to hold on to the deep time, and need to shape my everyday life to encompass it. Or rather, to enter it, as one does a door into enchantment.

12 Breakfast in Dakar

The courtyard garden is full of singing birds, an aural delight as I sip coffee and write my journal on the terrace of this old-style, slightly shabby little hotel. I can hardly believe I'm here, in a real African hotel. The gardener's sandals, sitting on the wall beside the kitchen door, set the mood: self-confident unselfconsciousness. I'm tempted to while the day away in this delightful courtyard with its colourful wall murals, hidden from the tougher reality of Dakar's streets. I wonder if George still runs the Acropole Hotel in downtown Khartoum, on the other side of the continent?

Nondescript

I cannot tell if it is me or the weather, but the days seem nondescript. It is dry and pleasant, chilly with a faint wind. The sky is either blue with some clouds or grey all over. Spring seems stalled. The primroses have bloomed, and a few celandines, but even though they have been around for weeks, no other flowers seem to have joined them, not even the violets. The daffodils go on and on, so early this year that by Daffodil Day, they were looking a bit bedraggled in their yellow town massings guarded by earnest ladies. I miss the usual drama, the light flickering over the hillsides, the rain lashing against the house, the occasional rainbow. The most extreme weather recently has been a hard mist wobbling through. Sullen spring.

13 Down in the City

Returning from my downtown ramble, needing a rest from hot sun and hustlers, I bumped into Latyr. I don't know how we met up, maybe I asked him for a direction or something. Anyway, he spoke English and we stood on the sidewalk for half an hour, talking. He's a small, prematurely aged, wizened man, fiftyish, I'd say. He used to work at the art museum and offers to guide me around the fish market and the souk, north of the city centre. He's on his way to visit a friend in the area, so we agree to meet later on when it cools down. We meet at the appointed hour and wander around the markets, Latyr explaining the comings and goings to me carefully. As sundown approaches – about seven o'clock down here – we head back and I invite him to join me for supper. We go into a neon-lit diner and get two plates of chicken and rice. Latyr eats with great concentration and then we talk for a long time. His story was strange. He wouldn't have told it if I hadn't asked. I won't tell it here. It was deeply personal and involved the spiritual realm of things. I felt reassured.

Moving Weather

Moving day to Ballintlea. Mags brings her van. Other friends arrive. We load up the cars and head across the mountain. The still weather continues, grey but bright with a breeze. I'm grateful for the dryness, the quiet. There'll be no dashing through rain or against wind. At the house, we unload quickly, and then turn to food, the first meal in my new home. We begin with chocolates, no surprise, to revive from the moving, and tea. I make fresh ravioli from the English Market in Cork while Biddy makes a salad. Herbs are brought in from the garden. Mags is admiring the house. Claire calls, and the table is reset to include her. The Mexican placemats are replaced by a delicate lace cloth from the linen closet, and the table looks suddenly more mine. We sit to eat, offer blessings and gratitude, toasts with champagne left by friends. We have a sprout course, then a walkabout in the garden before dessert, which is rhubarb pie with vanilla ice cream, chocolate applesauce cake, and a chocolate roulade, all with more tea. Washing up is collaborative, with Biddy and me coming and going, trying to understand why the radiators are not heating, although the fire is going strong. We never quite do, but the house is warmed anyway, and I say I will email the former owners for details. Outside, the weather holds, giving us mildness for all the ins and outs. Dusk falls, and everyone heads home, even me. I've determined I must walk across the mountain from Dunquin to Ballintlea before I can sleep there, and I still have a few days' work in Dunquin. I write now in Dunquin, most of my belongings, my Irish estate, across the mountain, waiting for me to come home.

14 Acclimatizing

I arrived into Mbour in the early afternoon, dusty and dirty. It was very hot. It had been a long wait at the bus souk in Dakar before the minibus filled up and then it took at least an hour to get through the traffic at Rufistique, the big crossroads south of the city, crawling along in thick clouds of diesel, scarves covering our noses and mouths. I walked the two kilometres out of town to the Hôtel Paradis – to test myself in the heat – and arrived dripping. The swimming pool looked inviting but it was still much too hot to bare my white pelt to the Senegalese sun, so I waited until five o'clock, then went down the beach. I'd forgotten that there's no privacy. I'll learn French quickly on this journey, or go completely insane from overexposure to people, in particular young men on beaches. But I swam with some kids in the warm ocean and watched the sun swell to setting before it vanished in the coastal haze.

Return

The wind is back, and with it the rain. The poor sheets have been on the line for two days trying to dry between showers which have escalated to storms. Rain-drenched, wind-tossed, they should give rise to interesting dreams.

15 Joal-Fadiout

Joal-Fadiout isn't far down the road from Mbour but it is siesta time all day long compared to the incessant noise and traffic of its larger neighbour. There's hardly a dog moving in the dust. The Léopold Senghor house isn't officially open at this hour but the curator has spotted me poking about and has decided to let me in, so I spend a while meandering in the cool, shady rooms of this former president's childhood home, looking at the many interesting photographs of his private and public lives. When I emerge, nothing has moved in the street outside. The light seems even whiter than it was an hour ago.

Wind Again

Tonight the wind slams into the house, the rain lashes the windows. I am exhilarated at the return of this weather, laugh when the car is pushed sideways, the grasses bent to the ground. When I come around the corner of the house, I'm wrapped in wind, and lean into it, a familiar friend. I think of the statue of the Islandman at the Blasket Centre, his coat blown back, his whole body a response to the wind. It's that kind of night.

16 Pirogue

At five o'clock in the afternoon, it's cooling down at last. There's a breeze now after a scorching day. Let's face it, it was a bit dodgy, really, to go out in Joachim's pirogue at such a late hour in the morning. The three-hour tour sounded great in theory: visit the environs of Fadiout, the Christian island across the bridge from Joal, constructed entirely on a cockle-bed; then go to the graveyard island and then, out in the middle of the watercourse, to the grain stores. I had hoped to get upstream near the mouth of the delta but we didn't set out until half past ten, and I had to quit and get off the boat at one o'clock, otherwise I'd have fried in this heat on the river. Even now, sitting beside the ocean in the evening breeze, I can feel my skin burning although I've been covered in that awful P20 chemical stuff since this morning's ablutions. I could swim at the Hôtel de la Plage but I think I'd still fry in this heat, better avoid it. Tomorrow, maybe. The beach here is pretty damn grubby, not at all inviting. Over in the bush behind the hotel, the guys are practicing wrestling. Others are running on the beach and doing press-ups. How do they train in this incredible heat? I need a hat.

Luminous

The fog that descended today lay over the land like a furled sheet. Not at all enveloping, it was in places thick, in others thin, and in the thin places luminous. All day, moving about felt dreamlike. The horizon was often not visible. From time to time, it seemed appropriate to turn on the car lights, then almost immediately they became unnecessary. It was a curious light, fluid, bright. An elevating foggy day.

17 St Patrick's Day

The caged pelicans in Mamadou's yard are reputed to dance but they just look miserable to me and they really stink in this heat. I didn't wake up early and then hung out indecisively trying to hatch a plan to go to Mbour to get money. This kind of currency does my head in: wads of relatively small money with big numbers on it. After Mbour, the next bank is Kaolak, in the interior. How can I do the delta wanderings without carrying a backpack full of bank notes?

It struck me that today is St Patrick's Day, so I walked back over the bridge to Fadiout at midday and spent an hour in the lovely chapel there, more to find cool lodgings without some young fellow hassling me, rather than to invoke the saint. Resembling a large gazebo, the church is open-aired, shady and full of songbirds flying in and out. Fadiout is a Christian village, Joal a Muslim town. I am like a Pentecostal missionary in this get-up of grey pants, seersucker dark-blue shirt and grey silk scarf covering my head but if I don't cover up, I'll be burned to a cinder. The P20 doesn't seem to do the job well enough for my nose and my feet. This puzzles me because it worked perfectly well in Cuba where my skin was exposed all the time, Cubans having no problems with showing off what they've got!

Walk

I am waiting for the day to walk from Dunquin across Mt Eagle to my new home in Ballintlea, the timing of which is dependent on my packing the house in Dunquin and finding a possible weather for walking. Today, fog sits on the top of the mountain, but the day below is bright with marine light. I finish packing, load the final things into the car so the house is empty, and decide to chance it. As I leave, the wind is at my back, and I turn several times to look again at Dunquin, the only town in Ireland in which, until now, I've lived, a town that is in my bones. As I climb higher, the fog becomes dense, the wind fierce. Dunquin disappears into the mist like some Brigadoon. I hear voices, and out of the fog appear six young men, German I think, all wearing huge backpacks and full raingear, stumbling, being knocked sideways by the force of the wind. At this point, I am still wearing only a heavy sweater with my jackets tied around my waist. No hat, no gloves. The young men look at me in some wonder as I climb past them. I suddenly realize I am being drenched by the wind-driven clouds and hastily put on the jackets, put up the hood, and begin to question my judgment in choosing this day. The fog becomes even more dense and I wonder how I will find the zigzag path that leads down to the lake. I slog on, find the rim of the cliffs above the lake, and the path by sheer luck. When I do finally reach the lake, I can see little more than a few feet. I decide it's unromantic, but the better part of wisdom to follow the road from the mast down instead of trying to find the cross-mountain path, the location of which depends largely on sight. It is by now about four in the afternoon, and I've no desire to spend the night wandering the mountain. I do not actually know where the mast road, which I've never taken, comes out, but I suspect Cill Dhorcha. However, at this point, I cannot even see the mast. I begin to remember all those cautions about going up the mountain in the mist. I am still unconcerned. I have a very visceral sense of where things are, both the place I've left, and the place I'm going to. I follow the lake edge to the water station, but still see no mast. Then the fog momentarily parts and I see it, head in that direction, undaunted by several fences to be climbed. I'm on the road soon, headed down. I do end up in Cill Dhorcha, and know the way from there. The fog lightens a bit, but comes and goes. In the absence of far views, the lanes become intimate, detail holds great clarity. I admire the primroses blooming, the heart-shaped leaves of celandine. Nearly in Ballintlea, I look up for a moment, and my house appears, its orange muted in this light. Almost home. A short bit more and I am there. Home.

18 Toward the Delta

The two hours on the far side of the river, waiting for the ferry over to Foundiougne, were white hot. The arid plain shimmering in the heat gave an impression that we had arrived at the river long before coming anywhere near to it – mirage, a strange phenomenon. Travelling down from Mbour was swift enough although I was sitting at the bus souk for about two hours beforehand. How do all those people make a living selling bits and bobs of cheap stuff around the market place? I notice that locals are more inclined to give coins to religious beggars than to street kids or to anybody else but it's still a shock to witness such poverty and disability, to hear the whispered plea in a child's voice, to feel ashamed because I am so wealthy by comparison.

Home

I walk out the door tonight. Below me, the sound of the sea. Above, the quarter moon floating in a starred sky. My toes curl with pleasure.

19 The Relief of a Strong Wind

By evening, there's a strong warm wind blowing down the Síne Saloum River: that's a relief after another day with temperatures hitting the 40s. How quickly it gets dark: within minutes, literally. The water is choppy now, the tide rising, splashing over the parapet of the *campement*, or hostel. I guess it will be high tide again around eight in the morning, a good time for a swim in the river. This is a saltwater delta, so no bilharzia, I hope.

Foundiougne seems like a sleepy enough town, smaller than I expected. I enjoyed sitting with the women having a boiled egg sandwich and instant coffee up at the marketplace around noon. Now it's time for supper. Standard fare is rice with thick, cod-like fish, or great hunks of chicken. Agnes has a well-stocked bar, so a beer or two out on the windy terrace might go down well before slumber. I'll never last 'til midnight when the Saturday night shindig starts. The dance gigs go on 'til dawn and then everyone crashes out on Sunday, unless they are churchgoing Christians who have to get up for the ten o'clock Mass. I don't feel confident to go along by myself; anyway, it's so hard to find one's way around in the pitch dark with no street lighting and I haven't figured out exactly where the ballroom of romance actually is. Still, if the wind continues to blow at night, if the screens are tight against mosquitos and if it's okay to swim in the muddy river each evening, then I shall stay here for a while.

A Day So Gentle

Then comes a day so gentle we remember summer. The rising sun wakes me early this morning, a marvel of brightness to begin the day. It stays all through, the light soothing, warming. Winter layers come off, sandals come out, skin turns red from sun not wind. In the afternoon, I open all the windows to the breeze, hear the leaves of the great plant in the living room clatter and the wind chimes sing, take a chair outside to eat lunch. After lunch, stretched on a rock in the sun, I nap. Still the Scairbhín to come, but today for a moment, summer.

20 Baobab-sur-Mer

It's not quite bright here until just before seven. From five o'clock onwards, dawn creeps in, birds are up and doing but nothing else happens around the *campement* until eight. Breakfast is left out with flasks of hot water for coffee by the night guard before he leaves. From seven o'clock until noon seems pleasantly hot. Then it starts to fry. Baobab-sur-Mer is also known as Chez Anne-Marie, the stately old dame who owns the place. Her hefty daughter, Agnes, runs the show, a mountain of a woman with a 'don't fuck with me' attitude marshalling a bevy of girls all dressed like hospital orderlies. But it's pretty laid-back, there's not a lot happening and they all seem to get along with her easily. Thérèse, her younger sister, is very friendly and goes out of her way to chat with me. I wonder if it's okay to hang my washing to dry from the courtyard bushes? I hope Agnes won't consider it a lowering of the tone.

The French fishermen seem to leave at dawn to go on all-day fishing trips with locals. Later on, they drink a lot of cognac after a whopping great fish dinner. They come here twice a year and obviously know everyone. We have exchanged pleasantries but I'm not up for hard boozing so they ignore me.

I went to the Palm Sunday Mass in the big barn of a church. It was the very long Passion Mass, delivered very formally, reverently, in French and in Serrer, the local language in the delta. The French nuns were watching the kids like hawks for misbehaviour or inattention. Men and boys sit on the right, women, girls and small kids on the left. Thérèse says that the renowned local youth choir is gone south to Casamance for the Annual West African Catholic Youth Day. They'll be back for Easter Day, though.

Now, after sundown, the water is indigo, the sky a lighter shade and the open-air dining room is light blue, with a fabulously multi-coloured batik roof. I nurse a beer and watch TV as an audiovisual language lesson. The soap operas are all Cuban or Egyptian imports, over-the-top melodrama of the worst sort. They repeat them over and over, just like a language lesson!

Heat

My new house is heated entirely from the peat fire in the living room. I have the occasional electric heater, and the alternative of an immersion heater for hot water, and the mysterious instant electric shower, but if the house is to be really warm, it must come from the burning of peat in the fireplace. When I first moved in, it seemed a hopeless and slow process. The radiators in the back rooms remained cold even after hours of burning, yet now, after a few days, a smaller fire seems to produce warmth all the way through the house. I tell myself this is because I am becoming in harmony with the house, but I suspect it is more the warmth outside. Even on the overcast days, the chill of winter has departed and the softness of spring arrived. Today, equinox, we slip toward light, and all the elation it brings.

21 White Heat

All day long there's been a white heat on the delta, the horizon smudged in dust. I wonder if it's this hot back at the coast? The visibly humid, wispy-clouded sky charmingly turned an exotic, flamingo pink shade after sundown, the plus side of the dust in the atmosphere. Despite the heat, I feel the need to stop, to rest, to find out something about the people here and make some contacts. Cheik, the young tailor down at the market, is an engaging character. I enjoyed having tea and a chat with him. He's fascinated by Normandy and has several maps of that territory. The egg and coffee ladies indulged me again today, not seeming to mind me hanging around their business. In the morning, I noticed a sign in the ditch outside town announcing WAAME/Project Mangrove. So I wandered in and ended up at a class for local mariculture farmers, mostly women from surrounding delta villages being trained in the cultivation of the mangrove tree: how to culture oysters symbiotically with the trees, instead of chopping them off; how to measure the salinity of the water as it changes through the year and the tides so as to maximize the oyster cultivation. The fellow giving the lecture was attended by a young lady who did all the social stuff – the register, the greetings, the questions. Of course it took forever because ladies kept arriving in dead late, then they'd have to be registered, then they'd have a chat with the others, and so on. But finally the teacher managed to show his charts of the monthly tide levels. After that, the rest was lost on me, as it was all conducted in Serrer, not French, as most of these women would never have attended school.

A Day of Quiet Rain

The rain comes softly today, no sound, just dots on the surface of the pond. It rains so gently it is almost not raining, but the parched ground is wet and a bit refreshed. I walked out in the garden with Anna, strolling, neither of us minding the damp. A cherished day, respite. A day to sit by the hearth and look out at the changing greys of the sky, the cloud caps caught on the peaks of the mountains all around.

22 Killer Heat

42 degrees in the shade, 50 degrees *au soleil*. Aagh! At four o'clock, I walked over to the market to get a few bananas. Twenty minutes later, I was dripping from every pore. The water in the river was still pretty low at half past five, but I swam nonetheless in the incredibly warm water, fish jumping around me in the mud. Then, finding that the plumbing was active again, I thought to

shower off the mud. The water gushed out boiling hot – out of the cold water tap. Now it is after dark and still roasting. Nobody here seems to sleep outside. Why? I'd really like to drag the bed into the yard and hang up the mosquito net under a tree, but nobody is encouraging this notion. I went down to the souk after dark for supper, wanting to try a chophouse for a change, and met up with Mamadou, a young student teacher who was keen to practice English. He introduced me to the Senegalese tea ceremony, a most peculiar ritual involving three different brewings of minute quantities of green tea with increasingly large amounts of sugar. The tea is brewed in a little tin pot, then poured into glasses. Just as one expects the glass to be offered, the pouring is done again. And again. And one more time. And then once more after that. The first cup is low on sugar. That's like death. The next one, after the brewing and pouring is done again, is sweeter, like life. The third, the sweetest one that takes a long time to get to, is like love. Subtle people, the Senegalese.

Long Weather

I wake this morning in a sun-warmed bed. When the sheer pleasure of this finally yields to conscious thought, I think 'laundry'. Yet when I finally do get up, I see dark clouds coming across Mt Eagle from the west. I cannot see how dense the cloud banks are, or if they are sporadic or continuous. I realize that in Dunquin I had become accustomed to looking out to sea for the coming weather. There, I could tell if a rainstorm was approaching, and if it would be sustained or brief. Here in Baile an tSléibhe, my long view is of the weather that has been, on its way to somewhere else. Today I look

*up at Mt Eagle, at the dark clouds across its ridge, and can only wonder
what the coming weather will be. Perhaps with time I may become adept
at combining wind, the quality of grey or blue, the texture of clouds, and
reach a conclusion. Perhaps birdsong comes into it, or the slant of a leaf. But
for now I can only start the laundry, hoping not to later have a houseful of
damp clothes brought in from the rain outside.*

23 Mind

It was a tough night, little or no sleep, and a constant
sensation of being bitten by creeping or flying things. I finally
slumbered at dawn and then woke, exhausted, after manic dreaming
and covered in gigantic bites. Now it is afternoon and I'm feeling
very queer. I think I took two tabs of doxycycline instead of one,
maybe that's causing the weirdness. My mind is battling. It's hard
to…what? No, wrong track. The mindset goes like this: 'What the
fuck am I doing here?' Bruce Chatwin said the only reason to travel
was motion itself. I think he was right. It's impossible to read or
write in this kind of heat so one might just as well travel, engage in
a way that doesn't demand much concentration or focus. Maybe I
just haven't acclimatized myself yet although even the locals seem
to be cribbing about the heat, insisting that it is too hot, too early
in the year.

I remember the initial weeks I lived in Sennar, Sudan, beside the
Nile: after the novelty had worn off and my mind realized that I'd be
staying there for at least a school year, it went berserk, wanting out,
loathing the awful choice I had made. Then it became depressed,
feeling utterly stuck, and then downed tools until Monica, my

colleague in the adventure, kicked my ass.

This is exactly the kind of mind stuff I'm experiencing now. Why didn't I opt for the Greek spring? Why didn't I go to Ethiopia with Monica, or somewhere with climatic options? The idea was to swim in a warm sea. How could I forget that a solo woman traveller will never get peace on a beach in a country like this? How could I forget the energy drain of endless verbal engagements in a foreign language? The beaches are grubby and full of depressed individuals like Elizabeth whom I met down at Joal on the beach behind the Frenchman's hotel. She sat on that log with me for as long as I stayed there, waiting. Waiting for me to deliver. She was no more than seventeen, I'd guess. Her husband had left her with two youngsters. She said she had no family there. She begged whatever she could get in a day, sleeping wherever. The older child was off on his own somewhere, fending for himself; the three-month old girl strapped to her back was in good health, she told me, thank God. Thank God. I admired her plaited braids and the pretty daughter, touching both, and we both laughed, shyly, as the sun evaporated over the ocean.

Grey Blanket

The wind has shifted round to what I think of as the usual direction and all day today I watch a thick blanket of grey clouds move across the sky from the southwest. It is a day of no obligation. I read. I nap. I watch the sky. Content for the moment to just be here.

24 Going with the Flow

It's after breakfast as I write this and there's a pleasant breeze coming off the delta. Maybe the heat will back off? What about using my time here to write something: a play, or more of the memoir? Anything at all to engage the restless mind. I know quite well its negative workings and I mustn't get into a discussion with it – that would be as useless as trying to outwit the local young-guns! Here I am. Trust it. Follow it. Don't resist the being here, the thing that propelled me here. Go with the flow. Maybe this is the WHY of the trip: to practice, to just be. Later, in the church, I meet the white-haired man I thought was a priest last Sunday. His name is Philippe and he is Breton. He visits here for three months every spring. He asked me about my trip and suddenly I burst into tears! Everything I am battling with in my mind poured out, like water out of a burst pipe. He was kind, pointed out that although he feels at home here, knows the people, he is always surprised each year at how much he doesn't understand about the ways of the people. He says Foundiougne is at least ten degrees hotter than Dakar, that perhaps I'd be more comfortable back up the coast at a place he knows called Popenguine. Then he went over to the tabernacle to pray – it is on the side altar as this is Holy Week – and as he left I cried, hating myself for not being tough enough to cope with the heat and the pushy young men down at the market, for being upset by poverty and depressed in myself. I stayed a while longer in the silent church, despite my unrest.

Downtown, I looked in to say hello to Cheik, who called for tea, and enjoyed a conversation full of laughter. At lunchtime, I stuck my head into Khadi's chophouse and met Ousman, the webmaster at the WAAME office. He studied computer technology in Montreal and consequently speaks some English. We lunched on *téboudienne*, fish stew baked with rice, the best one I've eaten so far. Despite the desperate heat under the tin roof, I stayed for another hour to chat with Khadi. I'd had a few meals there already and had gotten to know her a little bit. She explained to me that the young lads – the hustlers – mean no harm, no disregard, that their only income is from tourists and that anybody getting out of hand will be severely reprimanded by their elders. It's a rural town, everyone knows everyone else and everyone else's business. While we spoke, the Minister for Women and Social Affairs arrived from the ferry and was escorted by all the local drummers to the girls' high school. I looked in at the lycée sometime in the afternoon and felt sorry for the Minister and the staff who were obliged to look dignified in the sweltering heat, dressed up in their best.

At around six in the evening, Thio – the plumber at Le Baobab – brought me out on his motorbike to the salt flats. Women collect salt here in the incredible heat, then immerse it in pools of water to clean it. It rises to the surface a shade of coral pink, then it is sorted and sifted, killer work for these women whose hands must be raw after handling crude salt in this temperature. They sell the stuff in kilos to buyers who then sell it on to the processing factory up at Kaolak, the triangle between Foundiougne, Fatik and Kaolak being the main salt plain in Senegal. The salt pools deepened to rose pink as the gigantic solar disc disappeared into the dust-laden horizon. The motorbike was a bumpy ride but it is definitely a practical mode of transport. This is the time of day I love the most, when the light mellows to gold and gilds the bush.

Coin

> *Now, in the garden:*
> *the round gold coin of the moon.*
> *I stand still, transfixed.*

25 Birthday in the Bush

A cool, breezy morning at seven o'clock is a happy birthday greeting. I meet Sherif, Diallo and Abdallah down at the WAAME office and we drive out of Foundiougne heading south through Djilor, then on down through Toubacouta. They want to test the salinity at various points on the delta and to call in on some of their people. The landscape becomes more wooded as we leave Foundiougne. The bush is dry savannah woodland, watered from below. Mudflats and mangrove swamps shimmer along the delta's many watercourses; away to the east, more salt flats. As we go further south, tall kapok trees tower over the bush, vying with baobabs for sovereignty. There are red-assed monkeys with long tails, water eagles and many other birds of prey. We pass through small settlements and stop to buy mangos and bananas. This is surely a luxury birthday travel day: you can't beat air-conditioned, four-wheel-drive vehicles in the bush. They are designed for this kind of terrain, not for Dublin 4 or the suburbs of Los Angeles. I enjoy a pleasant sojourn at each stop while the boys do the business, Sherif or Diallo patiently following my questions asked in appallingly poor

French, sometimes pointing things out to me. Amazingly, I have a conversation about the World Cup with Diallo when we stop at the WAAME tree plantation. He's a big fan of Manchester United and their captain, Roy Keane, from Cork. I'm the first Irish person Diallo has met, though. Kind of breaks the ice!

Later in the evening, I sit in the warm breeze in white moonlight, wrapped in the green sarong for the wind is quite stiff now off the delta, the river water splashing over the parapet. I drink a beer and think what a fine birthday I've had with lovely people, all keen to include me in their daily lives. This is what it's all about. I knew this would be a significant journey. I wonder what will follow?

Sail

> *A single sailboat*
> *moves across blue grey water:*
> *Good Friday, Ventry.*

26 In Search of Cooler Weather

It's late afternoon, nearly six o'clock and still roasting despite a strong breeze off the river. If I sat out in the sun, my nose would be a complete mess. It's a red mess already but I can't risk it getting worse. I feel agitated again. I need to go on down the road, to move. The choice is simple: if I go south, I need to do it in one journey so that I can get to a bank at Ziguinchor. I've no interest in hanging around Gambia dealing with currency hassles and hustlers, I just want to get to Casamance. It turns out that Sherif is actually from the south and Ous lived in Ziguinchor for years.

They both assure me that the temperature there will be lower due to the greater vegetation in the region. Everything inside me urges a move to the south. I better follow this directive.

Downtown, there's lots of action as people arrive home for the Easter Holiday, followed immediately on Tuesday by the country's most important local Muslim celebration: *le Grand Magal*. This takes place up north at Touba, with people returning each year from abroad in their thousands for the celebration, just like our Christmas. Cheik the tailor is bubbling with excitement; he is heading off tomorrow. This will be his third *Magal* and he is excited about meeting extended family and friends. From my perspective, there's a transport hitch: every vehicle in the country is on its way to Touba. Will I be able to get to the south in a day, or will I get stuck in Gambia waiting for the Banjul ferry? This is like trying to figure out the weather at home in Corca Dhuibhne, an impossible task.

In the afternoon, down at Khadi's place, a kid arrives with plastic bags of *mafé*, peanut butter sauce, a gift from her Christian neighbours. For *Tabaski*, Islam's most important festival (called *Eid al Kabir* in Arabic), Khadi sends them a cut of her ritual lamb. She insists on charging me the local price for her wonderful meals: 'You are a regular now,' she tells me, 'so you get a regular's discount.'

I spend another hour with her, peeling onions.

Moonrise Over Cuan

In a day of splendid light, of saturated apricot sunset which leaves the sea at Brandon Bay pure light held by a dark band at the horizon, the moonrise

147

dazzles. Later, in the distance somewhere over Cuan, the moon appears as a deep orange sphere, its reflection glowing on the small arm of bay there. I wonder if the people who are resident there this holiday weekend are experiencing this light, or if it is a gift of my higher elevation. I go outside and sit in the red chair, just watching. Moon worship on Easter Saturday eve.

27 Mopping the Brow of Christ

Baobab-sur-Mer has been taken over by a group of French families down from Dakar. There are eleven huge landrovers in the yard. The men are French military servicemen wondering, perhaps, if they will be deployed to Côte-d'Ivoire where the locals and the French Military have a major disagreement about who is shooting at whom. It's too hot to go anywhere and too hot to stay in my room, so I'm sitting in the verandah writing this instead, trying to ignore my various bites which blossom like tropical flowers on my arms and lower legs.

The Easter Day Mass was wonderful. The jubilant choir had returned from Casamance. Adults and kids were being confirmed, babies baptized, elders receiving blessings, newly-weds too, an action-packed ceremony presided over by the tallest man I've ever seen. As the chief celebrant, he towered above his colleagues, lean as a pole-vault athlete, with an exultant, impassioned but comradely familiarity in addressing the congregation. I am struck by the prayerful attitude, the sanctity of the rituals here. Altar boys hand towels to the priest like Veronica mopping the brow of Christ.

Later, when the afternoon turns golden, I walk along the shoreline of the muddy river. I hope that going south is a good idea, that it really will be cooler there. By now I'm almost desperate for a dip in the ocean and, while I don't have high hopes that the Cap Skiring beach scene will be any different from places I've been along the Petite Côte, I'm very willing, right now, for a beach-type holiday.

Easter

A tender, still day beginning in bright sun, warm, slowly giving way to haze and colder weather. It is the day of the opening of Féile na Cásca, the Easter exhibit at the Máimín in Ballyferriter. Despite the fine afternoon, the windows are covered with paper blocking out the day. Inside, it could be November and raining, while outside the sun shines. Returning home through Dunquin, I look up to Mt Eagle, and there, to my amazement, three hang gliders hover above the ridge. From the house in Ballintlea, I can still see them, and reach for the binoculars. The three are stationary high above the mountain. As I watch, one of them drifts sideways, his sail parallel to the land. In Ballintlea, not a breath of wind stirs. I watch birds – a blackbird, a songthrush – come to bathe in the pond, dipping and shivering their wings. Not a ripple but the ones they stir moves on the water, yet high above some steady wind holds the three sailers aloft, tiny gods surveying our universe.

28 Transit

I rise in darkness, nurse my bites and get to the bush-taxi stop outside the WAAME office before six in the morning. That may be the only vehicle of the day heading south, everyone's gone north to Touba for *Magal*. The brisk, twenty-minute walk in the tawny, cool coming-to-dayness is an energetic antidote to the lethargy of previous days. It feels right to be on the move again. The van arrives and I find out it's headed all the way south to the Banjul ferry. Unbelievable good fortune!

The ferry depot was a frenzy of activity, as if a fire had broken out! I'd still be there if Pape hadn't hustled me along through the crowd pushing and jostling to get a ticket, for God alone knows the ferry schedule, but we were on the ferry within the hour and climbed to the top deck for the view of the great river delta as it meets the Atlantic. He had been sitting up front in the van out of Foundiougne and heard my enquiry about getting to the ferry. A quiet, polite young man, he had offered to shepherd me through the hazards of border crossings and buying tickets. On the Banjul side, he just pushed past the taxi touts and hailed a yellow cab for Serekunda. We passed by the 'Ali Baba Enterprise Co. Ltd.', 'Junction Vibes Music Distributors' and endless machine, spare-parts and repair shops with titles like 'To God be the Glory'. ENTERPRISE and MULTI-CONCEPT are big buzz-words down here. The Serekunda market was a maze of plastic sandals and hot-food stalls but eventually we arrived at the garage where Pape organized my ticket and said a solemn *au revoir*, my guardian angel for the day.

I bought tea from King Prophet Mohamed, enjoying his friendly banter in local English until the next *sept-place* was ready to roll. Then off we headed, bump by bump across the thirty-five kilometres of non-road down through Gambia, towards Casamance and its regional capital, Ziguinchor.

I found the Hôtel Perroquet in the late afternoon on the waterfront, a small, French colonial building with a tropical garden, a sleeping dog and very laid-back people having sundowners on the deck. White egrets traversed the silvery river, water lapped the deck, brightly coloured pirogues were moored just down the way. The air was balmy. I had a strong feeling that I had made a good move, heading south into Casamance.

Translucence

These still days have left a haze over the landscape, a translucence. Today it seems that rain is always in the distance, yet when I arrive at the distance, there is none. It continues to seem elsewhere still, often in the direction from which I've come. When I come over the Clasach in late afternoon, the islands are floating amidst pure light, the still water no colour at all. On Béal Bán, a distant dark grey sky presses the light down against a milky jade green bay.

29 Fleuve de Casamance

The pirogue wended its way down the Casamance River into the mangroves. On the far bank, in the mudflats, pink flamingos, pelicans, herons and egrets picked their way through breakfast, guzzling prawns and a hundred other delicacies spewed up by the great river delta. We passed a fisherman's hut, perched in the mangrove swamp. They fish at night and sleep during the day, dropping the catch into Ziguinchor before dawn. The prawn fishers have small, crude pirogues, nothing at all like the huge barracuda pirogues that go out to sea for two or three weeks at a time. I wonder how they carry enough fresh water? In the morning, we stopped off at a small island and spoke with a woman shelling and drying oysters. There was no fresh water well there, nor was there a cistern for catching rainwater. Every three weeks or so, they must buy sweet water from the mainland. Moored around the island were small yachts owned by French guys who hire them out to other European fishermen year-round, tax-free, no port fees involved. I gave the woman a litre bottle of Kirene mineral water. What the hell else could I do? This kind of thing makes me so damn angry.

In the afternoon, we stop at Afinam to avoid the strong afternoon heat and I visit the famous round house, a thick-walled adobe with cool mud rooms, the roof made of durable mangrove wood. This is a traditional Casamance building, totally different to anything one would see up north. In many ways, it feels like a different country. The vegetation is lush: coconut palms, royal palms, tall kapok trees, mango, acacia, baobabs, and many species I don't recognize. The villages down here have a different design, the buildings are square, not round, wrought of molded mud and with deeply sloping roofs. It is hot but less so than in breathless Foundiougne.

Rita and Willem, from Flanders, have been on the river with me all day. We enjoy dinner on the deck in the balmy evening air and I hear amazing travel stories from their time in India and Nepal. Willem is an organic grower and a committed ecologist. He told me about a recent court case in India in which an American-based multinational tried to copyright basmati rice! The Indian government won the day in court, fair play to them.

Breath

Can this stillness last? It has begun to feel as if the wind is holding its breath.

30 Ziguinchor

Ziguinchor seems like a pretty nice town, green, clean and relaxed, French colonial buildings, gardens and a curious quarter of modern, three-storey buildings beyond the pirogue berth. Teenagers were practicing basketball outside and the whole thing had a suburban feel to it. I guess these are the upcoming middle-class people in a very poor society. The downtown market is in a covered, concrete modern building. This is the first time I've seen decent fruit on my journey and I buy mangos and papayas to share with my Flemish friends. The main street is full of hardware shops, dry goods stores, the banks, the cybercafé and a bookshop with piles of newspapers and magazines, including a great quarterly journal about African politics by the BBC, with an African editor. I spent quite a lot of time at the travel agency, trying to nail down an airline ticket from Cap Skiring back to Dakar. Right now they are cheap because the airport at Ziguinchor is closed for repairs. I might as well avail of this and avoid the long haul back north going overland. Maybe I'll go visit St Louis, the old capital way north of Dakar? Today, I feel relaxed, willing to hang out at the bookshop and the travel agency talking to the ladies, waiting to see what happens. I like the feel of this place and the temperature is okay. I eat lunch at a place near the *rond* that has a Guinness sign over the bar. I tell them I'm Irish, from the land of Guinness, and that the best way to drink it is from large bottles, warmed by the fire! They think this is hilarious and they invite me to a complimentary beer. Later, I head back to the Hôtel Perroquet to share tropical fruits and sundowners with the Flemings in the balmy evening.

Still

Still still.

31 Overcast

At half past six the sky was overcast, but by breakfast time, the thin gauze began to dissipate, sucked up by a thirsty sun. The humidity remains high over the river although it feels several degrees cooler than it was up in Foundiougne. There's a peculiar light between the hours of seven and nine in the morning. The Casamance River is silvery-grey with a matt texture, not brilliant, probably because of the river mud underneath. The sky is a paler whitish-grey, causing a silver sheen on the river. Mangrove swamps ride the horizon line. By nine o'clock, the sun is breaking through. As I sip the second cup of coffee, I become aware of the whispering voices of two little children through the pillars of the balcony. The nice guy who minds the bar is also serving breakfast and as he clears the end table, he gives them whatever bread has been left. Why are you travelling, Trish? What is the urge that drives you out? Safety wants to stay home, not deal with children begging, guilt, boredom, heat and hassle. So what the hell are you doing here?

In the early afternoon, I arrived in Cap Skiring, a village with the trappings of beach tourism – lots of little bars, chophouses, batik stalls, the usual stuff. Walking back the road to where the *campements* begin, a guy in a jeep stopped, offered me a lift, said it was too hot to walk. He said he'd drop me at a place I'd enjoy. Le Falafu. Fine.

6.20 p.m. This is a really beautiful beach lined by palm groves, miles long. It continues on past the Guinea Bisseau border, three kilometres down the beach. The sea is choppy and only slightly warm in the strong breeze. What a relief to go for a long walk in a stiff breeze!

Curl

When I sit out on these still evenings in the red chair against the orange wall, I can hear the water in Ventry Harbour curl and meet the shore. And curl again. And curl again.

April

1 Sundown

At quarter to eight it's nearly dark. Sundown happens swiftly around quarter past seven. I went down to the beach and bathed as the huge sun disappeared. It doesn't sink red into the ocean but vanishes into a haze, never setting. The temperature is delicious at this hour, perfect for hanging out on the balcony, listening to the roar of the ocean below. In the afternoon, Erika, the owner of Le Falafu, invited me to join her and Moussa for coffee. Her braided long dark hair and heavy silver jewellery give her an exotic air, her body lithe and sinuous, a dancer's body. It's hard to believe she is Swiss. There is an intense energy about her that is curious and attractive. Moussa is the cook and mister fix-it for the *campement*. He has very beautiful almond eyes and an air of merriment about him. I feel very welcome here, as if I already know these people. Strange.

Moon-Inhabited

The dawn this day is a clear and moon-inhabited blue filled with birdsong.

2 La Lutte

Everyone is excited because this is the first day of *La Lutte*, the annual wrestling festival in the village of Kabrousse, three kilometres down the road. Although wrestling is the national sport of Senegal, the wrestling at Kabrousse is different, unique to the people of this particular area, spilling over the border into Guinea Bisseau. The people here are neither Muslims nor Christians: they worship the spirit world and have even declined to hook up to the national grid because they feel electricity may disturb the energy in the village and interfere in their communication with The Unseen.

The opening ceremony gets going around four o'clock when the great heat of the day is beginning to wane. There are hundreds of people there already when we arrive, standing in a huge circle around a clearing in the bush, the older women leading the clapping and singing, cheerleading the various teams as they arrive, boys and girls organized according to their ages, each age group wearing a particular colour. From time to time, various individuals go into the circle and perform a hopping dance, raising the energy around their teams, keeping things charged up while we wait for the arrival of the Fetish. The arena is surrounded by dry savannah woodland and by five o'clock the sunlight is somewhat filtered, although it is still quite hot out of the shade. The Fetish arrives out of the bush with its retinue, carried by the Fetish Priest, a tall, very thin old man. He goes to the centre of the arena and plants the Fetish – a tall stick with a short crossbar like a long sword – in the dirt. Moussa whispers to me to watch closely, that the Fetish will spontaneously catch fire and smolder throughout, but not burn down. The men have poured fresh palm wine and the Priest has drunk for the Fetish, the calabashes have been passed around and further incantations have been sung. The Fetish starts to smoke. The Fight is ready to begin.

Today, it's the boys' turn. The girls will fight tomorrow and the last day is the championship for the young men. Boys advance in pairs, challenging a pair from another team to fight. Each challenge is a swift affair, lasting about three minutes, or less. The idea is to get your opponent flat on his back on the ground. The arena is large so many challenges are happening simultaneously, clapping, drumming and cheerleading going on by different supporters all around the circle. Everyone is buzzing with energy, thrilled to be here today, thrilled to witness the skill and beauty of their fine young people.

When it is over, Moussa and I walk home through the bush, he pointing out various shrubs, trees and birds for me as we walk on dusty trails, the golden sun declining quickly now. This is a beautiful hour of the day, the sound of birds slightly echoing in the bush, the slanting light, the stillness. We stop by a house to greet some friends and then descend to the beach in the gathering darkness for the last half mile to the house, listening to the ocean, enjoying the light, cooling breeze.

Summer Skin

This morning as I sit outside drinking coffee, eating a scone, layer after layer comes off in the warmth of the sun. Tonight, my skin is glowing, the first blush of summer.

3 Dance

We missed seeing the girls fight. They had already finished when we arrived at five o'clock – they fought in the heat of the day, fair play to them! I saw the morning from the noon end, exhausted after last night's outing to town with Moussa. The *Orchestra de*

Sédhiou was playing in a local club and I was keen to get a taste of the local scene, minus the disco. We went at eleven, much too early, so we got the disco anyway but it was worth the wait because the orchestra was fantastic, playing long dance sets of up to twenty-five minutes: Brazilian *samba*, Congolese *rumba*, Cuban *son*, local *mbalax*, and the odd 1950s jazz standard thrown in for good measure! Equal to the orchestra was the style of the dancers: ladies wearing bodiced tops with leg o'mutton sleeves over long, tight skirts and extremely high-heeled sandals, all designed to show every curve of breast, hip and thigh. And the hats! The hats could be worn to Ascot! The men were pretty slick, too. Watching this lot dance, it's really hard for me to believe I'm in a Muslim society. The flirting, the parading, the unbelievably suggestive nature of the dancing, the hip-to-hip closeness of it all, are, well, quite a surprise! This is not the hip young international crowd of the Dakar nightclubs, fresh off the catwalks of Paris or Milan – although I've seen a few of them here, as well – but local enthusiasts on a regular night out, strutting their considerable stuff. I dance with Moussa, treading on his fancy white dancing shoes several times. They have long, tapered toes that curl up at the ends, for heaven's sakes!

At two o'clock, I begged to go home, exhausted. My white cotton trousers and blue silk shirt were soaked in sweat, my hair plastered to my skull, my head was spinning and I needed to fall down. A mile out of town, we came upon a get-together of about thirty people dancing in a circle. Two balafon players sat in the dust, sharing the big wooden instrument between them. The dancing was curious, wild hopping on one foot, the other foot doing an acrobatic thing of its own, individuals coming forward to do their particular dance, inviting someone else and then retiring to the circle, the balafon unceasingly in the background, everyone singing and clapping. Dust rising. People laughing, enjoying one another's style, flirting, showing off, just for fun. It was a gathering of Mandinka people, Moussa's people, so he entered the circle and strutted his stuff too, grinning with delight, before we headed off down the dark road again, avoiding gigantic potholes in the intermittent tarmac, our clothes drying now in the light breeze.

Distant Blue Vista

It is difficult to describe the peacefulness of these days. The sun shines benignly. If there is wind, it is little more than a breeze. If there is fog or rain, it is brief, often occurring discreetly in the dark. The nights are mostly chill and star-filled. The days give rise to dawn glow and distant blue vista. I move slowly through them finally, after the rush of the past two weeks. I walk barefoot across the lawn, feeling this land with my feet, taking root.

4 Cooling Wind, Warm Embrace

In the evening, I go with Moussa to Bakine, a *campement* that operates like an arts centre, where there's supposed to be dancing tonight. But nothing is happening, so we leave and go down to the beach, walk for a long time in the cooling wind and hold one another for a longer time in a tender warm embrace.

Slashing Silver Rain

Variability returns to the mountainside. The weather today alternates

between small intervals of calm sunshine and grass-flattening wind followed
by slashing silver rain. The Cuan caravans gleam white in the storm light.
The new island ferry remains anchored in Ventry Harbour. I race from
window to window catching rainbows, one anchored at Masatiompan,
another stretching from Brandon to just below the house. At sunset, peach-
tinged clouds drift across Mt Eagle from Dunquin.

5 Decision

Tears poured down, confusion reigned, an inner battle raged.
I didn't even register the heat. At sundown, I decided not to leave
tomorrow as planned. I will make the return trip to Dakar in one
long haul, and hope to make the flight on time.

The guys from the *mbalax* band have a gig tonight at the hotel near
Kabrousse, so we'll wander down there later on. They are living
here in the *campement* for the week – they come from up north,
near St Louis – and, as well as being fantastic musicians and dancers,
they are inveterate flirts, especially the incredibly beautiful El Haji
to whom I've given my silver sun and moon earrings. But it is
Moussa I'm staying for.

Sweaters Back On

Winter returns with a vengeance. Wind howls, drives sheets of rain into
whatever is in its way. The temperature drops. Everywhere, grey. In a
moment of folly, I washed all my heavy sweaters yesterday, and now they
stretch damp across the frame in the back room, destined to remain that way
for a few more days. To stay warm, I add layer upon layer, listening to the
wind howl through the vents. Yet it is good in its way to be inside and dry

with the rain beating on the roof and a fire in the hearth. Sheltered from the
storm.

6 Here and Now

It was pretty hot today, windless when I plunged in the waves
after breakfast. Later at Bakine it was a wild night. The sensuous
woman in the red dress beckoned me to dance with her, to follow
her steps. I couldn't take my eyes off her. Olivier's pronounced limp
vanished when he danced, his bulky six feet plus dreadlocks flying
in the air. Moussa whirled in his flowing robes, laughing, whooping
with delight. At three in the morning, exhausted and exhilarated,
we walked home hand-in-hand through the bush, in the starlight,
caressed by the warm wind blowing in off the ocean.

Fierce Squalls and News of Snow

All day wind has been flattening the grass between intervals of calm. Fierce
squalls of rain descend preceded by the roar of wind. The far mountains
disappear. The bay disappears. The stone fence disappears, and the world I
can see becomes small and luminous, dotted with the last of the daffodils, the
wild pale primroses and the cultivated ones coloured blue and fuchsia and
violet. White galanthus rise. Thrift is in bloom on the hill, the yellow gorse.
Bluebells in the shy corners. In between the storms, I pull the pale runners
of last year's nasturtiums, hoping for such abundance again this year. I begin
to prune away the dead fennel stalks, but stop, wondering if they somehow
deflect the wind from the tender new shoots at their base. A friend calls from
Dublin in the evening, and tells me snow is predicted soon.

162

7 Market

In the cooling afternoon, we walked to the village by way of the beach, through the tourist village and the fish market. I bought a bag of spicy Touba coffee for Sandra and a huge watermelon for supper. Moussa picked it out, so he had to carry it home! At dusk, I swam again in the warm ocean, not wanting, now, to leave this place, this person I'm just beginning to know.

North Wind

On the small table in the living room, I've put a map of this end of the peninsula arranged so that it lies the same way as the landscape I look at out the windows. A compass sits on top of it so it can be re-aligned if I happen to move it for some reason. This is such a folded landscape, with such a northern sun, I'm still, after seven years, never quite sure where I am, or where things I know are in relation to me. With the fixed point of the house, I hope to learn.

The front door here faces southwest, and I see Mt Brandon out the back room windows to the northeast. The windows of the long side of the house face southeast, gathering in the sunlight. On a clear day I can see Glenbeigh and the Macgillicuddy's Reeks from them. I know, I think, just where Slea Head and the Great Blasket are, out of sight behind Mt Eagle, where the sun disappears sometime after seven these evenings, and then casts its setting colours onto the clouds on this side.

From all this, I know that today's wind was a north wind, although one step outside and into its chill would have told me the same thing as the map and the compass inside.

8 Afternoon

Madame Kamara, Moussa's step-mother, sits under a tree shelling peanuts, watching Pope John Paul II's funeral on the television. I lie with Moussa in the darkness of his room, in the heavy heat of the afternoon. Before sundown, we walk across town to visit his mother's household and on the way pick mangos from a neighbour's yard – breakfast for Monica when I arrive in Dublin.

April Snow and Seagulls

This morning Brandon is covered with snow again, a light dusting, but a good way down the mountain. In the market, vendors are alternately protecting perishables from the heat of the sun and grabbing their booths against arctic gusts of wind. Everyone has gloves on, and when I meet Biddy, she is in her big winter coat with her hood up. By afternoon, the mountain is clear, and I find myself dozing at home in the early evening. The movement of a large bird catches my eye, and I see it is a gull. Soon others appear, all heading up Mt Eagle toward the lake it seems, a stream of them. Suddenly a cacophony of cries sounds, and I go to the kitchen to see masses of birds circling the mountainside. So far as I know, no field was opened today, and I've not, in my admittedly short time here, seen this before. As quickly as it began, whatever it is, is over, the gulls seeming to melt into the air. Later, I close the curtains against the dark and light the fire. It is cold tonight, but not as cold as it has been these past few days, this April return of winter.

9 Flight

It was still dark when Moussa woke me, when we washed

in the yard before going to the *Gare Routières* to get the earliest *sept-place* out of Ziguinchor for Dakar. Two hours up the road, the sun rose and the long journey embraced me into itself, a curious comfort to the pain of parting. Now it's evening. We made it to Dakar before sundown, returning by Kaolak this time. I looked out at the salt beds, water and salt pouring out of my own body as we passed through the region and I was aware of a different response now, a month down the line from when I arrived in this country. It just feels different, that's all. Now I sit in the airport lounge, writing, watching other travellers waiting to board flights, looking at the phone cubicles, wanting to call Moussa, to hear his voice but I have no phone card. The flight leaves after midnight. Another four hours to go. Other travellers seem so pressed and laundered, not a hair out of place. Here am I, in comparison, wrecked and grubby and overwhelmed.

Quiet Weather

A day of weather shifting quietly, soft as water flowing in a summer river. Fog came and went. Rain pattered. Sun dappled the hills. All this with little fuss, no dramatics. Gentle background to the day.

10 Lost

It's cold and wet at Dublin Airport. My backpack has disappeared and I'm feeling pretty damn lost myself.

Now

Now it's spring that has returned, mildness and pale sunshine. The long light in the evenings makes it feel like summer, and travelling to Feohanagh tonight, it seemed that every detail of the base of Masatiompan was etched in the slanting light. Tomorrow, Derrick comes to begin to teach me the garden. What to weed, what will stay. Once I've the tasks set, each day can bring time outside, hands in the earth for learning.

11 The Rain That's Not Falling

The weather is okay but I can't stop crying. All the rain that's not falling today is leaking out of me instead.

Trimming

The day starts warm and dry, dry enough for laundry on the line and grass cutting. Derrick arrives and we walk the garden plotting where the mower will go, identifying what can be trimmed. He sets off on the mower and I descend with the secateurs for clipping and my two hands for trimming. As we work, the clouds begin to gather and the temperature to drop. By the time he leaves, the lawn around the house is cut, paths leading to small sheltered places for sitting wind through the grass that will be allowed to grow wild, and a few small patches are incrementally neater, although it seems a substantial amount of last year's growth has been added to the pile inside the holding fences. The laundry has also come in from the line and I have learned how to start the mower and gingerly operate the strimmer. When the rain begins, I'm inside by the fire, warm, with a sense of having begun a task that will occupy me for years, if not the rest of my life.

12 Cold

A wet and windy day. Grey sky, black sea. Cold, inside and out.

Inside Gardening

Although the day is warm and dry, it seems that the indoor plants I inherited with this house could use some attention. I water each of them, the philodendron climbing a moss post, the Boston fern, the aloe in the living room and the cactus in the kitchen, the spreading prayer plant by the hearth and the giant Monsteria deliciosa *(yes!) climbing the wall. The only directions I was given was to water them once a week, but they are in need of trimming and dusting. Consulting a book on house plants, I learn I've been watering the bromeliad incorrectly, and so pour some water directly into its thirsty centre. I water the very happy geranium – a dark red Tomboy – I brought with me. It is thriving in the kitchen in the place it was casually set down when I first arrived. All of this takes a great deal of time, and leads me on to other dustings and cleanings. By nightfall, I've a sizeable bag of clippings for the pile outside, and all of us in the house feel better, ready for the flowerings of summer.*

13 Weather Change

What the hell am I doing here at Monica's place in Bray? Why don't I go home? I can't bear to go back to the familiar world in case the great weather change that has happened in me might drift away.

How Many Weathers Can a Day Have?

Today I woke in a pool of sunlight, drank morning coffee looking down at a gleaming Ventry Harbour, but before noon, the sky released lashings of sepia rain, with a swirl of wind to make it drenching. The afternoon drive to Tralee was wet still, but by the time I parked downtown, patches of blue showed, and then it cleared. Mid-afternoon, it rained again, then hailed in Farranfore. I entered a store through ice pellets and emerged perhaps ten minutes later to warm sun. Far in the distance, the sky was a deep carbon grey above glistening emerald fields, but none of the rain fell again until I returned to Ballintlea where I turned off the main road in light drizzle and then climbed past the loch turn a few minutes later in dazzling sunlight shot with slashing silver rain. More shiftings before dark, deepening blues and shimmering rainbows, soft golden light resting on the hills. Creamy clouds in a tender robin's egg blue sky. Now, at dark, stars shine above me, and I am off to bed, exhausted from the weathers.

14 Changing Trains at Mallow

There's a change of trains at Mallow. I cross the bridge to the shop on the far side of the long platform, hoping for warm coffee and maybe the *Irish Times* to warm things up and distract from the coldness inside and out. Mallow Station on a cold day is not the bleakest one in Ireland – that accolade goes to Limerick Junction – but the coffee is just finished and the paper is sold out. A young woman with toddler, baby and buggy struggles to negotiate the stairs to the bridge, so I offer to help. She says she's from Nigeria, living in Tralee. I tell her I've just returned from Senegal where people often helped me on my way.

Driving into Elusive Rainbows

I had the good fortune to be driving east late this afternoon, into deep grey storm clouds with the sun behind me. Several times rainbows appeared in front of me, not in the usual high arcing intensity, but as a low pale wash of shimmering colour scrimmed across the landscape, colour so faint it seemed to be almost not there. Yet it was.

15 Oblivious

Sandra enfolds me in careful affection in the mountain house. Surrounded by weather, I'm in the eye of the storm, oblivious.

Sunlight Wakes Me

Sunlight wakes me. When I open my eyes, there before me is a bright blue sky with a curving wash of dark grey, and in front of the grey, an illuminated white puff of a cloud. In the time it takes me to write this, the cloud is gone, moved west by the wind. I lift my head and see a golden apricot rain below the grey.

16 Picnic

On the way to the train at Tralee, we stop awhile at Pedlar's Lake above the Connor Pass so that Seán Kerry can shout and hear the echo coming back from the sheer walls of rock all around us. Sylvia and Bernd take lots of photos: this is their son's first visit to the place he is named for, a place they love. Further on down the road we spend an hour in bright spring sunshine in a sandy cove near Castlegregory where we eat our picnic, half-pretending that they aren't really leaving to go home to Germany. Caught up in my own drama, I didn't realize they had to leave today – I thought it was Monday.

Red Tulips

> *In a friend's garden*
> *deepred tulips celebrate*
> *her passionate path.*

17 The View from Sandra's Loo

Opalescent light glows over the dark brow of Sliabh an Iolair. Thin, wispy clouds process in slow motion across the emptying sky, bruised tones of khaki and olive green. The light seems to intensify although daylight is seeping away now behind the mountain but the moss and lichen texture of the hill is still visible against the coal-dark wetness of rock and the lighter grey of stone dried out by wind. This is the view from Sandra's loo!

Computer Weather

When there are computers, there is very little weather.

18 Dawn to Dusk

Woke at 6 a.m. to bright sunshine on the mountain. Slept at 6 p.m. in warm sunlight at Kinard. Later on, saw the Blaskets floating in luminous mist in a silvery ocean. Flat calm.

Eating Murphys Ice Cream Outdoors

Although the cautious weather predictions in Saturday's Irish Times *showed boxes with rain falling for a week, a partial sun hiding somewhere behind the precipitating cloud, today is glorious, warm and bright. In the morning, I trim old canes from the mint garden, my hands as they move sending up fragrance from the new growth, my back warmed by the sun. By afternoon, the weather has not done its frequent shift to cloud cover heading for rain. This mid-April day behaves like summer, and I move the red chair into a patch of sun outside. I remember that just a bit of a carton of Murphys* fanaile *ice cream remains in the freezer, and I go inside to collect it. When I come out again, a white sailboat moves across the deep blue bay. I spoon ice cream into my mouth, luxuriating, thinking of summer and honeysuckle bloom.*

19 Garden

There was a scattering of frost when I woke up but two hours later, the sun is well risen and is warming the caravan at last. The garden glistens, the greening well underway.

Glenbeigh Glowing

It is after seven at night, the sun still full out but about to go behind Mt Eagle. In the distance, Glenbeigh glows with a white luminescence, as if it were a mythical place, the hills around it hazed with the same pale light. I sit in the living room. The sun floods the windows behind me in the kitchen with a yellow warmth. The house casts a shadow in front of me. A bar of sunlight touches the cover of Colour, *a book resting on the end table, making each pigment represented there vibrate with intensity. The quarter moon rides high waiting for the sun's kiss of light. I know in just moments, when the sun drops behind the mountain, all this will shift, the blues deepening into the violet hour, when birds arrow into bushes for sleep.*

20 Between Two Mountains

The evening sun was a platinum disc above Sliabh an Iolair and in the inner folds of Mount Brandon to the north, dense thermals were rising, spilling over the ridges. No wind.

Crossing Mountains and Many Sunsets

After the sun sets behind Mt Eagle this evening, I cross the mountain to Dunquin, where it looks from Baile an tSléibhe as if it might be a bit overcast. I've left a still night full of birdsong, the aftermath of a sun-filled day, yet from Dunquin, bathed in rosy light, I look back to what seem to be dark storm clouds massed behind Marhin on my home side of the mountain. Driving, I see the sun set again, this time into the cloud bank far offshore. I go on to Ballyferriter, where the storm clouds now surround Mt Brandon, then turn to pass back through Dunquin on my way home. The sun appears briefly again, muted by clouds. By the time I've almost reached Coumeenoole, the air is suffused with peach light and I see the lower edge of the sun a deep glowing orange moving into an opening in the clouds. All along, an orange light has been reflected on the water. As a thin line on the horizon, as an oval out beyond Inishtooskert. I pull off the road to watch as the sun slowly passes through the clouds, slipping finally away. At home, the night continues calm. The storm clouds are nowhere to be seen. All along, it seemed the storms were somewhere else, across the mountain, but never there.

21 Tropical Sunset

In a limpid, pastel blue sky, the mountains are powder blue darkening to indigo. Way above, blue seeps away to luminous, eggshell white. As I ascend the Connor Pass going home from Tralee, a brilliant window of flamingo pink is thrown open over Brandon, then a molten orange sun flames through, giving the pastel world of the northern spring a cheeky, tropical flavour.

Teaching Me the Morning

This house is teaching me the morning as no lover, friend, or even husband could. Most people I've known have been early risers. Connected to the more obvious natural cycles of light, they often have little regard for my rhapsodies over darkness and moonlight-laced silence. They wake with first light, and by dark or reasonably soon thereafter, are ready for sleep. And of course we all know that early to bed and early to rise makes a man healthy, wealthy and wise, so all virtue argues against my habitual, not to say genetically ingrained, habit of wakefulness far into the night followed by sleep well into the morning. Here in Baile an tSléibhe, my bed faces a large window looking southeast across sloping fields to Ventry Harbour and then the Iveragh Peninsula in the distance. But if I am lying down, I see mostly just a sizeable slice of the sky. These late spring mornings the sun streams early into the room, flooding it with light, warming me, waking me. If I think to look at the clock, I often find it hours before my usual waking time. This morning I came awake at five-thirty, opening my eyes to a rose-infused sky, the mountains a deep, almost burgundy silhouette against it. I thought of a friend's praise of summer predawns above Mt Brandon, and rose from my bed to look out, to even go into the next room to look at Mt Brandon itself. Back in my own room, I could see the sun had still not yet risen. Should I watch a while, I wondered. Was this return of the sun linked to yesterday's many sunsets? I folded myself back into bed, thinking to watch, but alas

must have dozed, as next I knew, the sun was in the room, a golden patch
on the wall, and, when I looked, full up in the sky. I'd missed its slide into
day. I know now though that from my bed, I will see the first finger of light
on the wall, and can move to watch the entire rising. More and more often
here I wake in these early hours, predawn or first light, the sun indeed doing
what no lover or friend or even husband could.

22 Revelation

At nine in the evening, the sky above Ballymore is laden
with cloud forms; blankets, eiderdowns of gathered moisture in
shades of grey and textured hues of darkening blues; slight bruising
around the edges going vaguely purple, lightly, as if through a
sepia filter. The sea below is steel grey, the headland at Parkmore
across the harbour pewter, now, as the light refines, thins itself,
deepening all colour before blotting it out completely. I caught
sight of the moon, her hiding place suddenly revealed and, just as
quickly, concealed again. At first, I couldn't name the colour she
was wearing but then I had it: opal.

My brother joins me for an hour of silence in the growing darkness,
the yellow candle on the shrine playing on the sand picture from
Casamance, the southernmost part of Senegal from whence I have
recently returned. Returned? I don't know any more. I observe I
am not really present to what is happening here.

The wind has dropped from this morning's wet bluster and by
half past ten this April evening there is a cool nip in the air: the
Scairbhín na gCuach is in the weather wings, waiting to be fully
revealed.

Sea Indigo

All morning a clear bright line runs across the bay below the Iveragh Peninsula. The wind is strong enough to make whitecaps visible even from my mountain perch. As I drive to town midday, the line continues a white band. Below it, the water is indigo shading to green. Three distinct colours, intensely glowing.

23 Photosynthesis

It's a shining green world this morning in Ballymore. The foliage in the willow garden outside my window, buffeted playfully by the sharp, dry Scairbhín wind, is bursting with bright light: the magic, the energy of photosynthesis revealed in texture, colour and motion. Fascinating.

Distractions

Trish and I are inside working at the computer on Weather Watch. *We are sitting at my desk in front of a window that looks out across the fields to Ventry Harbour. As we work, scrolling and pasting, adjusting and editing our weather records of the last six months, the water below us shifts and changes and fills with light. Trish exclaims, and I look up to see the water a colour I can only call navy green, combined with a silver shimmering faintly tinged with lavender. We are trying to be diligent in our work, but the light is constantly distracting, mesmerizing. Suddenly I notice the time, and leap up, thinking we are late for an appointment. I am wrong about the time, but the leaping up has taken us into the living room, where we stand looking down at the water, which has somehow become even more spectacular than before. I conclude I was not wrong about the time. It is time to stop work, to*

*stop addressing the abstract symbols describing weather on the page, and to
stand and revel in the real thing spread out in such glory before us.*

24 Atmospheric Pressure

A glorious summer's morning and the full moon at 10 a.m.
hinted strongly at the first swim of the season but, just after Britta
and I got down to the cuaisín, around two o'clock, the weather
changed completely. For the rest of the day and through the
evening I've had a splitting headache and a nauseous, unbalanced
sensation. I think the sudden drop in atmospheric pressure sent me
reeling. Coupled with a full moon and an inner world blasted open
by recent events, this is a bit over the top! I'm going to bed for a
long sleep.

Two

*Two ravens fly over
deep in conversation.
Their voices descend
companionable
from the clear blue sky.*

25 The Values of Grey

I saw the dawn from a corner of my dreaming. It burned
crimson, a small island of livid colour in a sky dense with grey
cloud. I know an English painter called Mick who lives at the Baltic
Sea; he explained to me once how shades of grey create definition
for stronger colours. Swathed in my blue wool wrap, hugging the

morning coffee this damp morning, I admire the emerging yellow irises below the 'van and consider the values of grey.

Milky Day

The morning starts with its usual sunshine, although when I look back toward Cruach Mhárthain, I see mist. No wind gives a sign of how weather might move, but by midday the mist has spread across all I can see. Everywhere a veil blurs or obscures the landscape, a veil the colour of the pale pale blue-white film left on a glass of milk after it has been drunk.

26 Turn and Turnabout

It was a day full of dynamic weather changes. I woke to a cold, rainy morning, lit the fire, wrapped myself in the blue wool shawl and set to relearning the script for *Magpies*. At around noon, the sun was bursting the sky and I had to open doors and windows to avoid being cooked inside, although outside there was a stiff breeze driving in from the ocean. By evening, I was blue with the cold and lit the fire again. Now, just after midnight, it is raining hard, spattering like gunshot against the aluminium caravan, the usual advent of summer in Corca Dhuibhne.

The Glories of the Night.

Last night. Oh! Working late, I look through the glass doors and find below me a shimmering sea of moonlight dancing across the bay. The moon herself is hidden behind clouds, but casting light lavishly down. I open the doors and stand outside to look, drinking in the delight of it. When I finally go to bed at five in the morning, the clouds have cleared and the moon is still above Sliabh an Iolair, while the sun is beginning to brighten the sky in the east to a tender blue. I see a circle of light on the floor at the end of my hallway, just outside my bedroom. I realize it is moonlight coming through the round front door window. I kneel down into the light, turn, and find the near-full moon hovering round in the round window. I go to sleep feeling suspended in light, moon setting, sun rising. Glorious.

27 The Possibility of a Jungle

'April showers bring forth May flowers…' If the old adage is correct, and if the weather continues to carry on like this, then there's the definite possibility of a jungle bursting forth!

Hardly Looking Up

It is three-thirty in the afternoon, and I have been working at the computer since I started the day. Having missed the morning's sun, I began to concentrate on the screen during grey and rain. Now, hours later, I raise my eyes to the window and see the day is brightening. Mick's Blasket Island ferry is moored in Ventry Harbour, so no island access today. It is, in fact, a still day, bright again. As my eyes rest with relief on the landscape, I realize I've hardly looked up in all the hours I've been working. Anything could have been happening out there. The hare and her young one could have crossed the garden. The birds could have bathed and shivered off the water in the pond. The mountains of the Iveragh could have come and gone, and colours in the sky. Computer Weather inside. Grey.

28 Storm and Bluster

In the early hours, a full-scale storm was bashing the

caravan from the southwest and rain lashed against the aluminium like gunshot. I slept fitfully and woke late at nine o'clock full of quandary, unhinged so that it took a full hour to steady myself but the unsettledness prevailed throughout the day. Storm gave way to bluster, torrential rain to sunshine as the day increased and later, an early evening sunshine storm was blowing hard across Ballymore, the water down in the cuaisín all churned up, bashing dementedly against the perimeters of the swimming hole. Do I really go swimming down there in that torrid pool? Now, close to midnight, the only sound is the force of the ocean out there in the not so dark night. I wonder if it ever storms like this down at Cap Skiring where Moussa is?

April, Baile an tSléibhe

> Bees in the willows
> make a summer humming sound
> while cold rain slants down.

29 Luscious Still Dreaming

There is a perfect stillness this evening at eight o'clock. The mackerel sky has fled away to an opaque overcast, highlighting the green of grass, the paler green of the willows, nettle green, juicy montbretia greens and the black green of fuchsia bushes, all conspiring to overwhelm my computer-tired vision in a luscious still dreaming.

Janus Sunset

Inside working at sunset tonight, I stopped for a rest as the light faded. From the front of the house, looking southeast, it was a muted world, grey and soft. I stood a while looking out. When I returned to the other side of the house where I'd been working, I found a sky flaring rose, pulsing, deepening. I sat still watching as Cruach Mhárthain's curves were silhouetted against this passion, as the rose deepened and complicated, added lavender, and then slowly muted into grey.

30 Soundscape Saturday

This moisture-laden eve of Bealtaine, the only sounds are his lordship, the Ballymore cockerel, announcing his presence, birdies twittering on willow branches, the swish-swish of Britta's knitting machine and the occasional car heading into Dingle, amplified by wet tarmac; otherwise, the eternal rumbling undertone of the now quiet ocean.

No Mountain Day

Fog down. Mountain gone. Little more to say.

Bealtaine
Summer

May

1 Stormy May Day

The beautiful old Irish poem announces: 'May-day, season fair, perfect time of year' but this one is overcast, wet and very windy. Britta and I look out, reckoning it's much too stormy to go out to Béal Bán for the races this Bealtaine.

Moussa called earlier. 'What's the temperature?' I enquire. 'Getting hotter,' he laughs. Senegal: warm, hot and getting hotter. It's warm here today too, in the sense that it's not cold, relatively speaking! I've hitched the door open to let the wind circulate and although it's pouring rain, there's no call to light a fire to counteract the dampness. My hands aren't blue either, a real sign that this is summer weather, however wet.

The Kindness of Damp Weather, or: The Pages Are Falling! The Pages Are Falling!

I woke yesterday to my least favourite weather: fog, no wind, dreary drenching rain. It reminded me of winters in Oregon where such weather can go on, it seems, for months without respite, with no sight of the sun or dryness. Yesterday's weather followed several days of warmth with sun and brilliant light, and I thought with resignation of how the things for the Weather Watch installation would all have to be protected in plastic just for the move from the house to the car to the site, as yesterday was the day for mounting the exhibit for Féile na Bealtaine in Dingle.

Once there, Trish and I hung the first book in Lisbeth Mulcahy's archway, then watched the weather take it apart. Wind lifted and clattered the pages with our writing, loosening them. The damp of the wall and the gutter began to seep into the paper. Even as we triaged, changing to meet the weather conditions, the weather let us know we'd not taken it enough into consideration. The weather, the subject we'd observed and written about for nearly six months. Finally, while Trish was off problem-solving and Britta, who'd stopped by to advise, and I stood holding in place the one long book we'd actually managed to mount, the pages began to detach and fall one by one to the ground. We looked at each other in dismay, and she at me with pity. It was clear that the installation, so long worked on – and printed in the official Féile na Bealtaine program – could not be mounted in this space. Britta said then it was a good thing the day was damp as, had we done the installation in calm dry weather, we might have come in on the next damp or windy day to find the pages gone, blown around the town.

Trish returned. We took the book down, catching the pages now falling faster and faster. Dismay all around. But Trish took over, calling for hot chocolate and re-grouping, the end to guilt, and the necessity for a new space. This, in the very late afternoon of a bank holiday Saturday when all the town was crammed with artists mounting exhibits for the Féile starting the next day. Miraculously, she did find space, and a fine one at that, in the Díseart. We spent the evening clearing the room, installing and repairing, moving gingerly away from the dismay. Today I'm left thinking of the kindness of the weather in providing a damp day to show us the folly of our choice of venue, and to give us the chance to change.

2 Sky Sisters

The Sky Painter has put herself to bed at last, pulled up the

186

soft mauve and grey duvet of evening this second day of Bealtaine, ready for slumber at the end of a perfect day in the western world. Her older sister, the Big Blue, doesn't retire at this time of the year at all, preferring to hang out all evening until dawn, radiating her subtle light, flirting with those of nocturnal disposition.

Warm
Words cannot say the pleasure of the warm sun on the body in the garden.

3 To Everything a Season
Masses of cloud move high over Ballymore from somewhere north of Brandon Mountain, dense banks of pearl-grey thermals, gilded gold, rose and peach under the infinitely thin blue dome of the early summer's evening, flying swiftly southwards towards the Scelligs. After Sandra and Britta depart, I watch the racing clouds until colour and the visible world seep away to indigo. My friend Mark phones to tell me that he and Despina are selling his lifetime home and moving to Greece, her homeland, a revolutionary turnabout in their lives. Sitting in the darkness listening to his news, I find myself smiling broadly. I hear in his voice the confidence of someone deeply following his inner direction, knowing his own weather, his own season. I notice that I am listening very acutely in the silence, in the stillness of the advancing evening, for my own deep knowing.

Sunlight Floods
In late afternoon, I return to the room in the Díseart where Weather

Watch/Faire na hAimsire *is installed. The room is empty at the moment, but I remember it earlier in the day filled with friends and strangers who have come to wish us well. Images return. Of the backs of people several rows deep, all turned to the hanging books, looking, reading, lifting the pages to uncover our stories. I hear Trish's voice and mine rise into the room, strong voices, sending our words into the air, to the ears of the listeners. I remember the genuine applause, and the comments after, the excitement. It is a simple idea, writing about the weather every day, but it seems to have touched some deep place in many people. I stand quiet in the bright room, the only person there now. The morning's rain has passed. Sunlight floods the far corner where the spiral-bound version of the manuscript rests open on the music stand with Trish's wellingtons below.* Weather Watch *is launched.*

4 Dining Alfresco

Warm sunshine and wind abound this afternoon. I go down to the cuaisín to check out the possibility of a silent hour on the lizard rock before going in to prepare for *Theatre Shorts* but the wind is sharp, reminding me of the old adage: 'Ne'er cast a clout 'til May is out!' The south side of the caravan, however, makes a great windbreak and the pair of beat-up wooden armchairs come into their own again, decked out now with brightly coloured cushions, so that when Kathrin arrives she dons her denim miniskirt and we enjoy our pre-show dinner alfresco, serenaded by birds, wind and ocean rumble. We consider the nature of deep friendship, our friendship, and how it might be should I move to Casamance, so far away in southern Senegal, to join Moussa, for this now feels like the direction my life is taking, a strange and unexpected direction, a

tough route, but nonetheless one that is calling to me loudly.
Kathrin and I have become so used to the intimacy of dailiness, an exchange and familiarity so reminiscent of weather itself, that the possibility of its absence seems inconceivable. On the other hand, soul friendships cultivated in an intrinsic creative intimacy have nothing to fear from space-time events. With that sure knowledge, we celebrate our first alfresco dinner of the year in good cheer.

Is Maith

Is maith an scéalaí an aimsir.

5 Unravelling

Emerging from the loo-with-a-view, I notice that the Scelligs have vanished while the Iveragh, breaking up slowly now in the distance, unravels itself into an infinity of grey. A bumblebee, hunting for supper in the impossibly yellow flags, is the only thing moving ahead of immanent rain.

Floating

Last night at just about the time I was supposed to be walking into the theatre, I was in my living room watching the clouds. Earlier, I'd been in the kitchen where I could see clouds above Sliabh an Iolair coloured by the sun setting beyond Dunquin. Intensities of amber there. I puzzled again the name for that very faint tinge of warmth left on the grey clouds as amber fades, a curiously unhealthy colour. Healing Bruise? Still pondering I wandered into the living room where I saw the sky gone to dun blue. Floating above the indigo mountains in the distance hung several slender

189

clouds, ethereal clouds, clouds delicate as a baby's eyebrow. Palest grey against the deeply peaceful blue, they were underlined with a gentle white, stroked above with tender pinks. As I watched, the colours shifted ever so subtly, deepening to rose, touching lavender, breathing almost, each breath a slightly different colour. A bit to the south, pale peach quivered. I sat until the sky became a monochrome of greys. Elated. Replete. Still.

6 Clarity

Clarity, silently observing the proceedings, on a grey, misty day in early summer.

Mist and Marble

The clouds were everywhere today, often on the ground in the shape of a fine and drenching mist. Even though it did not seem to be windy, the mist swirled about, sideways, driving in a soft sort of way. I thought of clouds I saw yesterday as I drove up to Biddy's house on Slieve Mish. The line of the mountain was sharp on the horizon, and the clouds above it were dense and glowing white, their edges sharp too, clean sculptured lines. I thought of marble, not cloud at all. Tonight, I wonder how these clouds are all related, the fine mist and the dense white. If clouds have clans and species, subspecies and divisions. If they recognize one another, or argue, or intermarry. So much goes on we've no idea of, just above our heads. Or today, swirling round our bodies.

7 Light

The summer hopefuls sit outside Quinn's in Ventry at seven o'clock for sundowners. The sun, still high enough above Sliabh an Iolair, casts its evening rays upon us, sheltered here from the stiff Scairbhín wind as we enjoy our drinks and yarns. Later, when the sun dips behind the mountain, coats go on and eventually, admitting we are pretty damn cold, we head for the warmth inside, reluctant because it is still so bright. Summer, here, is not about temperature: it's about light. This month of May, Bealtaine, is high summer and this continues through June to the summer solstice. All nature is at its zenith in this period of maximum light, relative summer in this North Atlantic place.

Long Light

I arrive home at 6 p.m. after time in town, a day in which it seems both warm and cool, the temperature varying almost within yards. On the way in, I stopped at the Ventry store wearing a wool sweater over a t-shirt and encountered a young woman at the counter in a camisole. Jim walked out in his shirtsleeves, heading down to one of the houses by the water. At home, it seems by the time night is starting, but after I read the Times, *nap, unpack town things, and wander around the house straightening and cleaning, the light is still bright. At nine-fifteen it looks like mid-afternoon. Summer is well begun.*

8 Skylarks

Low tide on this new moon day was half an hour before noon; at 0.8 metres, the water seemed miles away, particularly at the far end of Ventry Beach. These days, the shorefront is thickly coated in rich green seaweed and I'm sorry to have forgotten shovel and bag to gather some for the compost bin and the garden. This thought is suddenly shattered by the sound of skylarks. I look up but can't spot them; they are nesting in the dunes between Church Cross and Church Farm, creating a gleeful racket on this coldish, sunny morning. The Scairbhín is blowing from the northeast, making the river behind the caravan park shiver on its way down to the shore. One of the beach dogs is bathing in the foreshore, grinning that waggy-dog grin. Maybe he's enjoying last week's joke from the Kerry County Council which prohibits the walking of dogs on Kerry's beaches!

Bees Knocking

The house is cleaned. The pie − apple-rhubarb-pear-plum − is baked. Mozart is playing on the radio. The expected friends have not yet arrived. I am stretched on the couch, drifting, admiring the clouds, grateful that the weather is fine for the first visit of these friends to this house. I have not yet heard from them on the road, so am slightly surprised when I hear a gentle knocking, then another. It's not the friends, but bees, sun-dazed, knocking tipsy at the windows on their way from flower to sweet flower.

9 Weather and Home

Home is where the heart is, they say. What a wonderful day to show friends one's home, a new home, a day of brightest sunshine and cold wind, this month of May when nature is at its most exuberant pitch, the mayflower bursting white out of hedgerows, yellow flags and celandine carpeting the lush greenery, willows flying in the sharp Scairbhín wind, Ventry harbour bluer than blue under an eggshell pale sky. On the way to Sandra's first dinner party in her new home in Baile an tSléibhe, I divert to greet Britta and Glen in their new home at Baile an Trasna above Ventry. The foundations are dug, this is their first day in the mobile home, the champagne is flowing. Home at last. On up the road past Ard an Bhóthair, sharp right after Church Farm, and up the curve of the hill to Sandra's. This is her first formal dinner party in her new home, a small gathering of old friends and new, much talk of ancestors, familial relationships, language, the weather, in particular the quality of wind. Orna recalls storms past, how the old people told her about a wind that comes from the northwest that sounds like a train. She has heard it, can vouch for their knowledge. It caused havoc in the district on Christmas Eve some years past. Going home to Ballymore around midnight tonight, the sky is aglitter with starlight, a complete panoply on this early summer's evening. Watch out! There's likely to be a heavy frost under such a cold, clear sky. Now I'm glad that I didn't get those seeds sown, after all, during yesterday's dark phase of the moon.

Bright Blue Weather

The day dawns bright and stays that way, although I'm told by Dave who rose at dawn that a bit of rain came through. He says he saw the drops on the surface of the pond before they appeared on the cement of the half circle that I'm rather loathe to call a patio outside the glass doors. A small cloud passing through. We drive from Baile an tSléibhe to Dunquin, visiting the site of each house I've lived in there. The ferries cross in blue but rough seas. Dave says he can't name the blue, and we agree that even if we had Ridgway's colour book, we'd not open it in the bright light for fear of fading.

I contemplate the idea that a copy of this same Ridgway owned by the University of California at Berkeley can no longer be opened because it has faded so much in the bright California light. Does this book still exist as a book if it can't be opened? With my copy, will I only want to compare things seen in dim light? As we move about the end of the peninsula in clear sunshine, I'm grateful for the weather, good weather to be showing friends from far away my new landscape, to be having them say I live in paradise.

10 Wind Shadow

On this very cold morning, a solitary heron is perfectly reflected in the still water of the foreshore at Cúilín in the wind shadow: a no-time, no-motion study.

Oh So Still

The wind is quiet these days, blowing a gentle Scairbhín from the north. In the garden, the roses seem to have suddenly sprung with buds, magenta in the front garden, white by the driveway. Derrick comes to cut the grass, leaving daisies and a ranunculus behind. High mowing. Dave, Rainie and I walk from the Clasach across Sliabh an Iolair down the zigzag to the lake and home, a long bright day with more light still. We race into Dingle for lamb chops, eat, visit Bob, are joined by Orna as we walk over to An Chathair Liath in the growing dusk. We marvel at the age of the structures, cross a field with cattle in it, and a bull, travel along a fuchsia tunnel, and then to home. Dark finally, clouds and a few stars. A letter from the man who was once my husband, the dishes, and bed.

11 Absorbing Blue

In the morning, the Scellig Rocks are immense on the southern horizon in a glassy ocean. Cloud cover of an uncertain disposition has built up overnight yet it is still quite cold. Overall, an absorbing blue, filtering light from sea and sky. No movement.

Rain Again

The moment the guests depart, rain. The sun-dazzle of the past days is gone. Instead, an evening of calm greys and birdsong.

12 Low Pressure

Intensity of filtered light and low barometric pressure: is this the calm before a storm? Today, I don't know where my skin ends and the weather begins.

Jubilant Haze

The swallows are jubilant today, swooping more than even swallows do. No wind to resist them, they are free to move lightly in any direction, sweeping down to touch the pond, curving over the stone wall, arcing above the field below. Moving, it almost seems, in amazement at the absence of the wind that both supports and resists them. In the distance, the mountains are hazed, as if a sheet of etched glass has descended between here and there, the birds making the patterns, the stillness keeping the haze in place.

13 March in May

The cold dry Scairbhín is overdoing it today. The skin on my hands is beginning to crack and they go purple with cold if I don't light the fire. The fire, imagine, at this time of year! Scandalous carry on. Nothing in me wants to go walking in this biting, easterly breeze. It feels like March in May.

A Wintry Day in May

I leave the house this morning wearing a linen skirt in acknowledgment of the month, and a heavy wool sweater in response to the actual weather. No bare feet and sandals this day, but a return to tights. Everyone in town mentions the wind, although at what is my usually famously windy house it seemed rather calm. Yesterday's haze continues, but with what Orna describes as a heaviness when she comes to visit in the evening. Even as it is cold, I do not make a fire, reading comfortably into the night. May, but not May. Summer, but not quite.

14 Skirmishing with the Wind

The wind direction changed today sometime around noon: the biting easterly Scairbhín swung around and lost some of its sting, if not its bluster. On a ramble with Kathrin and Donie, I huddled into a bunker just underneath Eask Tower, above Burnham inlet, glinting like phosphorescence in the slanting light. Filling our bag with sea spinach, we repaired to Ballymore, eager now for dinner after skirmishing with the wind.

Lessons in Flirting

All this day when I should have been thinking about the weather, a story of flirting kept coming to mind. It was a cold day, bright with sun. I did not see any flirting in the weather, unless it was the swallows with the sky, or with the water as they so briefly touched the surface of the pond. Perhaps it was something in the way the huge sun sank slowly into the sea and the sky turned rose. I remembered a sense that when Trish returned from Senegal, many of her Weather Watches seemed full of noticings of flirtatious activity around her. What I thought of today was an encounter I had some years ago with an eminent English writer. It came about that I was one of a group of people at dinner with him, and also who acted as his escort while he was visiting a city near where I lived. He had asked to see a particular wild orchid blooming, one he'd read about but never encountered. This had been arranged and some of us had travelled together and found the orchid, which caused tears to come to the writer's eyes. One among us thought it may have had something to do with the wife he had recently lost to a sudden death, but none of us could really know. It was perhaps simply the beauty of the orchid itself, rising fragile and pink on the shaded forest floor. I was an admirer of this man's work, and so was mostly rather quiet around him. As he was leaving the hotel where he stayed, we were standing together on the sidewalk. He turned to me and admired the silver earrings I was wearing. Naively, wishing to offer him pleasure, I unclipped one of them from my ear and handed it toward him for a closer inspection. He looked briefly startled, and declined to take it. I saw in a flash how inappropriate my action had been. His had been a courtly gesture, a very gentle and civilized admiration. I saw he was not admiring my earring so much as acknowledging that I was female and he male. The appropriate response to such a gesture would have been a slight arching and baring of the neck toward him, with perhaps eyes lowered. No more. No less. A moment indeed brief and graceful as the swallows' touch on the surface of the water. A downward curve, a touch, a rise. Pleasure to the bird. Pleasure to the water. Connection. Past.

15 Sociable Weather

The wind had the good grace to drop this morning in the lovely graveyard below Ballyferriter where John, our Ballymore neighbour, was laid to rest. A sociable, music-loving man in life, he was celebrated in death with beautiful songs and lilting dance tunes in the great magnificence of sky and ocean looking out over Dún an Óir, a place he loved. I followed Britta to her new homestead at Baile an Trasna for a brunch of fried eggs and the view of Ventry Harbour, followed by a gentle ramble around Slea Head in wind and sunlight with Peadar. Stretched out on beds of sea pinks, at eye level with a flock of twenty elegant choughs, we watched a seal way below us and gannets plummeting from the sky into turquoise depths in search of lunch. So much sky, so much sea, so much wind, so much energy. I phone Moussa to tell him about this day *amuigh faoin spéir*, explaining how it is still not dark although it's now half past ten, for this is the northern summer although I'm still lighting the fire in the evening. Down at Cap Skiring, it's a roaster at 40 degrees.

The Absence of the Green Flash

Yesterday as I left Biddy's new home, the sun was huge above the horizon, glowing orange. A few clouds hovered far out at sea. I thought this might be a night for a possible sighting of a green flash, something I've never seen. Years ago I read about this phenomenon, an eruption of green light occurring just after the sun sinks below the horizon of the sea. It is something I have watched for at every opportunity and latitude, hopeful even when it seemed unlikely. Since I left Dunquin in March, I've had report of two

198

green flashes there, and I think of all the sunsets I eagerly watched from its headlands without a single hint of green, even as the colours that did appear challenged the imagination in their naming. The recent sightings both happened on nights with slight cloud on the horizon, so this gave me hope yesterday, and I calculated where I might best find a clear view of the sunset, one not blocked by tree or hedgerow or house, and how quickly I might get there. I raced along the highway glancing more often than I probably should have at the quickly lowering sun. A turn for the beach at Carrigharoe left me literally hedged in until, speeding along the green boreen, I reached the main road again. Finally I did find a spot with a slight elevation where I had a clear view of the horizon. The sun seemed to melt molten into the sea. Alive with anticipation, I risked my eyes in taking long glances, but the sun was soon gone leaving no green behind. The air was suffused with rose, Brandon a dark silhouette against it. Clouds trembled with shifting gildings. I told myself to revel in the glory that was and not yearn for what was absent, but could not stem the disappointment. As I drove on again, I thought about courage and risk. Is it, I wondered, the courage, the Icarus risk, to stare long at the orange sun that yields the fountain of green?

16 Concert

Wind blows through sycamores in the grey overcast, bruised a pearly pink at this hour of the evening. The lovely altar window in St James' Church frames the musicians and the weather. Éilís translates the gist of a song for the international audience: 'You are my sun at night, my refuge in a storm, a shelter from bad weather.'

This Mildness

What is this mildness in the time of the Scairbhín? Today Ger, Kate and I walk up to the lake on Sliabh an Iolair in the gentlest of weather. Wind rolls across the curves of the mountain, but seems to end in sighs. We return to the house through Cill Uru watching light beam down on the slopes we just walked. 'Glorious Light,' Kate says, naming a series of slides from Ireland she once presented. Later, in moonlight, we stroll down toward the beach, our shadows preceding us. The night is quiet except for the murmur of the distant waves and the sleepy baas of lambs. 'This is usually a wind tunnel,' I tell them, but, wrapped in moonlight, they hardly seem to hear.

17 Cotton Wool Sky

There's a cotton wool sky high above me as I lie in the warm sand of the dunes near where the bridges cross the reed beds at the far end of Ventry Beach. The wind has a sting in it still, although there are signs of a change, but I lie out of its reach, horizontal. In this corner all is still: the multitude of small woolly clouds are stuck to the deep blue wrapping paper above. Only the sounds of a barking dog splashing through the foreshore and the faraway breaking wave of the outgoing tide cue my brain that something, somewhere, is in motion. I am utterly still.

Sunburned

I look in the mirror at my sunburned face and think of the day spent rambling. With Béal Bán in mind, we set off toward Slea Head, were distracted into Fán, admired the Scelligs faint on the horizon. Below on the highway strange cars raced along the road, tour buses waddled, cyclists rode, stunned, under the sun, and walkers travelled with their jackets tied round their waists. We did ultimately get to Béal Bán, wandered barefoot the length of it, and returned with pockets full of crystals and shells. As we walked, the scattered clouds coalesced to grey cover, the water shifted from translucent green to deep teal. At home, we lit the fire and settled in for sunset and conversation, an evening ending with pie.

18 Release

The rain came this morning, the sky's gentle release after three cold, dry weeks. The ground accepts it easily, relieved of thirst. The rain trickles down windowpanes, softly, insistently, my own face a windowpane for warm salt tears. Everything is fluid on this menstrual day: blood, rain and tears, moisture for body, earth and soul.

Beaded

After the days of still sunlight, rain returns. Just now, in the early evening, the fog has descended. For all I can see them, the Iveragh Peninsula and Sliabh an Iolair may not exist. The far headland is a faint shadow. The house feels calm in the beaded lawn, the stone wall a holding around it.

19 Wind and Silence

The wind gathered throughout the day and was blowing hard this evening as Kathrin and I sat, making space for inner silence. Sometimes, I find silence in the wind.

Shushing

Fog settles in, with a gentle shushing rain. Blair, visiting after five months in Ghana, talks about how good it feels to be in the cool grey again, sheltered inside a house with the small storm outside.

20 Wind in the Willows

The willows are dancing in the wind, skittering playfully in the airwaves. I have made my couch outside on the wooden chairs, hoping to lie down awhile in the wind and the sun. I need to let the weather flow through me. Somewhere I'm caught in an anticyclone, things are blocked up. The willows flex and bend lightly in the wind, fluidly, calling to me to pay attention.

Moonbright

Outside tonight, a moonbright night, bright enough to see in a blue the colour of dusk.

21 A Moment in the Here and Now

All is still in Burnham Wood, no wind there, sheltered by summer foliage. Down on the waterfront, I sit for a little while but the stones are cold; there's been no real warmth yet this May. A subtle sound flirts with me, interrupting the barrage of thoughts that are troubling my head: it's the delicate popping sound of seaweed releasing oxygen into the water, the familiar bubbles appearing on the still surface of Burnham lagoon. A gull flies low over the water, perfectly reflected. A moment in the here and now.

Blue-Laced

As we travelled across the Blasket Sound this afternoon, the colour of the water was a blue-laced black, the brilliant blue shimmering in strands on the surface.

22 Changeable

'Changeable' is the only reasonable forecast these days. This morning, I wandered with Britta and Tinka down the track behind Tig Áine's to Clogher Beach. It started to blow right on cue after we left the café, spitting rain and a wind that would hurt your head. Clogher was in full bluster, all that cubic tonnage of water throwing its weight around, elegantly though, well dressed in shades of turquoise and aquamarine. On the return, having been wind-blasted up on the headland, the rain stopped, the wind vanished and the suddenly warm sun made us peel off our coats. Along the stream, orchids glittered like amethysts after rain.

Shimmering

A shimmering, cold day of sun and sudden shower, rainbows arcing over Ventry Harbour. Trish, Blair and I sit in the May living room near a winter-sized fire, watching hail falling through evening sunshine bounce off the curved cement outside.

23 Writing the Weather

It's cold, wet and grey, this twenty-third day of May. There are other things I could say to expand that report but they would describe me, not the weather. The inner weather is cold, grey, hungover and frightening.

Ripple

With little sleep, I am up early, out, and have walked the length of Ventry Beach before 10 a.m. The wind is strong, pushing the waves back further than even the tide pulls, making braided cords of the crests. I free my hair from its clip, letting it skirl out. I am yearning for a grounding, for the cleansing wind. I walk with it and into it, move, stand still. I stay a long while. When I return home, I walk slowly through the garden, looking, stopping. Somehow in all the moving and settling, I still haven't found the plants. My eyes can rest on stone or shell, catch their infinite specific varieties, but skim over the plants, unable to stop beyond briefly. As I walk, I wonder if I should have been given the care of these lives. I stand at the edge of the upper garden, looking down at the lower which has been allowed to go completely wild. As I watch, the wind ripples through, bending grasses this way and that, their seedheads catching the light. No steady move in one direction, but arabesques. Dancing wind. I see myself as perhaps a stone in a river, affecting the current of the wind as it passes around me coming down from the mountain. I wonder which pattern might be mine.

24 Listening to the Weather

Sweeping veils of sepia-coloured fog are rushing in from the south over the jagged skyline of Macha na Bó to the left and the great mass of Brandon Mountain to the right, as I ascend the Connor Pass coming home from Tralee. At the top, I pull into the lay-by and sit awhile in woolly whiteness, listening to the patter of rain on the windshield and the wind rocking the car. I am tired, glad to rest here after a heavy inner storm. Today, I learned to listen up close to turbulence; listening took the place of being afraid, a subtle shift of attention. Up in this foggy eyrie, I am at peace, listening to the weather.

Ahead

In the glittering rain ahead of us, a writhing on the road. I slow the car and we see a kitten, its back legs thrashing, clearly hit. I stop the car, put on the emergency lights and get out. In the headlights, in the falling rain, the kitten is soaked and mewing. I move her to the side of the road and she burrows into the bushes. With a canvas bag as wrap, I capture her and hand her in to Blair. We are silent on the way to the house, wondering what we face. No blood is visible, but the kitten's eyes are wide with shock. She is sleeping now, or dying, I do not know. She would take no milk, either from dish or twisted and soaked cloth. Her breathing is occasionally ragged and congested, her head shakes oddly. We made no examination, as it was near midnight when we returned from the cinema, only wrapped her and put her in a box by the heater. It is, as Blair said, better than the road. It's the best we can do for now.

25 A Delicate Pink Suggestion

A day of heavy rain passed into an evening of fog. It was hugging the skyline at Kinard, edging closer from the Dingle side while maintaining its distance out to sea. Washing up after dinner at Kathrin's, I glanced out the only un-fogged window in her caravan to see a pearly pink glow over Dún Shean. Stepping outside into the damp, cold garden, we watched as the unseen sunset filtered through the veil a delicate pink suggestion, a suggestion that became a statement as it filled the gaps between fogbank and horizon line, then spilled over into the milky ocean below. Then it was gone.

Damp and Done

A day of drenching rain spent trying to find a home for the roadway kitten who awoke at dawn this morning whole and well, something confirmed by the veterinarian Eileen. It seems all day I ran from car to place, the kitten-containing cardboard box clutched under my arm dampening a bit each time. Tonight, the kitten resides at Mags' house in Ballywiheen which now shelters a mother cat, four two-week old kittens, a six-week old step-kitten, and last night's small survivor, judged about four weeks old. This is a temporary home while I take Blair to Shannon. On Friday when I return, I'm to pick up the kitten for whom I've still to find a home. As we settled her in at Mags', the kitten ended sleeping on my lap, tired from her adventures, and at ease in the shelter of my arms. She has a dash of black along her nose, continued more faintly under her chin, green eyes that look out calmly at the world, a delicate head and a brave heart. I think of her now sleeping trustingly, then think of the birds in their unguarded bathings by the pond in the sanctuary of my garden, and do not know what to do.

26 Calm

The May evening is utterly still under a grey sky dense with humidity. Mist spills out from low mountain tops and hillside valleys as I drive home from visiting Úna in her new home near Lispole. Starracín looms vertically through cloud near Flemingstown, a cloud bank that rolls way back over the Connor Pass. On the seaward side, there's little visibility, perhaps half a mile or so, then nothingness. We had lingered outside the house, marvelling at the evening birdsong, checking the Ordnance Survey map against the vague outline of hills and mountains in the shifting mist. Midges hovered, cunningly picking at us in the damp atmosphere, several degrees higher today, it seemed, than previous days this week. Around Úna's house, mature sycamores hang darkly in the falling evening. We establish that the big outline directly to the south is a mountain of the Iveragh, the next peninsula across. I had thought it was Caherconree but no, now I see it is a much longer outline since the mist had shape-shifted on the horizon. Annascaul is to our left, Caherconree further east, out of sight this foggy evening. There's no ripple on the water in Dingle Harbour; seaweed floats motionless on the glassy surface at Milltown Bridge. At home in Ballymore, the yellow irises and the arum lilies seem to glow as the evening increases. No need of a fire tonight. I wonder if that's the end of buying briquettes and firelighters? Is summer really going to happen at long last?

Aflame

Coming into Shannon tonight we find the sky at sunset deepening shades of rose and orange. The first blush, hardly apricot, is followed by a sudden burst of flamingo that throbs its way into a gaudy shocking pink. The colour-washed clouds are gauzy in the sky, veiled over a background of grey. Still, but almost dancing, they remind me of a description of the Northern Lights I once read: Tai Chi movements across the sky.

27 No Weather Report Today

Dreary

Is there anything so dreary as Limerick in the rain?

28 No Need to Water

Rain patters on the caravan roof, on the big windows. It's after midnight and the only other sounds are the tap-tap of my fingers on the keyboard and Sooki's creeping along the top of the sink, trying to be invisible, wondering where the hell the salmon went, for the smell still lingers…No need to water Derrick's plants, nature is doing it for me. The big green barrel beside his caravan is spilling over with rain water and there's a pile more up in that heavy sky. At the market this morning, Rosemarie and I talked about the state of gardens this May: frankly, it's now too late to be sowing summer veggies and salads; the earth has been too cold for germination up to now and anything that is showing up is quickly gobbled by voracious slugs. Someone else had predictions of an intense heat wave coming in July–August, the kind of heat that kills off older people. All I know right now is, there's no need to water.

Breathing

After yesterday's grey, sunlight and shadow return, the light breathing in the living room as I sit and read. Caught in the black and white symbols, I am sometimes startled by the bloom of light, look up to see the day passing silver then blue outside.

29 End of an Era

I sit in the courtyard of Mark's house, coffee cup in hand, dog at my feet, face to the summer sun at nine o'clock this Sunday morning. It's a hide-and-seek game with dark clouds and warm sunshine. There's a freshness in the air, a slightly damp sensation along with the intangible scent of wild roses. It is more than half a year since I have visited here and this is probably my last visit ever. The place is being auctioned at the end of June and my friends will leave to live in Greece. The end of an era. A mile down the road is the place of my childhood, Newtown Anner. Whenever I have come to visit this house, I have walked in the woods and riverside fields of my old home. But this is a fine morning to celebrate the here and now without nostalgia: the warmth, the roses, the coffee, the visit. From here on in, we'll be visiting by email.

Ventry Blues

The morning that begins in sunlight gradually greys. Far across near the Reeks, the clouds cast the water below to a deep navy blue with lighter stripes of marine. Near shore, blue green fades into jade. I look at the sky above all this intensity and see nothing but shades of grey.

30 Flirting

As I cross the field, shimmering light catches my eye, flirting with me. What's that, I wonder? Aha! It's the rainwater in the green barrel reflected against the aluminium of Derrick's mobile home. The image shimmers, flickering white flames in brilliant light. I look closer and see filigree webs strung from the rusted chassis, gleaming.

A scarlet plastic crate is alive with light energy, complementing the green barrel. All of this, couched in tall grass, wide butterburr and pungent nettles, gloriously parading verdant energy in sun and wind. Threatening cloud masses have gathered to the north over Brandon auguring more heavy rain after this pet day break. Still no need to water.

An Island Day

When I wake mid-morning, the day is bright and still. I look down to Ventry Harbour and see Mick's boat is gone, a sign that ferries go in to the Great Blasket today. Even in Dunquin, I did not have such easy access to this news, having usually to go to a nearby field and then stand waiting to see the ferry crossing. I like this connection to the Blasket at a glance from my windows, the way it re-affirms my ties to the other side of the mountain and the islands beyond.

31 Sensory Perception

Birdsong bursts from surrounding meadows and hedges, cows are bawling on the hill, early commuters flash past, a horn blows, alerting someone to his lift into Tralee. In the background, the hollow caw–caw of the crow. The sky is a blanket of grey-white cloud. Willows sway gently in a light breeze. It is warmish in a damp, sunless, Irish kind of way. Smells waft – I could smell the coffee brewing as I walked back from the loo a while ago. Everything echoes, amplified under the low sky. Sitting here with coffee and cat, listening to birdsong, I wonder and worry what I will do in Senegal. Maybe I'll learn to just BE.

Velvet Sky and Metal Sea

All of this strange day, the clouds hung thick in the sky, seeming not in the least cloudlike, but dense and velvety. They made a low ceiling, and underneath, the surface of the water was still and metallic, pewter as I passed by Inch on the way to Killorglin, bronze on the way back. When I finally reached home, the clouds had descended further, obscuring even my very orange house from sight as I came up the road. The air was full of water, but with none of the release of rain.

June

1 Crimson Dreaming

Ballintlea is shrouded in thick fog and it's raining hard when I leave Steve's studio. I can't see a thing and must manoeuvre carefully out the driveway onto the curving laneway, blind. We've spent nearly three hours trying to retrieve information from my computer via his studio systems, so, at half past two in the morning, it's time to call it a day. The sky is aglow over the crossroads at Ard an Bhóthair, the sodium street lamps around the little church reddening the sky in a foggy halo, leaking into the aqueous molecules. All of a sudden, the image of flamingos rising off Lake Naivasha, their tail feathers dripping red pigment into the crimson-hued lake in East African morning light, floods my memory.

White

I wake to a white world. Outside my stone walls, nothing is visible but white, the fog still settled in. All day, the white continues, no mountain, no sea, just white.

2 Special Effects

From Strand Street, the sky behind Dingle town is illuminated by filtered, golden light. It catches the eaves and roofs of buildings along the harbour front, all gilt now like paintings of the Italian Renaissance. Tourists pass along the pier, checking out menus in the windows of pubs, hoping for hot dinners and a cosy environment on this second day of June, an apology for summer. But something is happening now: the overcast is opening and the Lighting-Techie-in-the-Sky is doing wonderful things for our delight.

Possible Wind

The fog continues low on the ground. In the morning I can see nothing of the mountain beyond my stone wall, and only the faintest hint of the land stretching below me to Ventry Harbour. A drenching rain falls, but the fog holds back the wind, so I put the inside plants outside, their first spring bath. The living room looks larger with the prayer plant and the fern gone, the bromeliad no longer hovering in the corner. I think to move them to the back room for a while, where they will have enough summer sun and heat. I think of them outside now, these domestic creatures, and wonder if they luxuriate in the feel of the rain washing them, watering their pots, or if they quake in fear of slugs and possible wind. By late afternoon, the world is still white, but I can see the foot of the mountain, and the harbour out past Ballymore. I see Mick's boat is anchored. Despite the calm seas, not an island day.

3 Bank Holiday Blues

What masqueraded, at first, as a better day than yesterday, turned around and bit us in the arse mid-morning. In the Goat Street Café, I needed a hot meal and consolation. In the evening, I needed another hot meal and consolation took the form of congeniality and good cheer with Kathrin, up at Seacrest. As we ate, it sounded like winter outside, blowing and storming and carrying on. Did someone mention summer? Ha! It's a bank holiday weekend, so the weather is doing a holiday-special to frighten off the tourists.

The Incredible Length of June Dusk in West Kerry

The morning begins in strong sunlight, strong enough for napping in with thoughts of an afternoon on the mountain, stretched out perhaps in heather at Gleann Fán. As those thoughts are forming, so is cloud on the mountaintop, and the day devolves into a misery of rain and cold. By late afternoon the rain has let up, and the long dusk begun. At 10.30 p.m., I'm still watching clouds, currents of grey on the move. The dusk has been long enough for me to unload the car, unpack all the groceries, have two good conversations with friends, and check on another. To read the Irish Times *from front to back, to nap deeply enough to dream, then to wake and watch the clouds. It's still nearly three weeks to solstice, when it will hardly be dark at all.*

4 Slug

Sitting on the step, scrutinizing my little garden, I don't see much growth in the sweet peas I planted out two weeks ago, although the strawberry plants, previously pot-bound, have enjoyed the cold, wet weather and are now flowering. Comfrey, the blue geranium and foxgloves are also indifferent to these low summer temperatures. They are flourishing, along with enormous slugs. I am slow and sluggish myself these days, weighted down with resistance to life.

Things to Do Inside

When I lived in Dunquin, it seemed I was outside at least for a bit on most days. All around were short loops, down to the cuaisín, across Graig to Clogher Beach, along the cliffs and up past Gobnait's well, that I could walk in intervals when no rain threatened or fell. Here in Baile an tSléibhe, to walk is to start a long route, down to Ventry Beach, up to the lake, along the ridge of Mt Eagle, all a commitment to both time and weather. Days pass without an amble farther than the gate, but I think it is more the shifting shape of my life here than the landscape that keeps me in. I first came to Ireland for respite, knowing few people, an outsider in the community. My days were full of unstructured time when I could respond to a clearing outside, or spend the afternoon with no thought of needing to return home. I'd left all the everyday dealings of banks and insurance and bills, even friendships, in the US, tidying up details to lie dormant until my return after months away. Now that I live here, all these things live here too, calling for my attention indoors, keeping me from the mountains and the beach, keeping me inside with things to do.

5 Sunday Best

Ventry has vanished. Down on the beach, visibility is about one hundred metres in either direction. The littoral is disheveled today. Curly strands of bladderwrack lie along the foreshore like discarded tutus, brown-bodiced with golden frills; green sea lettuce and pink carrageen pattern the sepia-toned beach, more vivid now in opalescent light than in bright sunshine. A strip of beach, the foreshore, a parallel strip of water: nothingness on either side, yet so much to see, to wonder about! Why are there so many dogfish corpses in the shorewater today? I've counted fifteen already, plus one silvery fish that might have been bass. That one had a chunk missing, as if a seal had munched on it for breakfast. The black, bark-like substance along the waterline is peat, I reckon, the ground-down version of the peaty clumps you see further down the beach near the fen land. Close to the shore, but on the sandy bed, is a narrow carpet of reddish weed; the wavelets forming and breaking on the surface don't ever seem to turn it over. Everything is so still, so minute in movement this hushed Sunday. As the water fans out from the shore, it assumes a milky-green tone, becoming milky-blue near the pier, which all of a sudden vanishes from sight. There's nothing behind me now, no Sliabh an Iolair, no Cruach Mhárthain, nothing up ahead nor out to sea, only this narrow strip of beach and shore, a fascinating clutter of organic life showing itself off in a coquettish manner: Ventry Beach dressed in its Sunday best.

Bank Holiday Weather

It is a bank holiday weekend, so naturally the weather is wretched, as it was for the May bank holiday too. Someone did mention vaguely that Easter was fine, although that was so long ago it may not be accurate. The fog sat low on the ground, obscuring even Ventry Harbour. The rain teemed down. Trish arrived at my door, her clothes mottled with wet spots after a walk on the beach. Maria arrived for her first visit with her hood up, her feet soaked in crossing the few yards between car and door. The rain did let up for a brief meander through the garden, then poured down again as I dashed for the car and a dinner with friends in town. When I opened and closed the gate, the tracks of the road were running with water, as they were when I returned home several hours later. A typical bank holiday day.

216

6 Clearance

The sky has opened up in the south, out past the Scelligs, and seems to be pushing the dense cloud cover away inland. The temperature shot up overnight but not enough to burn off the overcast. Donie and I walked along the Slea Head track, lightly attired in a clammy warmth, bemused as fog chopped and changed the familiar landscape into all manner of weird visual effects. The entire middle section of the big Scellig was obliterated, leaving a flat lump on the ocean with two curious shapes apparently hanging in the further distance like pieces of a jigsaw puzzle scattered about. Now, both islands are the vaguest outlines on the horizon but they are intact, the jigsaw complete again. After coffee at Slea Head, we walked back along the road in misty rain, enjoying the motion, delighted to have walked the lovely trail and greeted the mountain. If nothing else has prospered in cold gardens, at least the foxgloves are delighted with the mist and fog: their elegant purple frames line the roads, ditches and hill trails, bowing graciously in a formal, old-fashioned kind of way. In the evening, I watch the Valentia lighthouse winking at me across the bay in a completely bright sky at this hour of ten at night. For days, there has been no sky, no bay, no Iveragh, no Valentia. Maybe there's a change coming, at last. Maybe the real summer will roll in now. Maybe we'll lounge soon on these rocks, like lizards, soaking up the sun. Maybe. I won't put my wellies away yet, though, just in case.

Cloud Play

All day the clouds have swirled around the mountains, curving into hollows, curling over ridges. The lake on Mt Eagle looked as if it had become a

217

cauldron, clouds like steam rising all afternoon. On the far blue mountains of the Iveragh, morning clouds made a blanket over the peaks, flat-bottomed and embracing. By afternoon, the clouds had lowered to the water, leaving the peaks exposed. Whenever I looked out, a cloud was dancing with a mountain, until, when Danny, Máire and Orla left, we stopped amazed at the gate to see a thick white mist held in the bowl of the Clasach, with the merest wisps, frail fingers, embracing the ridge stretching to the east. Their car left so slowly I knew they were enjoying the light and the shaping of it. I stood a while too, and when I turned back toward the house, there, hovering to the southeast, three perfectly curled clouds floated high, holding the last faint tinge of pink in the sky.

7 Sandra's Cure

Clearance did an about turn overnight and grey overcast was the order of the day, although fog and rain had, at least, moved on. As I write, this evening, it is quite windy, yesterday's warmth forgotten. I've just lit the stove and, earlier, cooked a big dinner of fish and spuds. The wellies stand sentinel at the door. Lots of people hereabout seem to have a feverish, bronchial bug, not helped by the prevailing damp weather. Sandra's cure for Britta was a gigantic portion of two hundred per cent buttercrust fruit pie with a half-pint of cream. Britta had to go home to sleep it off! If the weather keeps on like this, Sandra will have to bake hard, every day, to ward off nasty bugs in the ether.

Lily

> *Water lily blooms*
> *in the pond: white spiked petals*
> *hold a golden heart.*

8 Transformation

A not very promising, warmish morning transformed itself into a real summer's day at noon. By mid-afternoon, I was on my bike clad in sandals, jeans and green t-shirt. A question arose in my brain about the possibility of a swim but the breeze said, 'No, get on the bike!' It's a proper Irish summer's day with sufficient wispy cloud cover to restrain the sun's natural exuberance, a perfect bike day with little fear of being sunburned and not too much sweat going uphill. Yellow irises gleam elegantly in green willow meadows looking altogether different than on luminescent, overcast days. Same fields, same flowers, different light, different weather. What about us, then? Are we like plants, subjectively different according to light and weather?

Sky Blanket and Full Sun

This morning when Biddy calls, I report a blanket of clouds over the sky, a uniform covering of grey. Before I finish my shower, the grey has dispersed, leaving the sky blue and the day bright, even glaring. I put in laundry to hang on the line. The day unfolds in reading and the garden, but by early evening, the blanket is forming again. As I come up the hill from Ventry, I see the circle of the sun like a full moon through the clouds, so muted I can look straight at it, as I might at the moon. The laundry hangs utterly still

on the line. Not a breath of air stirs in the night. No stars are visible. Sky
blanket covers us.

9 Sickle Moon

Around two in the afternoon, my brain thinks it is too hot
out there. I laugh incredulously. Hot? Are you joking? Remember
forty-three degrees in Foundiougne inside the Siné Saloum Delta?
I cycle up to Ballintlea and get cold working on Sandra's computer,
absorbed in the study where the afternoon light is obscured.

Later, we sit in the dusking light with wine and mackerel pâté,
fascinated by the shaft of light on the brow of Sliabh an Iolair, rocks
and boulders highlighted like sculptures in an exhibition. What
about photographing the hillside every day for a year to catch the
light line? All the while, swallows dart and play over the pond.
Later again, I turn from my writing to see blue-filtered twilight
streaming into the kitchen, the new sickle moon overhanging a
dense cloud bank where once was mountain. We halt the car at
the crossroads onto the Clasach above Ard an Bhóthair, admiring
Cruach Mhárthain darkly impressed above thickening fog, the sliver
of moon sharp against the indigo sky. What a weird and wonderful
weather world!

Bees Hum

Bees hum amidst the magenta roses, the white water lily in the pond opens
to the sun. A blackbird strolls in the lawn gone wild, sure of his cover. On
my shelves I have a book in Irish that I hope some day to be able to read.
In a chapter on the weather is the name of a wind still except for a faint

occasional stirring like breath on a cheek. That's the wind this morning.

10 **Light**
At eight in the evening, blue black water, translucent in the cuaisín, reflects in dappled patterns on the grey rocks of the tide pools. I am shivering, can hardly hold pen to paper, my skin all goosebumps after only five minutes in silky ocean water, my first plunge of the summer. An hour later, the brilliance of the day begins to leak away, the sky softens to an eggshell hue and cows in the hillside field are gilt-edged in slanting evening light.

Summer Morning

I slide the glass door open to this summer morning and birdsong. Only the faintest breeze stirs in the day. I wander outside, my nightgown thin and diaphanous around me. At the edge of the pond, I look down into the golden heart of the water lily, kneel on the mossed stone to dabble my fingers in the water, then rise and slowly walk back toward the house, my feet feeling the softness of the uncut lawn. Off in the distance, thick clouds fold themselves around the curves of Mt Brandon, spilling into, filling, the valleys below. I think that tonight I will sit by the pond, watching for the reflection of the crescent moon to appear. I bring the súgán chair out into the sun to write. As I begin these words with the date, I realize that, had I still been married, today would have been our thirty-eighth wedding anniversary.

11 **Invoking the Goddess**
Tunnels of leafy green in dappled sunlight, the Sulane River at Baile Bhuirne gurgling and bubbling below us as we hang

over warm stones watching trout from the bridge. They hang loose in the slipstream, waiting for flies. This is Gobnait's country and I invoke the saint's blessing on Kathrin, Donie and myself as we wend our way eastwards this lovely summer morning to the meditation practice at Bandon.

Warmth

In the warmth of the afternoon, the coral poppy released its petals, dropping them to glow in sunlight on the wood of the living room table.

12 Song

There's a mist that appears from the west,
E Hine
Where the mountain below meets the mist from above,
E Hine
E Kui E Mareta, He Puna Roimata, Ingaro Ki te Po,
E Hinenui Te Po.

Listening to this beautiful Maori song as we travel home from Bandon through the golden noon across lush tree country, I try to sing along, to learn the shape of the words, but I am choked with tears. Something is evoked at the deepest level of emotion. Kathrin suddenly turns to me, 'Please sing for me sometimes when you go back to Senegal,' she asks. Tears stream down my face for the rest of the journey home.

Alphabet of Ballintlea

My garden seems full of birdsong, the morning wakings, but also just a steady commentary throughout the day. Blackbird or Wren launches into a complicated song. The pheasant coughs, someone cries out two notes. The ravens still pass in conversation overhead. I think back to the days of the brouhaha over the dawn chorus, and all the commentary explaining the function of birdsong, how it marks territory, how it will diminish as summer goes on and mating moves into rearing. Not here. The birds continue to sing, often it seems in sheer celebration of the day. The scientific attitude would have the song be purely functional, but I wonder how humans would feel if all their output of narrative, literature and myth and tale, were defined as 'seeking a mate' or 'marking a territory', which I suppose in some ways it could be considered to be. I remember a postcard I once received with the simple words: 'All art aspires to the condition of birdsong'. Then I think of writing things down. Last night a friend gave me the website www. bzzzpeek.com where, she said, I could find the way animal sounds are recorded in different languages. I've not seen this yet, but I imagine how a single recording of birdsong might be transcribed. How Irish with its broad and slender consonants might interpret it, or Russian with its access to the wonderful letter for a slurred zhhh. Do I hear what an Irish friend hears? Or a German? Or a Japanese? Once a friend came into my house and whistled – twice – a new birdsong he'd heard. Aside from being amazed at his ability to do this, I now wonder if it is the cadence, the music, that is the essence, and not any representation of it. And then I wonder at how these abstract figures on the page can possibly capture the silver bend of the grass as the wind moves through, or the precise lavender shading of the Iveragh at sunset. The dappling of clouds over the mountainsides or the gleam of small beetles moving across the surface of the pond. The golden heart of the water lilies, the purple rise of the iris, the velvet red and amber-tinged cream of the rose petals in slanted late afternoon light. I know what I see when I write of these things, and even some of what I feel. But what can a reader come to know, one who hasn't the alphabet of Baile an tSléibhe?

13 Perspectives

From the top of the Connor Pass, the Scellig Rocks far out at sea are huge and glistening on the horizon. They seem much larger than usual but it's a trick of the light and the weather, I suppose…unless, of course, they really are the gateway to Tír na nÓg, as the old stories say, in which case they wouldn't be subject to normal physical laws but to the desires of the unseen, magical world. Valentia Island, the Iveragh Peninsula and Bolus Head seem stuck on with Velcro under a sky vaguely the same blue-grey shade but more vibrant in texture. However does that Lighting-Techie-in-the-Sky draw up the tech spec, I wonder?

Maps

Four large maps are taking up most of my living room floor. Numbers 70, 71, 78 and 83 of the Irish Ordnance Survey, they represent the world I can see from my windows, and from high on Mt Eagle above me. After three months here, I am trying to learn just where I am, what the name of that mountain directly across Dingle Bay might be, and how all this folded landscape fits together. Tracing my finger across the maps, I name the places I've walked here: Béal Bán, Cruach Mhárthain, Com an Lochaigh, Graig, Clogher Beach, Binn an Choma, Sliabh an Iolair, Gleann Fán.

Loch Cruite, Glanteenassig, Aughacasla Strand, Com an Áir, Bearna na Gaoithe, An Sás, Loch Dubh. Illauntannig and the Great Blasket. I remember the bright days of walking, my body coming to know the land. I name the townlands I've lived in: An Cheathrú, Baile Ícín, Baile na Rátha, and now Baile an tSléibhe. I see the places I've yet to go. The stone fort high on Mt Brandon. The slanted road up a mountain above Loch an Dúin. A particular configuration of rocks along the slope of Mt Eagle. I imagine what it might be to know all the convolutions I see in the greens and browns and creams of the maps, even the uniform blue of the water. How it might take a lifetime. I begin with the mountain across the bay, learning its name: Cnoc na dTobar.

14 The Sensual World

The sky tonight is low and dense, layered with purple clouds flowing in rapidly from the southwest. It looks like we won't make it back to the car park before the heavens open but then the dynamic changes, something else has happened up there, so we head up to Quinn's for a leisurely pint. Britta and I are playing midsummer but it is still quite cool for sitting outside. As we walk back up to Baile an Trasna, a cleft opens in the thick sky and the setting sun pours through in flat bands of golden light, reflected in the petals of a thousand yellow irises in a swampy field near Britta's new home. Cows bawl, ravens caw, Tinka's tail spins like a propeller in that happy, waggy-dog way. We have walked the beach and found delicate, lemon-coloured shells like babies' fingernails. At home later on, I squat outside to pee as fat raindrops begin to fall. The white arum lilies glow eerily in the gathering darkness. The earth is suddenly pungent, has opened herself to the rain like a lover. The smell of bread baking in my mother's kitchen wafts into memory.

Name

Bob asked me if the house had a name, and I answered that it was Tigh na Gaoithe, House of the Wind, but its summer name is Encantada.

15 Texture

A thin film of rain sweeps across the hollow of Ballymore from the southwest. The temperature has risen overnight so anybody growing spuds had better spray them fast before blight sets in. Cut hayfields lie pale yellow on the hill, uncut meadows still high with summer grasses and buttercups. I love the field behind my caravan: tall red dockweed overlays the lush green like Indian silk, that emerald green with a reddish sheen in the weave. The lighter green stalks of irises bend the light, the yellow flowers glowing mutely in silver-grey piercing light. The hollow diminishes, the light pressed into the thinnest gauze. The hilltop has vanished.

Goldfinches! In the Garden!

The lawn was cut yesterday, and the birds seem a bit disoriented, wandering across the sheared grass where once there was a forest of plants. No more casual snacking from plantain flowers above their heads, or dipping into dandelion bowls. Last night a blackbird seemed to be wondering where she was, and just what had happened to her territory. Tonight though, she had switched from vegetarian to meat-eater, walking around with a succulent slug dripping from her beak, a slug that no doubt had once taken cover in the high growth, and now wondered too what had happened to his world. Such a simple thing, the mowing of the lawn. When faced with a lawn, we do it almost without thinking. It's something one does. Neighbourly and neat. But here in Baile an tSléibhe in my garden, I see directly what effect it has, on those I can see, and those I can't. I try to imagine my own world mowed, and am startled at the thought. As I was watching all this eating and meandering, two goldfinches flew into the olearia. Goldfinches! The amazement of their ruby heads, their flash of bright yellow. They, it seems, like the lawn mowed, as I've not seen them here before. There's something in this, of give and take, and loss and gain. And flexibility in a changing world.

16 Blur

Trees bend wildly in the strong southwesterly as I ascend the Connor Pass, strutting their high summer foliage like Senegalese women at a dance. Soon, all is lost to a grey-white pillow of fog so dense I can barely follow the curve of the road, no car tail lights to lead me on up ahead. I crawl along at twenty miles per hour, wondering at the tricks of that Lighting-Techie-in-the-Sky: he's lighting the pass from below, a much whiter light rising than the one positioned above in the grey dome. When I emerge lower down on the Dingle side, yellow and pink houses break the grey behind impossibly green hedgerows. This morning, I was angry at the weather, reckoning we were in for a traditional Irish summer – green fields, grey skies and pale skin. It seems like we haven't had one of these for a few years. Later, I realize that the anger is my own. The weather is just being itself.

Internal Weather

I am reading Stephen Levine's A Gradual Awakening, *and come upon this passage:*

> *As awareness more deeply penetrates the flow, we experience that our natural condition, our natural state of being which some call wisdom-mind or Buddha nature, is like the sun which is always shining, always present, though often obscured. We are blocked from our natural light by the clouds of thought and longing and fear: the overcast of the conditioned mind; the hurricane of 'I am'.*

It's foggy today, with the sun trying to break through.

17 Grace

Under the humid overcast, wild roses cascade down a wall almost hiding a Marian shrine tucked into a niche. Our Lady smiles benignly, her cheeks lightly blushed, her light blue gown a compliment to tumbling pink roses breaking the grey-green plains of Munster for just an instant as I drive by on my way home from leaving Sandra to Shannon airport. She's high in the blue blue sky somewhere over North America by now, bound for Portland.

Above the Clouds

Up above the clouds, sunlight, to travel from home to once-home in joy and astonishment.

18 Sap

In hedgerows around Ballintlea, high summer plants ooze sap, sticky and white like candyfloss in cloying dampness. Cobwebs glisten underfoot, reflecting diaphanous light from the low sky. My head is in the clouds. My feet are on the earth. In between, sap rises with the temperature.

Market Weather

I wake at 6 a.m. this first morning in Portland, doze a while then rise while it's still early. It's a cool summer's morning, and I think of the farmers' market under the trees downtown. I arrive to a lushness of summer spilling over all the stalls. Greens of every kind, crisp from the field. It's berry season, the last of the deep red strawberries, small and misshapen and sweet. Blackberries already, raspberries and blueberries. I'm dazzled by the abundance, just strolling for a while until my first purchase of dry-roasted hazelnuts, followed by a jar of peach lavender jam. I quickly add new-laid eggs, lettuces, basil, a cucumber, some cheese. Even though it's early, I stop for a sausage sandwich smothered in grilled sweet peppers and onions, finding a park bench in the sun to eat it. I gather a bouquet of sweet peas, so deep a purple they're almost black, another of peonies, and then some bachelor buttons that remind me of my grandfather's garden. I get two raviolis, one filled with crab, the other with pancetta and favala beans, and a cream chardonnay sauce to put on them. Although I could, I do not get wild mushrooms, organic beef, handmade chocolates, French pastries, artisan bread, olive oil, walnuts or wild salmon. All this richness comes from the area around the city, most of it from small organic farms. I take my full bag to the car, and return again, wandering, looking, drinking in the play of light under the shifting shade, the summer coming into fullness.

19 Headache

Up on the Slea Head track, all is deeply silent. I trot along the familiar path fleeing this headache that has cut through my morning like a jagged knife. At the stream I pause, drawn to the playful melody of mountain water tumbling over stones. Hearing the water, I am no longer listening to the headache. On that note, I decide to stay awhile. I lie down on a warm boulder and feel the air, the summer sun, the singing stream and the scent of ferns flowing through me. When I awake, the headache has receded although the shape of it still remains. Resuming the trail, I follow the intricate stone wall to my left. Not far above, mist hugs the hillside in a clammy embrace. Tall purple foxgloves are breathing with me as I walk, loving the damp humidity.

Storm Light with Volcano

When I enter Powell's, the giant bookstore not far from the house in Portland, it is a clear, warm summer night. When I come out again after an hour or two of browsing, the air is suffused with amber light. I look up to see a double rainbow in a high arc vibrating over the city. Lightning flashes below it, the product of an obvious storm heading this way from the east. I stand astonished as the glass of downtown skyscrapers glows with the same amber, then rose, then a colour close to a new bruise. In the car driving, I keep turning for glimpses of the storm behind me, glimpses that appear in breaks in the trees, at the openings of streets. I feel I am racing a downpour, and the strangeness. As I move along, I pass groups of people clustered on the streets, looking back toward the storm, pointing and talking, not sure of anything but amazement. When I cross the freeway bridge, the light becomes an eerie suffused rose blue, and I hope someone is photographing this. At Burnside, I see the tallest building in the city, its lights suddenly all on, a glowing white tower against the rose-grey sky. I do arrive home before the storm, and later receive a message from Darcy who has been with her husband John on the top of their tall building, watching not only the storm, the light, the rainbows, the lightning, but Mt St Helen's, the volcano north of the city, which she tells me has been erupting in the midst of all this energy two days before the solstice, an almost midsummer night.

20 Summer Solstice

This summer solstice turns out to be damp squib. Glen, however, being a true Aussie, stokes up a barbie in Anke's wet garden under two huge beach umbrellas. It's Dave's 60th birthday and no better man for a party! He treads about barefoot, beaming all over, greeting his friends, impervious to lousy weather. The barbie hisses and smokes as rain trickles down in thinning twilight.

Sips

Back in the States, I have access again to my books of poetry. At Powell's yesterday, inside while the storm gathered, I found a new Ted Kooser, where this morning I read these lines:

> *'I was alive and looking
> the right direction…'*

which seems to me to be the story of Weather Watch *and all its gatherings. I am reminded he has another collection called* Weather Central, *which of course I must look at, remembering it holds some lines of poetry that I can actually quote. In a poem called 'Old Dog in March', Kooser is watching his elderly dog on the steps outside. As the poem ends, the old dog lifts his head and*

> *'...he sips the cool, delicious,*
> *richly storied wind.'*

21 Restlessness

I can't muster the energy to celebrate midsummer. This dull, sunless weather is unnerving and I feel crushed by an on-going sinus headache. Sooki, dashing up and down the caravan in short spurts, seems to pick up on my restlessness. I need to be quiet, to relax my mind which is roller-coasting off into the future, wearing down my nervous system. I so wanted to enjoy the summer before heading off to Senegal with the swallows when autumn comes. Will I ever discover the experience of being fully present in the here and now?

City Sky

I go outside to try to find the moon, and find myself confronted with a city sky. A deep luminous blue background fronted by clouds lit to a peach colour by the lights of the city. In a small opening, I see parts of what I call the Big Dipper, called the Plough in Ireland. The only evidence of the moon is an intense paler blue aura behind some clouds. Tall buildings stand blocking where I think the moon might be. I walk out to the street for a clearer view, but can see no more. I rest my hand on the ancient redwood nearby, asking it to greet the moon from its heights, this full moon of solstice.

22 Dressing Up

High tide at half past five on this day of the full moon is a rough affair, far too choppy for swimming although the day is glorious and the southwesterly deliciously warm. Maybe tonight's the night for the annual airing of the sexy red linen dress! By nine o'clock, coming up to party time, the red dress idea is dead in the water: that wind is really strong now and Laura's house at Fahan is slap-bang in the lee of it. Mike is stoking the barbie out the back when we arrive but the great outdoors soon loses its appeal and a parlour party ensues. Will that damn dress ever get an airing this year?

Storm Light

This afternoon as I sat reading in the rose chair I plan to bring to Ireland, the light dimmed to that pale sepia that precedes a storm. It did indeed rain, huge drops hitting the leaves as hard as hail, making a large shusshing outside. Lightning flashed, then deep thunder. I read on, snug and dry amidst the downpour, congratulating myself that I had not taken off as I might have on a series of walking errands that would surely have caused me to be drenched. I had made phone calls I was waiting to be returned. I was sporadically cleaning various parts of the house. Mostly, though, I was enjoying reading with the storm outside.

23 Rites

At Teampall Geal, the bright temple in the townland of

Cathair Bó Sine, we circle the well in the lower field, drinking the sweet water as Father Ó Fiannachta leads the prayer before walking up the hill to the bonfire where we will throw our sticks into the flames, casting off our sins and ills. Then the old shaman-priest calls out to the world and all things in creation. He calls to the wind and the rain, the sun and the frost, clouds, mountains, pasture lands, the ocean, all the animals, humankind, the birds and insects, and after each is invoked, we shout, 'Give praise and thanks unto Him!' Then he calls out every townland and headland in sight, peppering the prayer with information about the origin and meaning of the names, for this is his own country and he knows the place and meaning of each rock and watercourse as if he were as old as the place itself. At the temple, praise songs are sung and then it is time for refreshments. Toose, our host, has driven his little tractor up to the fire and hands out tea, whiskey and lemonade with bars of chocolate. The little kids sing in clear, bird-like voices and tin whistles ring out merrily as people chat and exchange news. It has been a humid, overcast, headachy kind of day but at ten o'clock, a pink shade slides into the sky and a most spectacular light show begins. The pink deepens to rose, the mountains and peninsulas turn indigo, the ocean a metallic blue, and dense cloud formations on mountaintops and on the horizon become opalescent. Chris and I wonder at a strange pink cloud that seems to leak over the ocean. All of a sudden, we realize it is a rainbow, a pink rainbow in the midsummer's night and, as we watch, some of the other colours tune in as the surrounding heavens turn ever more rosy. The arc is complete and astonishingly high, rising over Dingle Harbour, sinking over Ventry. We stand on the hill watching this for half an hour, awestruck, thrilled. As I head down the hill, Peadar is playing rhythmic tunes with a red-haired girl as Niall jumps over the fire.

Weather

Perfect.

24 Slumber

A golden day tapers to palest lemon light. The dark nipple of Cruach Mháirthin silhouetted on the western horizon slides into the softer belly of Sliabh an Iolair as dragon's breath rises from below. Hush! The Goddess slumbers.

Rustling

It is after one in the morning, a mild wind rustling the leaves of the trees out back. In the light from the building next door, I can see the silver maple moving, and only imagine the ash and the ailanthus. I wonder why in all the years here, I have not learned to distinguish their sounds one from the other. The wide starred leaves of the maple must surely have a different tune from the more slender and elongated ash. The sway of the ailanthus would call forth a different cadence again. If the winged maple seeds are set, they would add to the rhythms, or the first hint of the ash's red berries. The weather continues perfect, the air warm to the skin, but not hot, the slight breezes contributing to the shift of light. So perfect though, there's hardly anything to say about it at all.

25 Summer Breeze

'Summer breeze makes me feel fine, rolling through the caverns of my mind.'

I can't remember who sang that song way back in the '60s but it's the right song for today. I went out on the bike to air aching sinuses and an aching mind and remembered, somewhere along the way, to look at sky, sea, hedgerows and stones. Sandra is in Portland eating peaches. I'm writing this Weather Watch in her front room in Ballintlea in the falling evening, the door flung open to the breeze. I still have the damned headache but my mind is loosening up, hoping to see the frolicking rat near the lily pond. The smell of windfalls in my father's peach house is wafting with the breeze down the caverns of my mind from long ago.

Who Can Say?

Who can say anything about weather like this? Pleasant to be in, light filtered through trees, warm, a gentle breeze. Nothing to battle. All ease. As we walk uptown from Powell's, we see a thermometer registering 84 degrees, but that is in the sun, and we are in the shade, much cooler and feeling no stress from the heat.

26 Paradise

I have to push the bike hard against an insistent southwesterly breeze that hits me side-on as I round Slea Head. My guardian angel must be on the job today, otherwise I'd probably crash the bike, so fascinated by the green colour of the water up ahead at Coumeenoole that I'm not watching the winding, windy road at all. This could be the front cover of a holiday brochure advertising Mauritius, Hawaii or some other exotic sunshine destination. (Admittedly, I am wearing a fleece.) There's no surf, just wavelets rising gently out of green water then seeping into the golden sand at Coumeenoole...oops, better stop this train of thought, it's beginning to sound like that damn travel brochure. Where translucent cove water seeps into the deeper ocean blue, greedy gulls flock and squeal around a small cabin cruiser – the guys must be fishing from the boat. The boat seems immobile but the strong breeze is visible in the tell-tale white horses riding the surface of the water. Down the road, I sit in a wind-free seat outside the café, nursing this Weather Watch. Hot sun, fresh breeze, a good cup of coffee: this has to be Paradise. I wonder if the other people here know where we really are?

An Irish Kind of Day

The perfect weather turns to rain in the afternoon, a steady downpour, which doesn't stop us from walking to the Japanese Garden up the hill in nearby Washington Park. When I offer an umbrella, visiting Orna reminds me we're Irish, and should spurn such things. This is a landscape of huge trees which it takes rain a while to penetrate, so for the beginning of the walk, we're merely damp. Even in the Japanese Garden, we're sheltered as we stroll over the moon bridge and among the irises blooming by the pond. We stop to watch huge koi glide orange black indigo gold in the water beneath us, and sit a while listening to the waterfall. As we rest again in one of the cedar shelters tucked away under the trees, I am soothed by the gentle patter of rain on leaves above us, a sound I almost never hear in Ireland. As we

leave, the rain intensifies, but not enough to keep us from slowing through
the exuberant rose garden to admire. Farther down, we pass again by the
reservoir which is low, and an intense clear deep green, a jewel on this grey
day. We arrive back at the house soaked, but still we walk out later to dinner
in the scent-filled evening, not even noticing any more that it's actually
raining. An Irish kind of day.

27 Morning and Evening

Silver snail spume glistens on the doorstep in golden, early
morning light. Away in the distance, the Iveragh Peninsula is but
a hazy suggestion. High grasses behind the pond dance in a light
breeze. No sign of the rat. In the evening, as the great disc of the
sun slides behind the mountain, a slanting ray cuts across the ridge
into the cleft of the lake, illuminating thermals rising after the heat
of the lovely summer's day.

Pervasive

The rain continues in a pervasive drizzle. This does not precisely stop us
from moving about, but it does slow us down. The day is dim, never really
brightening. We drive downtown, but hunch under hoods, or just dodge drips.
The rain has fallen long enough and heavily enough for the trees to offer
not shelter but these steady drips. As I drive back to the house, I see Orna is
napping in the backseat, and Bob is nodding. If the sun were out, I'm sure
we would all be energetically striding about the city streets, but as it is, we're
sleepy, quiet, wanting to nap. Oppressed by the grey and the humidity, we
wade through the day.

28 Heavy Weather

Breathless. It's trying to rain but can't quite get there. I swam in the warm cuaisín before supper, an antidote to the tension headache that makes my neck feel like steel. The midges are biting under a pale mauve sky.

Some Possible Clouds

As the weather here continues grey and still, a bit oppressive, I unearth the Audubon Guide to North American Weather *that has been resting on my Portland stairs. As I page through photographs of cumulus clouds, none of which looks like the other, I wonder if I will have track down a guide to European clouds, if, like birds, the species of clouds in Ballintlea vary from those here; if I will one day spot a cloud that is clearly off course, blown in on some winter gale, never before seen in those parts. I wonder if I should start the West Kerry Cloud Watch for all the possible sightings, and if there are endangered clouds as well, clouds possibly threatened by the thinning ozone. Then I think to imagine a way to make cloud prints, maybe by tracing the cloud shadow on a hill, or with tracing paper against a window. We could make our own guide then:* Some Possible Clouds in Ventry and Its Surrounds.

29 Fragrance

In humid evening air, the fragrance of honeysuckle and newly mown hay wafts into the caravan. It rained so hard last night that my sister couldn't sleep: Mo's not used to hard rain on a tin roof. Looking at this morning's dark overcast, I didn't expect her to get to the island but, as it turned out, she had a lovely walk there and saw the visiting dolphin, the resident donkeys and the seals on An Trá Bhán. I'd given her Tropical Jungle Formula to shield her against the midges but she never saw a single one! Absorbed in stories about the family, we almost miss the spectacular sunset but manage to get to Ventry Beach just in time to celebrate its final flush. We walk to the river and back and then it's all over for another day.

Summer in the City

Just after last night's cloud whimsy, late on a warm summer night, blinds raised, upstairs windows open, the doorbell rings. Before I think, I cross to the door and open it slightly, standing behind it to see who's there. A young man begins, 'Ma'am I…' and suddenly the energy changes entirely and he is trying to force his way into the house. He is fit and strong and I am afraid, afraid enough to push fiercely against the door and to scream at the top of my lungs for help. The manager of the townhouses, Douglas, shares a wall with me. Even though it is late, windows are open. I've often said I feel safe in this small complex, that if I screamed, I felt someone would come. I scream 'DOUGLAS! HELP!' at the top of my lungs, hoping he's home, hoping he's awake, knowing the man pushing at the door is stronger than I am. Suddenly his arm darts past me and grabs for my purse which I had dropped beside the door when I came in earlier. He takes it and runs. I start to run after him, realize the folly of that, and return to the house where I stand flushed, with my heart beating. I do not know what to do, try to evaluate whether this rates a call to 911, the US emergency number. I do call, and am told a policeman will arrive shortly. Then I phone Douglas, who answers, and tell him what has happened, ask if he will come over *when the policeman comes. Douglas tells me he did hear screaming, was not sure from where, went out into the courtyard where he could see me by then on the phone and our neighbour Don across the way cooking in his kitchen. Don often plays films late at night, and Douglas wondered if he would need to ask him to turn down the sound, if that's what he heard. The policemen comes. I do not let him in until Douglas arrives from next door. I am apologizing for my stupidity and lack of caution, but the policeman, who no doubt agrees with me, says I did the right thing by shouting and also by not giving chase. Douglas stays with me after the policeman leaves, just talking. He's been away since my return, and I tell him about Ireland, showing him pictures of the house, pictures that were miraculously not in the bag where they've been most days since I've been here. Nor was my passport in the bag, my address book or reading glasses. Another policeman comes to fingerprint the door. Apparently there have been two other similar incidents in the city this night, and the police feel that since force was used, the man may have a record of prints on file from former arrests. They fingerprint me for comparison, and I think of Bob and Orna and Orial just gone, that their prints may well be on the door too. I lower and lock all the windows, lower and close all the blinds. After a while Douglas leaves. I wake a friend in the now middle of the night to talk a bit. I do the dishes that I hadn't yet done. I do not put out the trash beside the back door as I usually would. I do not go down into the basement. I try to remember what was in the bag, and phone to cancel my credit cards. I try to read, and fall into an uneasy sleep around 5 a.m. with birds beginning to sing outside. I wake early to the phone. I mostly stay inside. At midday my phone rings. A woman a few blocks away has found my bag. I go, not without a shiver of paranoia, to retrieve it. Everything is there except the money, about $100 because I'd*

241

*just been to the bank. I carry the bag home gingerly, not wanting to touch
it. It's sitting again just inside the door where it was last night. I'm grateful
it was there to be taken instead of entry to the house. The house is stuffy
with the windows still closed. It's due to be very hot today, but no windows
will be open tonight to the cooler evening air, or doors propped open to allow
any possible breeze to enter. This has always been a safe place, which is why
I thoughtlessly answered the door, but it's the city. I try to look at this as a
lesson in awareness, and breathe.*

30 Night Lights

At midnight, a freshening breeze is stirring things up. Ursa
Major and Cassiopeia are fairy lights in a sky much lighter than
indigo. Clouds, incandescent lanterns in the twilit blue dome, play
hide-and-seek with their luminary playmates, light years away.

Summer in the City Too

*Last night I met Alyce at her townhouse downtown in the Pearl District
and we strolled through the summer city streets to Park Kitchen for dinner.
As it was a warm evening, the wide doors of the restaurant were open. Our
table was half indoors and half outside. In the park across the way, under
tall trees, people were playing bocce ball, their occasional cheers at a good
throw filtering over to us. Beside them, a casual basketball game was in
progress. We sat a long while, catching up, and then walked back in the long
summer dusk, Alyce showing me the new meditation park and pointing
out buildings completed since my last visit. The high and graceful arc of the
Fremont Bridge was black against an incandescent blue sky, a sky tinged
with faint persimmon from the sunset. I had on a sleeveless top, and felt no*

need for a sweater, the air soft on my skin. This soft dusk and glowing sky are graces of the summer city, as much a part of city pleasure to me as the equally glowing December dusk when snow falls gently through the blue.

July

1 Mí na Samhradh

Today is the first of July, *Mí na Samhradh*, the month of the summer. What can I say? It's great weather for ducks!

Summer Here

The rain of the past few days has fled, leaving the first day of this three day holiday warm and sunny. Fourth of July here can have just about any weather from cold rain to intense sun and heat. People flock out of the city to the mountains and the beaches. Giant fireworks displays rise over even small towns. I heard the first firecrackers – ah, some just now – go off earlier tonight. When I was a child, we spent summers with my grandfather in Chicago, and were allowed to touch only the sparklers, thin rods that make a steady fizzing sound as they burn and, well, sparkle, with a scent I'd recognize anywhere, particular to them. My grandfather had charge of the larger fireworks, the rockets that arced whistling high into the sky, exploding in showers of light. All along the street, each house sent up its own display, celebrating the founding of our country. It was a more innocent time perhaps, and always warm and clear.

2 Weather and the Warrior

'A warrior always returns to the fray. He never does so out of stubbornness, but because he has noticed a change in the weather.' —Paulo Coelo, referring to an *I Ching* commentary: To persevere is favourable.

Weather in the City

Amidst the streets and buildings, unless the weather moves — as rain or wind, the flicker of light through the leaves — it's hardly noticeable. This afternoon downtown, I looked up to see above me a patch of clear blue sky, a piece of white cloud ragged at the edge I could see. I was struck by the intensity of it, by the beauty of a world with a sky that blue on this day.

3 Still Blowing Hard

Lunchtime and it's still blowing hard. All morning it rained and howled but now great masses of cloud are being pushed away towards the south, out over the Iveragh and the Scelligs, leaving Ballymore with bright sunshine for lunch. It could become a proper summer's day yet, if the wind piped down and the warmth of the summer sun was left to ripen, unimpeded. I suspect, though, that lunch might prove to be a quick, risky affair but sweet-tasting, nonetheless.

Moonless

Yesterday I purchased a chart I often have with me, one that shows the phases of the moon through an entire year. It is arranged by month so that at a glance, I can tell just where the moon is in her journey from dark to full to dark. In Ballintlea, the moon is so frequently visible, even in spells of bad weather, I hardly need such a thing. Here in the city, since my return I have seen little more of the moon than its bright edge above one of the tall buildings in the neighbourhood. The chart tells me that tonight the sky will hold the next to last sliver of the waning moon, and that my birthday — which is often very near full moon — will this year fall just before the first quarter. As I write this I remember a birthday — I don't know which — on the Salmon River in Idaho. Was that the year the moon was so bright it woke me from sound sleep at its rising? That time, coyotes howled nearby, and then came up the hill where I was awakened, moving silently, the pack breaking to flow around me, as if I were a rock in the river.

4 The Colour Purple

In Sandra's mountain garden, flower shades of purple, blue and mauve rise majestically to cloudy grey skies. Purple loosestrife bends over the cloudy pond and hebe flourishes blue and mauve in tall grasses. There's blue geraniums still and foxgloves flanking stone walls and blue field scabious peppering the meadow. Underfoot, beds of self-heal are soft and discreet in violet dresses and dark-leaved cloaks. Under cloudy skies, these shades of purple seem underlined and in deepening summer twilight, seem to pulse as light seeps from the garden.

Pink Sky at Night

I leave Ger and Kate's house at the coast very late, hoping to avoid streams of traffic returning to the city after the holiday weekend. I begin the journey through a narrow forest road thick with trees. My lights touch ferns and foxglove. The air is fresh with the breathing of trees. Above me, the sky is rich with stars. As I approach the city, the stars fade in the light, a pink glow that ultimately entirely suffuses the sky with pale colour. I pass along a corridor usually thick with traffic, tonight almost empty. Gas stations still open after 2 a.m. dot the highway, lit to glaring with lights. Every sign along the way is lit, and close to the city, no space is dark. Gas is $2.17 a

246

gallon, about €1.78. As I drive, I think with anger that this is one of the reasons my country is at war, so the lines of large cars I travelled with on the way from the city can have cheap fuel. So gas stations can stay open twenty-four hours a day. So lights can blaze through the night on every insignificant business – open or closed – along the way. It's Fourth of July, Independence Day, the birthday of my country.

5 Discomfort

Dampness infiltrates my brain, bones, mucous membranes. A nicotine grey overcast incurs vague anxiety and the smell of slurry, spread on recently mown hayfields around Ballymore, forces me to close all windows to escape the nauseous stink wafting on the strong southwesterly.

Promise of Rain

Late afternoon, the sky clouds over and the light is tinged with yellow. Everything indicates rain, possibly a cleansing summer thunderstorm. But now, at near midnight, no rain has yet appeared. Outside, the leaves move restlessly, waiting. Inside, I move from floor to floor, restless too, wanting the release, the coolness, the promise to be fulfilled.

6 Is the Sun Up in the Sky?

I pause for a walk on Ventry Beach in the morning but soon give up the effort because I feel cold in the strong wind. Last night, I made a hot-water bottle and put another quilt on the bed. Is the sun up in the sky anymore?

Oh Dear! Oh Dear!

Oh dear, oh dear! The reports of weather in Ventry are so dismal, I wish I could transport you here, where it is summer. You could go out for walks in the warm sun, and then come back to suggest where I might move next in this snarl of possessions. I find myself sometimes just standing staring in dismay at all the accumulations. Think accumulations is related to cumulus? Could this be today's Weather Watch? It is.

7 Sweat

On a ferny hillside field above Dunbeg Fort, moisture clings to my body, drips down my nose, as I pad along the Slea Head track in cushioned silence. Only the crow way above and the ocean way below leave aural traces in the mist. The ferns seem to sweat.

City Summer Deep Translucent Blue

Dinner tonight was at clarklewis, a restaurant on the east side of the river, the side opposite to mine. Maggie and I sat at a table beside a wall open to the dusk outside. As night fell, a gentle breeze wafted in while heat from the kitchen area behind us kept us warm. The sky went that city summer deep translucent blue. The occasional train ambled through the city streets, whistle blowing. I was facing out, and could see the cars go by, freight mostly, moving slowly, the silhouettes of the empty cars black against the sky. We ate radishes with salt and sweet butter, scallops with shaved fennel, halibut with summer squash and shark with thin green beans. A glass of soave each, and bread to dip in deep golden olive oil. For dessert, a bing cherry tart with a buttery top crust and whipped cream, and a blackberry pannacotta. Deep strong coffee and good conversation. As I drove back to Vista near midnight, the sky was a deeper, still translucent, blue, with just a single star shining bright enough to pierce the city lights.

8 Weather Here and There

Looking up from the computer, I'm shocked to register blue in the prevalent grey sky through the window of the theatre office. I jump up for a better look and yes! there's an opening at last. Cloud is rolling off the side of the Connor Pass leaving a pleasant view of green fields bejewelled with stone walls, sunshine dappling the picture as we roll into a late Friday afternoon. Down in Casamance, in southern Senegal, Moussa tells me it's raining, the rice has been planted, the mood is cheerful. I told him this morning that I need to wear wellies to go up the field to the loo. We laughed. Nobody's talking about the weather in London today, only yesterday's bombing and the latest body count. In the voices of people interviewed on the radio, there is a stoic and determined resolution to get on with things, regardless. Londoners will continue with the summer, whatever the weather.

Rain

Just as the weather clears in Ireland, rain arrives here, and with it, chilly weather. I look out to see a falling mist that soon turns into drenching rain. Even so, it is dry under the redwoods, their tall tops soaking in the water, keeping it there. Another dry patch holds underneath the pear tree outside my door, and as Ger and Kate leave, we stop to admire the tiny pears forming amidst the branches. This is my first actual goodbye from this community. All the other meetings have had a promise of another time, but Ger and Kate go travelling next week, and will not be back before I leave for Ireland. A sadness holds us, and I realize the distance that will be between us, a long airplane flight across a continent and an ocean. These departing days, I feel the richness of my life here, with friends stopping by, offering to help with the move, delighting with me in my happiness in my new home. We skirt the issue of distance. I realize how precious these friends who saw me through turmoil are. I have no doubt that the move to Baile an tSléibhe is the right one, but that does not staunch the sadness of the knowledge of the riches I leave behind.

9 The Water at Caherdaniel

The water at Caherdaniel is the same green as Britta's eyes: sundappled. We glide through the water laughing at Tinka who splashes water into her mouth as she swims, barking with excitement. Caherdaniel is a sheltered cove with various nooks and crannies according to the architecture of the cliffs. Behind us is the deeply wooded estate and small national park of Derrynane. We walk through woodland and high summer meadow to get to the water. Today it resembles a lake; the opening to the ocean is small and now it is bunged up by a thick white cloud bank like a stopper in a bottle. Above, all is cornflower blue. There's a high in the Atlantic but it can't seem to burn off the incredibly high level of precipitation after last week's constant rain. There's nothing to suck it away either, no wind, so it hangs, gathering and swelling as moisture rises out of soaked hillsides. We are golden after six hours on Caherdaniel beach, rejuvenated, refreshed. Not a jellyfish in sight!

Featureless

A strange grey featureless day, all spent indoors until evening when John and Darcy come to pick me up so we can travel south to the suburbs where John will play the saxophone in a Japanese restaurant where the TV is showing Sumo wrestlers. We go inside while it is still daylight, but inside where we are sitting, it could be any time. The sound in the room is rich and gorgeous: John's saxophone, a piano, drums, and later, a large bass fiddle. The music is mellow tonight, geometric and often playful. Applause greets the end of each number. The movements of the Sumo wrestlers sometimes seem in syncopation with the jazz. Eating sushi, I am smiling at the wonderful strangeness of life.

10 Ballymore Picnic

Wendy lounging under the willows; Adrienne horrifying Kathrin and Britta with stories about various biting and flying insects in Hawaii; Tinka's tail spinning like a windmill, her doggy face wearing that quizzical 'wonder who'll throw the stick for me' expression; Donie dressed in his new bushwhacker shorts and hat; me padding in and out of the caravan with plates of smoked salmon, pineapple, salad. It's a Ballymore picnic day, too hot for roaming, too hot at this point in the day for stretching on the hot rocks below. The water level will be batheable again at five o'clock. What a languid summer Sunday.

Missing Weather

Here in this city house, I see only slices of sky, surrounded as I am by trees and tall apartment buildings. When I drive, traffic commands my

attention, leaving not a glance at the sky which does sometimes unfold in
vistas in this hilly, river-bisected city, but rarely without some man-made
structure – a smokestack, a bridge – in outline against it. In Ballintlea,
I am always aware of the movement of the weather, which direction the
clouds are travelling, how the grasses are bending to the wind. Even on the
busiest days, there's time for the weather, for brief meditations on its state
and manifestations. In Portland, the weather is distant mostly, muted, going
about its life far from mine.

11 Lost

Crenellated black rocks glisten in early morning sunlight
at this hour of high tide. I move through still cold water as if in a
dream, the rocks ahead of me at Parkmore Point suspended as if
they might simply float silently away at any moment to the south,
towards the Iveragh Peninsula, lost in the convergence of sky and
sea, a hazy dreamscape way in the distance.

Distant Weather

I was outside the city today, and able to see the sky, but somehow could
not make contact with it. The day was clear, the sky blue, the many clouds
sometimes tinged with the faintest amber, sometimes apricot. What is it
about the Irish weather that makes it so immediate, so present? In Ireland,
I feel wrapped in the weather. Here in Portland, I feel like a spectator seated
far away from the main event.

12 Hot Rocks

In the golden evening light, I curled up on the hot rocks

and maybe fell asleep awhile to the sound of the cuaisín filling up towards high tide. Later, Patrick's angular form perches on jagged stones as he casts his line, then he shouts out, 'Trish! Look!' and holds aloft a fine silvery pollack. Supper. Then a strong breeze moves in and I'm shivering after the last swim of this very hot day. Time for jeans and long sleeves.

Filter

The wind does not seem to stir in these weeks. I know it can come racing down the Columbia River Gorge and thread its way through the city, gathering, narrowing, speeding between buildings like water in a rapids. Tonight, though, the leaves hang breathless on the trees, still. Nothing to chase the city soot away, to clear the air. I can see the soot on the windowsills, feel it in my body. Sinuses and lungs feel thick, clogged, filtering the airborne particles the wind doesn't clear away.

13 Weather Clues

No dew on the grass early this morning, no sense of dampness late last night, no excess of moisture anywhere about: all clues pointing to an unusually high temperature and plant life sucking into itself every available drop of liquid nourishment with nothing left lying about. There's a change coming, though: today's sun is lightly veiled in a gauze of wispy cloud and a warm breeze is a welcome visitor. Riding my bike to Slea Head is effortless in the tawny evening. I glide along, my skin deliciously warm, the air so dry I'm not even sweating. The rhythm and airing of the bike ride, and a later swim off Ballymore rocks at high tide, is more appealing, somehow, than the sociability of Ventry Beach. As I cycle west, the haze increases. There's no Iveragh, no Scellig Rocks, only the Blaskets palely described in an ocean marginally bluer than the pale, powder blue sky. The outline of the Dead Man hangs in the distance, its substance erased by a thick fog bank rolling into the Sound from the north.

Moving Weather Again

As I am driving up Burnside Street, I notice that clouds are moving across the sky. What has been a largely static landscape is now in motion. I look more closely and see that the trees are moving too, the leaves of the maples glimmering in the afternoon light. Outside now in early evening, I hear the shirring of the wind through the trees. The youngest branches of the silver maple toss and bend. The air is fresh. A birthday present from the sky.

14 Edge

It's overcast again but a warm wind saves the day from lethargy. At the lower edges of the cloud, an intense glare pierces the atmosphere. So far, there's no rain, just the grey blanket overhead. I'd love to wrap myself up in it and go to sleep for I can't seem to think straight. Some kind of weather low is troubling the edges of my inner sky.

Second Sighting of the Moon

So much of the city sky is blocked by buildings and trees that I usually have to resort to my moon chart to know what phase the moon inhabits, but last night and tonight, the quarter moon rode high in the late afternoon sky, catching my eye as I walked about. A friend seen from afar, and missed in these city weeks. When night came on, the moon lit still more, the sky behind it glowing cobalt above the black silhouettes of the highrises, above the tips of the redwood trees.

15 Still Lake

Up at the lake on Sliabh an Iolair above Cill Dhorcha, all is still this evening after a very hot afternoon. I lie on a flat rock looking up at the sky, the wispy clouds, listening to the ravens and the sheep, all echoed here in the amphitheatre of this mountain lake; occasionally, the swish of the line as Patrick casts into the lake. The fat pollack he caught last night provided a fine dinner this afternoon: now he's hunting for brown trout. I like this green-eyed fisher nephew. Lying on the rock, I see nicotine-coloured clouds moving onto Brandon Mountain. We are elevated here, way above Ventry Harbour, so that viewing Brandon from an upside down angle, it doesn't look very high, an optical illusion. But weather is moving in over there to the north. Later, as we walk down the track to the village, I notice the warm air and the abundance of light at this late hour, although we are now nearly a month past the summer solstice. Peadar has juicy apples and chocolate biscuits stashed in the car, a fine picnic to end our evening at the lake. No trout tonight. Patrick caught a few but released them; he thinks they haven't much to feed on in this lake and have perhaps mutated to cater for this, remaining small in size. I cast my eye on Brandon again, wondering if we'll adventure there tomorrow, pass by the waters of its still, dark lakes. Let's see what weather arrives with the dawn.

Traffic

As I drive north along the freeway to Seattle, taking my work to the University of Washington, I encounter massive amounts of traffic. Through Tacoma, a solid five lanes in each direction slowed to 20 mph. In between the north and southbound lanes, work is progressing to widen the road still more. A sign says, 'Your tax dollars at work'. I cannot imagine driving through this every day, or what it must be like at rush hour when it is now only one-thirty in the afternoon. Each car has one driver. Two in a car qualifies for the more exclusive 'carpool' lane. I do not understand why citizens do not rise up demanding adequate public transportation rather than more roads. The sky far above is bland. It's having nothing to do with this beyond an occasional drop of rain, offered perhaps in futile hope of some cleansing. By the time I reach Seattle, it's given up clouds altogether and gone to sepia haze, hardly sky at all, but an extension of the exhaust fumes rising.

16 At the Top of the World

At the top of the world on Sliabh an Iolair we can see all the places that Patrick has walked during this visit to Dún Chaoin. Everyone tells him, 'You've brought the good weather with you' and it's true, it has been a spectacular week of golden sunshine and warm temperatures, perfect for rambling in the hills and headlands and for fishing, his favourite pastime. Patrick has a different rhythm to me and Peadar; we are swift movers, able to get up and go in an instant while Patrick is a dreamy kind of person who moves slowly, so we leave him to the fish and climb rapidly above the lake up to Binn an Choma, from where Peadar hopes we might see whales. No whales today but we admire the aerodynamics of the nut-brown kestrel who is rolling and hanging on the thermals; then the local flock of choughs barge in, gliding and passing in the stiff northwesterly that hits us well clear of the lake, forcing me to don the fleece. Later, we pick our way down the side of the basin above the lake – it's a lot easier than I thought, but also a lot bigger than it looks from below – and I lie on hot rocks for an hour listening to the swish of Patrick's line as he hunts for the brown trout I've requested for dinner. Before I write this Weather Watch, late in the evening, Moussa calls and I tell him I am full of air and sunlight, that I wish he could walk here with us on the top of the world.

When I go back to Casamance, we will walk in the bush, hand-in-hand, for there are no mountains, not even hills. Maybe someday Moussa will come here and walk on the top of the world with us and then feast on Sandra's sweet cake and coffee down below in Ballintlea. Sometimes dreams come true.

Down in the Basement

Whatever the weather might be outside, I'm down in the basement dealing with an internal storm. Years of accumulation face me in unopened boxes. It seems I sort and sort, carry and dispose, and still the mountain left is formidable. The Myth of Sisyphus surely took place in a basement, came from some similar moment in a life. The sun does shine outside. Summer breezes stir, and leaf shadows dance. I have only the view through the rather grimy windows, and the intervals of going from the basement to the recycling garage, which means up the steps, out the kitchen door, down the steps, unlock the gate, key the code into the garage and dispose into the appropriate bin. Then repeat. And repeat. And repeat again.

17 Ventry Regatta

Choppy water in Ventry Harbour makes the going tough for the *naomhóga*: they are getting hammered side-on, making it hard for the oarsmen to cut a clean swathe through the water. The cloud bank that piled up behind the Blaskets during the heat of the past days has busted in over the west, cutting the top off Sliabh an Iolair by mid-afternoon, the harbour now a matt-black body of shining water except for the tropical jade hue between the pier and the beach proper. That northwesterly breeze is sharp, so I'm happily surprised to find that it's warmer in the water than out of it! After the racing is done, we all repair to the village for pints and music, valiantly sitting outside despite increasing dampness. It's just possible that it will clear up and become another golden evening... But as Britta throws her third bull's eye in the horseshoe competition, dampness turns to actual drizzle. I hop on the bike and head for Ballymore, leaving sociability to the real party animals.

Is There Weather?
Another sorting day without one step outside. At least I was on the ground floor and not down in the basement. Outside, I could see sun. It was predicted to be 90 degrees today, and I suspect it came close. I was lost in a world of work, sorting through the photographs and teaching notes from the past five years. I was pleased with many things, feel the stirrings of more work to come. I just have to finish with these boxes and get back home.

18 Warm Wind

In the early evening, I lie on Ballymore rocks, the warm southwesterly wind caressing my skin. Banks of curious cloud shapes threaten to smother Sliabh an Iolair. Sunshine is just a memory but this day of warm wind is a subtle pleasure in itself, like a long, deep kiss.

Heat

A friend recently wrote from her home in Utah, 'It is 109 degrees — so hot that it is invigorating.' I cannot comprehend this. At anything over 80, I wilt. Over 100, I faint. Last night while sorting I found a set of pictures from my childhood. There I am, my two-year-old self, bundled in snowsuit and hat, standing in about two feet of snow, laughing hugely, clearly delighted. In all the summer photos, I seemed to be in contact with some kind of water, frowning a bit, no doubt at the sun beating down on my head. In one of the pictures I was about five, stretched out on my stomach holding on to the side of a small portable child's pool, kicking furiously, the water rising in a fine strong plume from my efforts. Suddenly I remembered that pool, a coated canvas about eighteen inches deep, green with a metal frame. I remembered the smell of the canvas heated by the sun, my nose so close to the edge for the hanging on. And the effort and pleasure of kicking, even though I was travelling nowhere with it. It was a few years before we would move to the lake-filled country where I grew up, and my father would teach me to swim. Then summers would consist of only bathing suits. We each had three, for morning, afternoon, and evening. This was before bathing suits dried quickly, and my mother would not let us sit around in them wet. We always wore dry clothes for dinner, but then often changed for a twilight swim, the lake gentle and the water warm, the air soft on the skin. It was hot here today, near 90 if not above. I am fatigued, but don't know if it's the heat, or the weight of all my belongings, the density of the memories they hold.

19 Forecast

'Damp conditions in the southwest will move in over the country by nightfall.' So said the evening weather bulletin on RTE Radio as I drove up to Ballintlea to check some measurements for Sandra. I could hardly find the bright orange house in the gathering mist. It takes the sting out of it to think that the rest of the country is in for the same medicine.

Outside

I finally got outside today, and then hardly noticed the weather. The heat has abated somewhat, a gentle wind sprung up. The sun was out pleasantly. I crossed the river, but didn't really see the water. I mostly kept my eyes on my tasks, moving from lists and phone calls to lunch with a friend to the lab to drop film off to the dentist for two crowns to the art supply store to check on flat files to the camera store for storage boxes and film. I managed to schedule the packing and pick-up for the Irish shipment for Thursday, the 28th, the transfer of the rest of the household things to storage the next day. The two Toms come tomorrow to take away the small couch, and Darcy perhaps to help with the chaos in the basement. I'm planning to put the weekend visitors to work taking books to Powell's to sell, and cleaning out the garage. They're old friends, and we've done work together before, planting and painting. I've talked to the people who will take the car, and must find the title somewhere amidst my files. Gene will provide transport of the remaining household goods to the community storehouse, where they'll be distributed to immigrants arriving in the city. I have to call about insurance, meet with the representative from the moving company, and, oh, see friends. Phone and utilities to cancel. Account addresses to be changed. And, oh, see friends. None of this will get done if I don't go to bed now and get some sleep.

20 Cloudscape

The top of Sliabh an Iolair is covered by a thick, pearly-white eiderdown of cloud. Above that, motionless layers of cotton wool. Further above, ominous rain clouds, slightly bruised in colour, move across the dense sky in a gentle southerly wind. In the distance, the Iveragh is sliced in two like filling in a cake by a long low spume of dragon's breath, the Scellig Rocks a vague suggestion on the horizon. As the summer evening deepens, the crazy Sky Painter dips into the colour palette, introducing pastels of purple, peach and apricot onto the background canvas of eternal eggshell blue on which she paints her swirling cloudscape.

Bearable

The heat has returned, but a breeze and the shade of the trees makes it bearable. In the midst of the day, I go to the farmers' market for the makings of a pie I plan to make for Cort and Dave this weekend. The Wednesday market is in the downtown park blocks, at the museum end, near the Performing Arts Center, the Oregon Historical Society and the First Christian Church. As I leave, carrying bags filled with peaches and nectarines, blueberries and blackberries and raspberries, some fine dark cherries, I pass the entry to the church and suddenly remember a night when I stood outside greeting friends who were coming to hear my then husband speak. It was sometime in the fall, a crisp night. I had on a long brown knit skirt with a matching brown knit sweater that buttoned up the back, and some sort of heels, if not boots that time of year. Many friends had come, but I remember most seeing Laura, whom I'd known since she was two, approaching, moving into the light of the entry from the dark of the trees in the park. That night, she was just engaged, glowing, wearing a pale grey suit of a fine wool with a slight sheen, her red hair expertly cut to just below her ears. I saw her fully as a poised young woman, sure of herself and her beauty in that moment, emerged from the girl I'd known. This afternoon, along with the fruit, I carry flowers. Pale lavender-dusted sweet peas, a summer bouquet of snapdragons and pincushions and yellow marigolds, and a huge bunch of montbretia that reach far above my head, reminding me of Ballintlea. The porch of the church is in sunshine, leaf shadow moves in the breeze. I find these moments as I'm leaving this city where I've lived for almost nine years, and visited for nearly forty. I walk back to the car smiling.

21 Full Moon Weather

Full moons are tricky, there's no knowing what'll happen emotionally. July's moon came to fullness at noon, a heavy, humid day with mounting cloud banks. How many times today did I think to myself 'Damn! I hate having feelings!' wishing I could function like a normal automaton and not burst into tears every couple of hours for no fathomable reason? It's like there's no body or skin to wrap oneself in. Impossible to keep anything out, impossible to keep anything in. One hundred per cent emotional permeability.

During a quiet hour back west, Imelda lit a candle and each person chose a crystal, symbols of awareness this foggy, full moon afternoon. At the later hour of the high tide, hot summer sun burned a hole through the mist at Ballymore and I basked there with Adrienne, salt tears coursing down my face, helplessly, thankful to share the hot rock with someone else who understands the peculiarities of moon energy. An hour later, a titanic cloud bank had cancelled the sky behind Cathair Ard and in the evening, as I left the theatre at Cúilín, mist was pouring down the hillsides into the town. The moon is veiling her face.

Full Moon in Portland

Last night after I turned out the lights in my bedroom, I noticed that the light on the Venetian blinds was not the usual rather pink city glow, but laced with silver. When I looked out, the moon was sailing low and near full in the sky, visible to me between the tall condominium building uphill, and the top of the redwoods. Old friend. I've been missing her these city nights. Glad to have her casting silver light across my dreams.

22 Fire and Rain

The hedgerows and waysides of the peninsula are aflame with blazing orange montbretia, energy in motion this overcast, seemingly motionless day in July. Raindrops glisten silver in the fires after an invisible, inaudible shower. Or maybe it was just passing mist. The harbour is like glass.

Visiting Weather

Friends arrive today, and the weather becomes perfect again. Last night's rain has washed the air, freshened the city. Cort has come from Idaho, where it was 105 degrees a few days ago, and as we walk through the city in sun-shimmered air warm enough to be comfortable, but not too hot, he exclaims about how beautiful it is, how refreshing. In the evening, after Dave arrives, we walk out to Carlyle for dinner through a gentle cooling breeze. It is almost as if the city is giving these days as gifts, so that when I remember the departing days here full of tasks and friends, I will remember with them the graciousness of the weather to visiting friends.

23 Relief

When the rain comes mid-afternoon, I am able to begin an article about Jan Garbarak's music for *Africa* magazine. It has eluded me for months for, although I love the music, I couldn't find anything to say about it, any way to describe the complex purity of the instrumental compositions.

The rain has brought with it a refreshing warm wind, blowing away the intense, headachy humidity of the morning. The tide was the second lowest of the year – 0.6 metres at 1 p.m. – adding, perhaps, to the tension. Unable to focus on anything, I boiled water and scrubbed the caravan floor, then washed the walls, a slightly hysterical rejoinder to the vacuous feeling of the day. It worked! The rain came and energy flows again.

Down in Cap Skiring, Moussa was cooking up baked fish stew when I called with my clenched-teeth report of tension and scrubbing. We had a good laugh and then the rain came. Relief.

Last Market

This sun-filled Saturday, we head for the farmers' market for lunch. So close to my departure from Portland, I'm looking for little in the way of anything other than immediate food, so we – Cort, Keats and her friend Morgan, Diane, Colette, Dave and I – pass quickly through the booths laden with blueberries and heirloom tomatoes, the first peaches, local cheese, wild salmon. Dave and I settle on sausage sandwiches smothered in grilled onions and sweet peppers, while the others go off for slices of pizza as we join the very long line beyond the booth. We begin in front of a stand selling plums, pale yellow tinged with green, stacked in boxes. When we finally have our sandwiches, we join the others at a nearby table. All around us, people are gathered under the shade of the huge trees, eating, listening to Andean music being played on one of the stages, chatting, watching people pass by. It is a lush environment, this sun-dappled park. Most there look prosperous. Most are white. Colette, who is five and Chinese, notices with excitement when a Chinese woman on a bicycle goes by. Families with children carry balloons, well-behaved dogs on leashes amble through. I have only one more Saturday in Portland before returning to Ireland, and I wonder if this will be my last farmers' market for a very long time, if ever. I know I am in some way looking at, participating in, a version of the American Dream, but I feel no regret in leaving. The girls return with handmade ice cream sandwiches in flavours of chocolate mint and lavender lemon. The pipes of the Andean music play behind me. Nearby, some Native American men, having sold all their salmon, begin dismantling their booth. It is nearly two o'clock, and time to go. Without a backward glance, talking and laughing, we stroll away, on to the next adventure in our day.

24 Batik Sky

The evening sky over Ballymore reminds me of a beautiful batik dress I once owned, washes of pink over a sky-blue fabric. I bought the cloth in Nairobi and a young Ethiopian seamstress back at Gedaref, Eastern Sudan, crafted the lovely dress. It was plain, cut just at the knee, with elbow-length sleeves. In Sudan, men usually do the tailoring. They look at you, no measuring, and you take what you get. But the Ethiopian lady knew about woman stuff. Tonight, I'd love to wrap myself in the coloured sky and go dancing with Moussa Kamara.

Location, Location, Location

After a day of farewells, I walk down to the corner grocery for something to eat. It's too hot, and I'm too tired, to cook, so I go to the deli counter. I bring home a slice of lemon pepper salmon, a pasta salad with spinach and walnuts, some thin parmesan crackers. I see a brick of Kerrygold 'Irish Swiss' cheese, and, homesick, ask for a few slices to be cut. I carry this all up the hill thinking about the days just past when we have gone to the market downtown, eaten at several restaurants, and wandered in the largest bookstore in the country, all within walking distance of my Portland townhouse. If one of us had become ill, the hospital is about a dozen blocks away. Should we have wanted to walk in the Japanese Garden, it's just up the hill. In the neighbourhood are stores selling household goods, hardware, magazines, soaps, clothing, antiques, stationery, and art. Not to mention coffee in every conceivable manifestation. As I walk, downtown glows golden in the late afternoon sun. If I walk a bit farther, I could see Mt Hood, over ten thousand feet high and snow covered, floating on the far horizon. The brick townhouse where I live is small and elegant, surrounded by a garden now in bloom with lilies, hydrangeas and deeply scented roses. The last of the roses climbing the front of my house are in white bloom. The first of this season's pears are beginning to fall from the tree outside my door. In the garden are four enormous redwoods, a fine and ancient chestnut tree and a flowering cherry. The front dogwood was lost last year to disease, but one still grows out back. This is a beautiful and eminently liveable place, yet I have few qualms about leaving it for Baile an tSléibhe. The qualms are all around friendships and distance from them. I find I can easily let go of this splendid city location for my small orange house on the mountainside overlooking the sea, its location no less splendid and dear.

25 Still

Ballymore is in a quiet mood this evening. No wind, no movement. Cows are painted on the hill field. Deep echoes resound in the hollow. I stand with Sylvia in the front field, admiring her baby son Thomas, who is now waking up to the outside world. Oh look! A gannet nose-dives into the ocean, just outside the swimming hole. A small flock is wheeling and diving, so there are probably mackerel around. Midges are biting, too. Hmm. I have to think again about no movement.

Partings

I am up early this morning to take Darcy and John to the airport for their trip to Santa Fe. As I walk to the car, it is chilly, a definite tang of fall in the air. All last week, Darcy has been, with exquisite tact, helping me with the move. She knows me well enough to take the bags of things to be dispersed with her when she leaves, allowing me no chance to reconsider my decisions to part with things I should have parted with long ago. If all goes as planned, she will not be returning from her travels until after I have left for Ireland, so the parting at the airport will be for a good while. Yesterday, I left the airport sobbing, having said goodbye to Cort, having seen his turn and wave from behind the glass of the terminal. We do not know when we will see each other again. Somehow, even though we haven't this time seen each other for the year I've been in Ireland, this parting feels more final, as he rarely travels to Europe, and the next trips I will make to the States will likely be to the east coast where my mother, who is eighty-five, lives. I am realizing how deeply attached I still am to the community here, and how important it has been to have a residence in Oregon, even though I have been living there less and less. I still have no doubts about the move to Baile an tSléibhe, but this is hard, this saying goodbye.

26 Swim and Shiver

Early morning high tides are still a challenge in July. The water is pristine but cold, for the sun hasn't warmed either the water or the rocks in the swimming hole; the water itself is still variable in temperature depending on deep ocean currents and isn't reliably warm until September. I don't care. I'd rather move through translucent water and feel cold for an hour afterwards than forego the beauty of the moment when the body glides through the ocean.

Hasty Weather

Weather report: hot. Hasty because the shipping to Ireland was moved up a day, and I've done nothing but boxes for twenty-four hours. No sleep. Little food but what friends brought. Bone tired. And hot with it. Seven in the morning and it feels like the day will be what my parents called 'a scorcher'.

27 Rain Coming

It looks like there's a change coming. The evening seems to be closing in too soon, the overcast darkening to a nicotine stain. Underneath, apricot is turning to rose above Sliabh an Iolair. The rocks of the cuaisín are warm now, the tide is coming to fullness and children's voices echo around the swimming hole full of excitement and adventure. The Cork gang are here for their holidays, the third generation enjoying the rock pools, the freedom of the campsite, the long summer evenings. Up in the yard I met Derrick. He'd just driven in over the hill from Castlegregory where it was raining when he left. I wonder if Sooki knows rain is on the way?

All Weathers

As a respite from the packing, in the afternoon I leave the crew at it in the house, the sound of tape pulled from the roll rending the air, and cross the river to pick up a year's worth of slides. When the house is quiet again, I sit at the computer looking to see what I've done. Suddenly the russet of Fán in fall fills the computer screen, and I remember the changed hillsides, the warm sun and chill wind of that day. On another day, a pale pink sunset hovers above a crumbling slate roof. Golden afternoon storm light suffuses a room. Daffodils bloom in the spring lawn. Montbretia glows in late summer glory, backlit by the sun. Hydrangeas emerge a tender dew-dappled green, and appear again in faded russet, hinting of burgundy. All the seasons are there, many weathers. I am grateful for these images on this sweltering day when it seems a chore to even move, and the sun is so hot it hurts.

28 Indecisive

The weather couldn't make up its mind in the afternoon, couldn't decide whether to wear a sexy summer dress or a gloomy overcoat, throwing off one and donning the other every few minutes. The ensuing light show at the beach was entertaining, though, as if the lighting designer in the sky kept changing the filters. Later, I heard there was torrential rain all day in the east side of the country and further east, in Bombay, the monsoon flooding has brought the city to a standstill.

Bruised

After sunset tonight, the sky is a pale bruised apricot in colour. Delicate and beautiful, but at the same time sinister. Perhaps that latter is because I haven't slept beyond a nap in two days, and I said goodbye earlier to Tom and Linda's dog Vinnie, who is seventeen and failing.

29 Tinge

There's an autumnal tinge in the air. I've been aware of it every morning this week but couldn't bear to mention it. It's only the end of July, for God's sake. Hmm. Just remembered we're approaching a bank holiday weekend. Hopefully the weather is just doing its usual thing to frighten visitors off and will revert to an appropriate summer mood on Monday evening when they've all gone home, soaked.

Weather Perspectives

It's a crisp Friday morning after yesterday's heat. The haze is washed from the air by a cool breeze that gives moving dappled leaf-shadow on the cream-coloured wall out back. Trish writes of the tinge of fall she's felt the past week in Ballymore, saying she couldn't bear to mention it. I felt the same tinge a few days ago in Portland with elation. I love the fall, the slide into winter. I grew up in a country with four distinct seasons. Summer heat has always enervated me, spring never impressed. Winter cold exhilarates, December dusk with snowfall holds one of my favourite lights, a vibrant blue grey. In the long winter nights, I can be warm inside, working and reading, fill my lungs with good clear air just before I sleep. It's the fall I love though, bringing with it a relief from the summer heat, leaves turned red and gold showering down through the slanted light. Even on the near treeless Dingle Peninsula, the hills turn a beautiful russet, glowing. It's the fall I love, with its sense of sharpened pencils, ready for new beginnings.

30 Airing

The willows and tall grasses in the wild garden dance and sway in the warm southwesterly wind. The air courses through the house, whispering gently of Sandra's return. Each rock on the shoulder of the mountain leans nearer, watching the house with longing. Yes! I whisper back to the wind and the mountain. Yes! She's coming soon.

Balmy

A hot day slides into balmy evening, and Sheila and I eat outside. We've know each other nearly thirty years, but have not seen each other for a year, and have

much catching up to do. We take our plates of salmon, beets with gorgonzola and
walnuts, tiny balls of mozzarella, and wild rice salad with mint out back. We've
already had some celebratory champagne, and have a bit more chardonnay with
dinner. As the light fades, Sheila points out the sky to the north, which is a
vibrant blue, with still a hint of sunset's gold at the horizon line. We stand
leaning against the fence a long time, admiring, feeling the warm summer air
on our skin.

31 Sky Painter

The Sky Painter applied clouds in thick oils today with a
rough-edged knife, oils in whites, greys and slate black. Way above
them, she whipped up a cotton wool blanket then, just for fun,
ice cream cones just above our heads, moving gently like cartoon
figures. All on a canvas of infinite blue, like a dream.

Burning

The enervating heat continues as I try to organize things for the departure
on Friday. The days are short. My lists are long. Sheila has come up from
the river to help this weekend. In the afternoon, we hit an incredible low, as
we look at the work still to be done and realize how long it may be before
we see each other again. I decide to walk out for some lunch to revive us,
but the walk to the deli is through streets burning with sun, a sun so hot it
hurts. When I return, the house is only marginally cooler than the outside,
but that margin is important. As layer after layer is stripped away, I begin to
think of burning some of the final papers – papers I don't want to keep but
don't want to simply consign to trash – in the fireplace. I cannot imagine
adding more heat, even in the cool of the night. But I cannot imagine any

other way to deal with these things. One full day before the next set of movers. I can only hope to fit in some sleep. The archivist in me cringes at things discarded, holes in the record of a life. The person I am learning to be in Ireland tries to trust that the important things are carried in the heart, not stored in the attic. But, oh, to let go of the pale linen skirt I wore one summer in Manhattan. Or the kimonos I brought back from Japan. Without them, will I ever think of those times again? Do I need to?

Lughnasa
Autumn

August

1 Lá Lughnasa

Lá Lughnasa, the first of August. I can't shake off the fatigue I've been feeling for the past few days but neither can I stay in bed. I have no peace with that. Instead, I almost run to Slea Head and back along the track. Humidity is high. The dense sky is mirrored by ocean, bands of light reflected in the glassy water, shades of palest peach and champagne with slightly mauve undertones. By the time I get to the café, my energy is right up again and I head back up the track. Amazingly, the dense cloud cover has passed over within the hour; I can see it floating over Brandon now like Darth Vadar's great black spaceship. There must be strong wind in the upper sky. I pause to watch the nut-brown kestrel hovering in the airstream, playing with the breeze, a true sky–dancer, and catch fleeting sight of the choughs above Binn an Choma. I arrive back to Ballintlea and suddenly, my internal battery is flat again. Two pots of peppermint tea later, I am collapsed outside in the warm sun, with no juice for anything. I lie there, surrendering to the tiredness yet unsurrendered to inner unrest.

So Far from Lughnasa

Trish sends a Weather Watch mentioning Lughnasa, and I realize I've entirely forgotten this first day of fall. The heat of the past days in Portland has broken a bit. The skies are overcast, and the trees move in a small restless wind. As I write, pale sun breathes bright and dim in the room. In

Ireland, I would never forget this date, forget to mark the passing from one season to another. Here in the city, so far from a true connection to place — the land, the sea, the sky, the curve and colour of the hillsides — it passes as another summer day.

2 Starry Night

We stand outside under starlight while my friends have the last smoke of the evening before heading home. Fin and Barbara are visiting from Berlin and are camping in the front field. Britta is here with Tinka and they're off home to Baile an Trasna. Sooki is curled up in my bed, having had the last of the cream that went with the strawberries for dessert. We've had a lovely evening together. The visitors spent the day on Sliabh an Iolair and are wind- and sunburnt to prove it. They don't mind about the possibly cold night. They've got a good tent and down sleeping bags. If it rains, they can bed down here in the caravan. After they've gone off, I stand outside to say a private goodnight to Cassiopeia, my favourite constellation, twinkling at me from the heavens. Good night! Sweet dreams!

A Day with Neutral Weather and Little Food of Note

For the move of the first boxes, my 'Here Be Dragons' files, to storage, the weather is blessedly mild, a brief respite from the heat. The weather boxes in the paper though, show the return of temperatures in the nineties in the days I will pull all my belongings from the upper floors and into the basement for their final moves. The bed went days ago, the dining room table. Today, the desk. The house grows more spacious as its elegant bones are revealed. In the early evening, I wander to the back courtyard for dinner, a barbecue given so those who live here in this shifting city neighbourhood will meet and know each other, a way of making community against the increasing threat of crime. I am soon to leave, but visit with neighbours in the softness of the summer evening. Grilled chicken and sausages, hamburgers. A selection of salads, one with wild rice and blueberries, another with beans and diced summer vegetables. Bags and bags of chips. For dessert: pies of peach and apple caramel, a dense chocolate cake, a yellow cake with whipped cream and blueberries, all from Costco. We sit awhile in shorts and short sleeves, children playing with yo-yos and balloons, this mild night just before the new moon.

3 Changeable

I tell Barbara that the only weather forecast here is 'changeable', that anything else is a lie. When I wake this morning at seven, bright sun is pouring into the caravan. At eight o'clock, the downpour begins and continues for the best part of an hour. Then sunshine returns and continues, on and off, throughout the autumnal day. That is the pattern of the days this week as the month of Lughnasa begins. Fin and Barbara are cosy in their watertight tent and down sleeping bags out in the front field. I'm cosy wrapped in my blue wool shawl with Sooki on my knee as I write the Weather Watch this evening. The evening sky is cloudy. The air is fairly warm. No sign of Cassiopeia. I wonder how watertight that tent really is?

Indoors

The predicted heat did not entirely materialize today, but I stayed indoors anyway. On the phone mostly, a respite from the packing and the sorting, resting for a moment in friends' voices, and on the good work done yesterday. The large afternoon wind rose just on time, swirling the branches of the trees, gently rattling the windows in their frames. The day was an oasis in the leaving. Calm. Gathering for the next assault on the possessions, which will be tomorrow when Kate comes with her large car we can fill, hoping the heat stays at bay as we dash around town dispersing.

4 Closing In

Visibility from Milltown Bridge was about 100 feet this evening at seven o'clock. There was no sign of the far side of the harbour. In Ballymore, the sky rose up like a blank wall just beyond the cuaisín. It was pissing down, very warm and the wind was rising. I excavated the Berliners from their tent and we decamped to Quinn's in Ventry where we had a hearty pint and a lot of talk about books. Out of the corner of my eye, I was aware of a television programme reporting about the food crisis in Niger. By the time we left, the rain had stopped. Hopefully it will have blown away by tomorrow evening when the Dingle Races begin.

Heat Again

The heat has returned to the city, and I slow down in my tasks, unable to function well in the midst of it. Everything seems to take longer, and the air to be thicker. Each step up the hill or out to the car seems to be taken against a wall of heat. Kate has come in from her forest home at the coast to help with the packing, and we load the car to travel around the city dispersing goods to various charities: Dress for Success, William

Temple, Oregon Community Warehouse. As the burden of my possessions becomes lighter, I still feel the weight of what remains. When we return to the emptying townhouse, I stretch out on the couch, dizzy with heat. Dizzy with dispersal and life.

5 Tingling

After swimming in the evening high tide, my skin is tingling in the cooling air. The incoming water is cold, pristine, although the day has been golden. Half an hour later, my fingers are numb, my salt-scrubbed body wide awake. Time for the blue wrap and a protein dinner.

Cool of the Night

I'm in the midst of another all night session, clearing the upper floors of the house so the painters can begin their work tomorrow. This afternoon, the couch left, moved two doors down for a visiting father. The townhouse, once so dense with object and memory, echoes now. Boxes and bubble wrap line the walls. I took the last of the flowers out this evening, but a candle still burns, one of my pear candles, glowing on the mantel in thanksgiving to this small house that has sheltered me through much weather for seven years. Even as it's late, it's easier for me to work. The night is cool. The air drifting in through the open windows stirs and releases the heat gathered through this intensely hot day. A day so hot that in the afternoon I could barely move, lethargic as I went about my tasks. I have no air conditioning here, and the way to stay even slightly cool is to open the windows at night, then shut them as the heat builds and the sun comes in the windows. This works mostly, although it makes for an airless afternoon, and after days of temperatures above the nineties, the brick begins to absorb the heat rather than act as a buffer against it. I am yearning for Baile an tSléibhe, for the clear air and the wind blowing in across the sea. I am yearning to be done with this task of farewell, and to be, finally, home.

6 Diamanté

Cobwebs embroidered with raindrops adorn niches and nooks outside the caravan, diamanté jewellery brightening up a foggy summer's day.

Far Dawn

As I worked my way through last night, I was soon greeted by an exquisite dawn, delicate lavender-rose shading to apricot. I thought of sunrises over Mt Brandon at home, so immediate, the sky so suffused. Here in Portland, it was a distant band of colour seen between the edges of two tall buildings. Exquisite nonetheless.

7 Hum

In warm, windless air, bees work double shifts this still afternoon in the nasturtiums and buddleia while I sit on the step, listening, not inclined to move. Hum.

Basement Weather

Last night I left the rooms of the Vista house empty, and stayed with friends. Their guest room window opens to a koi pond in a neighbour's yard, and thus has the 'babbling brook' feature, the water circulated for the fish. I slept long and deeply, waking before the alarm to a grey sky, the first hint of any rain in a good while. At Vista, Kelly and I have coffee and pastries in the back yard, nothing being left in the house to sit on. And barely to eat from, for that matter. By the time I descend into the basement for the chores of the day, the sun has come out. With just two respites, the rest of the day is underground. I walk out in the late afternoon for a hamburger, and then Gene, Maria and Aidan come by to pick up things for the Oregon Community Warehouse. While Gene wrestles things into the car, Aidan – who is soon four – and I sword fight with some twigs fallen from the ash, or the silver maple. It is peaceful in the yard, dusk falling, the air fresh. The rain never did come, but as I write, the sprinklers have gone on, watering the gardens. Which means it's well past two, and I should be crossing town to my babbling-brook bed.

8 Signals

When I turned my back to the island, a long spume of dragon's breath crept up behind me and chased me over the Clasach to Ventry, where it got bored and went off after somebody else. In the faraway Reeks, an Apache sent up smoke signals. I wonder what they meant? Then, at the hour of the high tide, a ribbon of palest blue mist separated ocean from sky, gently unfurling itself against the line of the Iveragh Peninsula and on out to sea, veiling the lower halves of both Scelligs and vanishing, then, into nothingness. The air is warm under a dense duvet of cloud. It's the kind of night when there might be phosphorescence in Ventry Harbour...or, at least, curious dreams.

No Weather Report Today

9 Anticyclone

Nature is holding its breath, waiting. The low sky, stifled, is trapped under the pressure of an anticyclone. Only the ocean rises and falls, unperturbed by the apparent absence of air.

It Takes a Meitheal

It's my last day at Vista and I've been up all night, begin the day by driving east into the morning sun to Tony and Maggie's for a shower and an hour or two of sleep. By the time I leave to return to Vista, the sun is hot on the side of the house despite the early hour. Friends have been calling with offers of help. Tony last night phoned to say if I was in a pinch, I should throw things into a box and bring it to their garage where it could be sorted later. Just this suggestion eases my panic, and I soldier on, weeping at times that I cannot do this, but never pausing in the work. Alta has offered to take things to the charity shops, and she arrives early with Karen and Charlie in tow. They exclaim over my things, assembled in bags on the lawn. Karen and Charlie are just moved in, and gather some of my household goods for their new home. Darcy arrives at ten, with food and good energy. Tony and Maggie show up later, willing to work. Kelly comes with her friend Fred from Miami to take away her green table. At two, slightly delayed, the movers Earl and Tim arrive. They prove to be wonderful movers, strong, efficient and cheerful. Slowly the basement empties into their truck. I lead them across the bridge to the storage place, and while Earl and Tim expertly fit everything into the space, Darcy and I go to Tony and Maggie's nearby to unload some of the boxes from my car. We end up having gin and tonics and curry and watermelon. Summer food. When we return, the movers are just finishing – with space to spare! We praise them, and return to Vista for the last of the boxes. Everyone else leaves. I sweep the basement, smudge the house, speak my gratitude to the rooms, to the struggle and joy they held. To the rosebush climbing the front of the house, to the pear tree beside the door. To the long winter table of Nollaig na mBan, to the picnics on the lawn out back. To the redwoods standing guard. I close the basement window, pick up the last bags and go. Joy fills me. At the privilege of having lived in this graceful place. At the hurdle completed for moving on, home to Baile an tSléibhe. Back at Tony and Maggie's, we have hot chocolate, and Maggie has placed a finish line across the door to my room, with Congratulations! on it. I walk into my room, the babbling brook room, and stagger into sleep, joy in my heart, joy in my aching bones.

10 Sure-Footed Weather

The weather didn't put a foot wrong today. It was golden throughout and when evening came, as we sipped drinks on the patio of Club Havana and listened to the band, my thoughts wandered to balmy evenings in Cap Skiring dancing with Moussa...

Beyond

> Beyond exhaustion
> I only notice the sun
> and oh! then the stars.

11 Overview

As evening comes, dense clouds move in from the west and soon, the sky over Ventry Harbour is swirling and tumbling, full of wind, announcing the break-up of the anticyclone. The cliffs of the distant Iveragh Peninsula, sharply illuminated by long beams of filtered light, seem within hand's reach of Sandra's front doorstep on Sliabh an Iolair.

Dispersal

The day is a perfect summer day, clear air, warm but not hot, a slight breeze. I have stayed the night at the coast at Ger and Kate's, and have a leisurely morning, waking to no alarm, sitting a while in the hot tub tucked in amidst the trees outside, clearing out and adjusting things in the car. It is the day of dispersals, of the release back into the wild of the rocks, feathers and shells that have inhabited the Vista house. I have four boxes and an extra handful of feathers. Two are stones, one feathers, one shells, collected from all the places I – and friends – have been these past years. Their proper home seems to be by the sea, and I am heading for a beach I know, one I've walked along, whose dunes I've climbed, where I've seen vibrant rainbows. Aside from my history there, it has the advantage of being very close to the road. The stones are heavy and I am tired, the boxes a bit unwieldy. I park, descend to the beach, shell box in hand, and tip it out. It looks natural there on the sand near the dune grass, and only someone knowledgeable looking closely would know that some of the shells are not native, are in fact from another ocean altogether. The feathers are next, and they scatter in the wind, a few of the larger ones catching to stand upright in the sand. I bring the stones down, one box at a time. Mixed in are pieces of crockery, two small clay works by a friend's son, and two rather unsettling pottery pieces with intaglio infants. Again, they do not look out of place. I offer gratitude to these fragments of beauty that have sustained me, and then leave them to walk to the water's edge where I stand looking out at the Pacific wondering when I might see it again. I stand a long while, the water lapping over my feet. When I turn to walk back, two people are sitting on a log just in front of my dispersal place, as far as I can see noticing nothing amiss in the presence of African feathers on an Oregon beach. The woman is photographing the man, and I wonder if some of my arrangements will be caught by her camera. I pass by them, pass by the dispersals, return to the car, and drive north, lighter by far than I began the day.

12 Wind Rising

The wind is rising, steadily gathering energy all evening and now, at midnight, becomes the backdrop for dreams. I think of whirling dervishes as I head for bed.

Parting Weather

The days continue pleasant, slightly warm. I am nearly numb with this process of leaving. Today I ate lunch with one friend, had tea with another, both of whom have been dear friends through the past years. Both say they may come visit in Ireland, but I don't know. The partings have too many tears for that hope to prevail. I run errands, close bank accounts and a safe deposit box, still have not turned in my change-of-address form to the post office. The residual piles await me in the garage, and I spend the night re-entering the place of too many decisions and fatigue. Above me, the Perseid meteor showers pass their peak, but too much city light keeps me from seeing them. Only the huge half moon and Venus are visible, the rest of the sky a pinkish haze. Day after tomorrow I leave for Ireland. The final tasks I still face seem beyond the time I have to do them. My fatigue is enormous; my yearning for Ballintlea is sometimes all that keeps me going.

287

13 Slumber

Warm air, dry grass, gentle overcast, occasional sunshine: perfect weather for slumbering all afternoon by gently rustling willows. Bone tired.

No Weather Report Today

14 Firelight

As the tide rises to fullness, the faces of campsite neighbours and friends are illuminated by firelight as we gather with Toni to celebrate his birthday this warm, calm evening on Ballymore rocks. The children, sure-footed, poke around the rock pools. Tinka, sure-nosed, pokes around the fire interested in the cooking chicken. The murmur of conversation rises gently with the tide, ebbing and flowing against the growing indigo of ocean and sky and Toni's lilting fiddle tune. It's nearly dark at ten o'clock.

No Sleep and Fiery Dawn

As Maggie drives me to the airport, the morning sky glows fiercely rose-orange, gold. Mt Hood is a massive lavender silhouette against the sky, and Mt St Helens is huge even with its diminished shape. I've had twenty minutes of sleep, from 5 a.m. when I fell fully clothed onto the made bed until 5.20 when Maggie knocked on the door. It is enough to get me to the plane where I nap and read in a middle seat, none of the landscape below on this summer-hazed day visible to me. As the plane lifts off, I think with some astonishment, 'I've done it!' The Vista house is empty of my things, the new tenant already moved in. My belongings are dispersed in several

288

directions, the last batch still in Tony and Maggie's garage stacked with neat post-it notes designating their destinations. Yesterday, I mentioned Bob and Orna's visit, which now seems forever ago, early in this Portland time, with so much happening since. I've addressed − at least in part − my mound of possessions. I've wandered the farmers' markets and seen friends, gained weight from so many lavish meals. I've said emotional good-byes again and again, to friends, to places, to objects, to animals, to my car. I've lived in a cloud of gratitude for gifts I've been given through all these things. I've seen my once husband for the first time in the seven years since our divorce. Again and again, I've practiced the river-running adage of the safe way to navigate a rapids: face up to what you want to avoid. I write now in the Atlanta airport. In two hours, the plane is scheduled to lift off from the land of my birth and take me to the new land I've come to love. Even as I look forward to this intensely, still, I'm at the moment stunned by the enormity of it, at the enormity of what I've done. Am doing.

15 Absolutely Still

Everything is absolutely still. The garden breathes deeply into advancing darkness. I sit on the step, listening. At a quarter to ten, I can no longer read the print in my book. Suddenly, the colour has gone from the brilliant nasturtiums, buddleia and fuchsia have absorbed the light. It is unusually warm, as was last night, and I don't want to go inside, to give up the evening...but the Weather Watch is calling. I wonder if Sandra's padding around the Ballintlea house, or even padding around the mountain, or if she's fast asleep, book in hand, moths flitting around her reading lamp, smiling as she dreams into the mountain again.

Assumption

Home.

16 Hide-and-Seek

All of a sudden through blanket overcast, a great orange moon appeared, as if someone had flicked a switch. Just as suddenly, it went out again, like a pin-pricked balloon. What? Where? How? It's a game of hide-and-seek played by the coy, coming-to-fullness moon and the warm west wind. The white morning glory flowers are shining outside, reflecting the moonlight.

Swallows Diving Over Me

Finally, finally back in Baile an tSléibhe, I fall asleep peacefully in the midst of the utter quiet and darkness of the night. I do not wake until well into the afternoon, and then, after a few hours up, poking here and there at unpacking and settling in, I take the white blanket out to the lawn by the pond to nap again. It is a day of perfect brightness. A wind has come up, lifting the closeness of the day before. Huge clouds move across the sky, their shadows dappling the mountains across the bay. In the bay itself, white sails make small dots in the blue. A gauze of cloud swirls high above the banked clouds. I turn on my side and sleep deeply, waking to find I am no obstacle to the activity of the swallows. As they swoop in to the pond, they fly low over me, their deep blue and rust and cream feathers clearly visible. A tightly packed flock of small birds whooshes suddenly by. I lie in the lawn in the afternoon sun, the softness of the blanket under me, the sky blue above me, swallows in the air, content.

17 Foul
'So foul and fair a day I have not seen.'

—*Macbeth*, Act 1, Sc 2.

Rain and First Fire

I wake to rain this morning, feeling the parched earth revive. The pond is beginning to rise, aerating after the dry spell that left it with the bright green growth of eutrophication, too little oxygen. The coolness is welcome on my skin. I put a sweater on over my t-shirt, remembering the recent days in Portland where the heat was so intense. By the time Trish arrives in the afternoon, the house feels chilled, and I start a fire. I know it's only August, and that I should not yield to this summer coolness, which is really, after Lughnasa, autumn coolness here. The fire is not for warmth though, so much as for comfort, for warming the hearth of home.

18 Perfection
The tide is high in the later afternoon, spilling over the great rock pool in the cuaisín at Ballymore, submerging the great bases of the cathedral rocks, filling the swimming hole to the brim. I swim out to where the cuaisín meets the open water and bob about under a cloudy sky, sunlight filtering through in dappled light. The salt water is fresh, not warm, not cold, velvet against the skin. I must follow my heart and go back to Moussa down in Senegal but how shall I willingly leave this place, this elemental beauty?

August Flames

I descend from my hillside into town through an alley of montbretia in full bloom, their orange blossoms flaming as I pass by quickly in the car. The entire way to the main road is rich with flowers, blood red fuchsias, purple loosestrife, creamy meadowsweet, and even the bright yellow illegal ragwort. It seems a day full of the generosity of the earth, the clear sky, the mild breeze, the end-of-summer richness. I would not want to be anyplace else but here.

19 Full Moon, High Tide

The tide thunders into the cuaisín under an overcast sky. I sit on the rocks, shivering a bit in the strong breeze, my head throbbing as if steel rods were embedded in the back of my neck, fit to burst into tears. But they don't come. Instead, I throw myself into the frenzied water, submerging my whole self in the salt water of redemption that won't flow from inside out. That comes much later in Kathrin's loving embrace as we wait for the moon to rise over Kinard's headland. Full Moon, high tide, strong emotions: heavy weather requiring prayers of compassion.

Perfect Coin

> *Perfect coin of moon*
> *rising above the cloud bank:*
> *August fullness held.*

20 Low Water, Low Dream

At midday, there's no water in the great rocky basin of the swimming hole, each stone and boulder visible at this zero tide, then masses of gelatinous seaweed fronds stretching away into low water, the squelching, sucking sounds of marine creatures marooned on rocks, waiting for the ocean's return. I lie under the overcast, listening, but the static of discord and argument in my head ruins nature's aria. No wind, no movement. Low water, low dream.

A Good Day to Be on the Water

By morning the scattered clouds the moon floated through last night have coalesced into a sky blanket, dulling the day. Yet by eleven when I return home from getting the Saturday Irish Times *at the Ventry store, the sun is beginning to break through in wide pale bars reaching to the land. The water is utterly calm. It seems it will be hot. In An Daingean it is the first day of the regatta, and I think what a good day it will be to be on the water.*

21 Blow-In

A warm wet wind has blown in overnight leaving a foggy overcoat hanging on the coastal doorjamb. Such a nasty, anti-social habit, especially on a regatta day. They'll hardly be able to see the numbers on the *naomhóga* today in Dingle.

Picking Blackberries in the Fog

The clouds have descended to make a foggy day, one occasionally dampened by soft rain. It is warm and humid, the kind of weather that seems to want a fire to dry things out, but which a fire would make too hot. In the afternoon, I take a bowl and go out picking blackberries for two small tarts I plan to make, adding the berries as garnish to nectarines and plums. I wander along my lane, choosing only those berries that fall off into my inquiring fingers, hoping they've gathered sweetness from the summer sun. I dawdle and admire the luxuriant growth, the honeysuckle and meadowsweet, the fuchsia all in bloom. I eat a bit as I pick. The mountaintop above me is shrouded in mist, its sides covered by a thin veil. I pick more than the few berries I need, lured by their abundance. Somehow the small bowl of glistening blueblack berries I carry home seems more luxuriant to me than all the booths with mounds of fruit at the farmers' market back in Portland. What I hold in my hands is sufficient, nourishing and enough.

22 Song

Heard on The Mystery Train, RTE 1 Radio, tonight, driving home, Bob Dylan in a live recording sometime in the '80s, going down a storm: 'The answer, my friend, is blowing in the wind, the answer is blowing in the wind.' From Kathrin's caravan high up at Seacrest in Kinard, we watched as day gave way to sunset, as two distinct bands of colour stretched out on either side of Cruach Mhárthain, golden apricot veering north towards Ballydavid, delicate rose pink spreading south towards the Scelligs, and not long afterwards, twilight. It has been a perfect autumnal day, with warm sunshine, lots of wind, some heavy showers and now, after dark, stars twinkle dimly in a stormy-looking sky, the waning moon hidden behind masses of heavy cloud, silvering the edges. Will she show herself, or not?...The answer, my friend, is blowing in the wind, the answer is blowing in the wind.

The Weight of Vegetable Matter

The day dawns clear, each blade of grass etched in the morning sun, the bay shimmering in the distance. I decide in the afternoon it is a good day to weed. I have been away most of the summer and the garden has gone completely wild. Even the small patch of lawn I arranged to have mowed is dotted with flourishing ragwort. I wanted to know what would happen if the land was simply allowed to do what it pleased here at the edge of the wild mountain, and, as anyone who has studied evolution could predict, I've returned to find that strong invasive plants, not necessarily native, are running rampant, and the pond is in a state of eutrophication. Even though I planned this, I feel I have been negligent. As I work in the yard, I find rosebushes choked by grasses, small heathers overgrown. I can find nothing of last year's luxuriant growth of nasturtiums which have been unable to return under the onslaught of green. Today I decide to begin by removing one weed – whose name I don't know – from the beds in the lawn. It is a tall slender weed, gone to seed, but dominates the beds making them look raggedy. It pulls easily, but I am almost defeated by the midges who seem to inhabit the moist ground I disturb in my pulling. To move into more open ground, I begin on the ragwort, which Trish has told me is both unneighbourly and illegal, poisonous as it is to cattle and horses. I feel these plants – which are dotted everywhere across my field – must go, but I also remember a conversation begun with Bob who tells me its Irish name is buachalán buí, *and has some association in stories with the fairies. I am once more reminded of how little I truly know of this land, even as I've been learning the plants and birds. I pull the ragwort up anyway, hoping for the best. I take bundle after bundle down to the plant pile. I am astonished at the massed weight of these plants. To carry them, I throw them on to a folded sheet, gather the ends together, then lift, supporting the bundle with my arms. They are surprisingly solid, a true dead weight, when I carry them. If I judge by my elderly dog who weighed sixty pounds when he became infirm before he died and had to sometimes be carried, I've transported about 240 pounds — over seventeen stone in the measure of this land — to the lower field. The enclosure has been overgrown by bedstraw, and each time I return covered with those sticky round seeds attached to my clothes. In fact, seeds are everywhere this end of summer month, and I wonder as I work how I, childless, failed to participate in this seemingly relentless drive. I have worked for hours to pull the ragwort before it goes to seed, and as I pull, I feel the resistance of each plant to letting go, its drive to continue life. For a respite, I turn to the pond, where I begin to net some of the eutrophication growth out onto the land. It proves to be a dense lime-green slime, also very heavy, sometimes bowing the metal handle of the net as I lift it out. It is finally the midges that defeat me. I return to the house covered in bites, my hand burning with the sting of nettles I failed to see. Even the dock has not calmed it. As I come in, I catch a glimpse of myself in the glass doors. I am wearing knee-length leggings and wellingtons, a t-shirt. My hair, pulled back, is escaping its tie. I look somehow as if I belong here. I think it's a good sign that I've encountered the hare twice in the afternoon. For a moment, the second time, we stood and looked at each other before she took off at a run toward the gate.*

23 Brewing Up a Storm

The wind has picked up in the last hour and now the rain is here too, pounding against the caravan walls. The willow grove looks ready to lift off, its branches flying wildly in contrary motion in all directions at once, doing a wonderful dance. The wild air is very warm and I bet the ocean is too, but I won't be checking it out! Sooki is pestering me as I write the Weather Watch. She smells like gone-off fish. I wonder where she's been lurking all day? I have a feeling her belly might be brewing up its own storm and won't be surprised if something is regurgitated later on...

A Tour Before the Storm: in which the water goes from grey to bluegreen to marine to mauve to sepia to glass green and back again. Trish tells me a gale force 10 storm is due this evening, and I head out for Dunquin to check an address before the force of it hits. The water below me in Ventry Harbour is a dark grey. The bushes in the lane as I descend from the house are tossing, but only lightly. The waves in Dingle Bay show whitecaps, and as I turn around Slea Head, I can see foam building from the waves crashing into Coumeenoole. Few cars are out, although the wind is not yet fierce. I collect the name of the B&B I wanted, and head along into Dunquin proper, where I take the small road that goes past the pier. The Sound is bi-coloured, a strange mauve at the horizon, with waves breaking high over the headlands near the cuaisín. I think to head in a loop toward home, want to see how the waves are breaking at Clogher Beach, but only find them mildly churned. Something is going on in Baile an Fheirtéaraigh, as all the street is lined with cars. I go on to Béal Bán, where I find the tide high and the wind skeining foam backwards from the waves. Despite the slight rain, I decide to walk a bit, make it only as far as the causeway, and return to the car with my hair soaked through and the raindrops being driven into me like needles. The wind coming strongly from the southwest has caused the surface of the water to be in a constant shiver at its passing. I return to Baile an tSléibhe by the old roads, small lanes lined with turbulent branches. Only in the pocket below the Clasach are they still, and by the time I reach home, the wind is everywhere around me again. As I write it is late, near eleven. Wind moves around outside, but not with great force. I'm yearning still for a gale to arrive, to shiver my skin as it did the water at Béal Bán.

24 Nature's Baptism

Underneath my bare feet the wet foreshore resembles the fresh mackerel I just bought for supper, the sand pattern like the inky stripes of the fish, the metallic blue of the autumnal sky reflected in the sand puddles the same colour as the mackerel's sheen. My feet move swiftly along, bathed in the warmish water, calm now after last night's storm and bluster. It didn't come close to the Met Office's projected Storm Force 10, although the rain came down in heavy cloudbursts throughout the night. As I approach the far end of the beach, near the graveyard, the heavens open right on top of me. There's no escaping, so I decide to relish it, raising my face to the heavy rain and throwing back my tight shoulders. Rain water above, salt water below: nature's baptism.

Wind That Moves the Clothespins

I have no dryer, and so things must be hung out back to dry. Because the clothespins are plastic, I just leave them clipped to the line when not in use. No matter how they're spaced when I leave them, they inevitably end up clumped together at the north end of the two lines, near the posts. I wonder about this, imagining the wind meeting and nudging each small surface until all have moved as far as they can go. Or it might simply be that the wind keeps the line in subtle motion until a jostling moves the pins on. The north side is the downhill side, but I doubt that gravity is a factor in this, though it may be. I've noticed this vaguely for months, and sometimes on other clotheslines. It's time to start a sharper observation, to see what I can see.

25 Sunburn and Soak

The autumn day is a complete tease, going from sunburn to soak in seconds, utterly unreliable, except in its unreliability. While we were in the theatre tonight, it seemed to me that the wind was getting up again but now, much later on, all is calm on the southwestern front.

Billowing Rain

When Biddy calls from Tralee at ten in the morning about coming back west, I tell her it's a brilliant day, the sun shining, the bay a glimmering beaten silver. By the time I leave to meet her in town at two, heavy raindrops have begun to fall. As I drive in, the clouds open, and I pass through billowing wind-driven sheets of rain. I think of the tourists in the last of their summer holidays, disappointed. I think of the bicyclists who started out in bright sunlight, now being buffeted by wind, drenched by torrential rains. In town, the sun shines, but when I leave about four, the storm is beginning there. Umbrellas, hoods go up. By Ventry I'm back in the sun again, return home to a tranquil sky.

26 My Unweathered Friend

Heading into the market, I meet Sandra heading out. Among her treasure is a little posy of sweet pea from Rosemarie's stall. Such heavenly scented delight. The posy suits Sandra's girlish energy. Ten days back on the mountain have sloughed a few decades off her, at least. Wind and rain, which usually weathers things, has restored her vitality and made her shine with youthful vigour on this fresh autumnal day at the market. She's so happy to be home again on her windy mountain, rediscovering the garden, the pond, the wild creatures there, the weather, the sky, the whole show. Sandra, my weather, but unweathered, friend.

Half Moon Rising

When I look out the window of a darkened room, searching for the Northern Lights that might be visible tonight, I see a glowing half moon rising through dark sculpted clouds. Most of the sky is clear though, thick with stars. I decide to go outside to watch a while. The Plough is resting on the horizon above Cruach Mhárthain. Capella is flashing her colours brilliant as any diamond. A satellite, small moving star, crosses overhead. I think again of the description of the Northern Lights as Tai Chi motions across the sky, moving veils of light. A recent sun storm has sent radiation pulsing toward earth, radiation so strong that the lights may be visible even this far south. I lie a while on the blanket, eyes north, but admiring too the Milky Way, its net of stars. One faint wash of pale light crosses the sky, barely noticeable. The midges discover me. I finally go inside, thinking to try later. As I write in the lighted room, I see only darkness outside, and the half coin of the moon still glowing.

27 Home

As I cycle up the hill from Ventry, heading home to

Ballymore, the cliffs of Valentia turn a deep rose pink, illuminated by a flattened sunset under the low, overcast sky. Each crevice and sweep of rock is visible, sharply defined, and further on, the whitewash of the Valentia lighthouse seems to glow. By the time I've pedalled to the top of the rise, the colour has faded away so that the only thing of note, now, is the winking neon light in a matt-blue, featureless headland away to the southwest. The swallows were swooping low over Sandra's pond this evening. The game seemed to be who could swoop the lowest, cut the water, but not get wet above the breast. They played this game over and over, each one fluttering and flapping like a wet dog as it sloughed over the still water. Earlier, Sandra had said she expected them to be gone any day now. I watched them, fascinated, through warm salt tears, and knew they have no cares about home – where it is, or how to get back there – that they just follow their nature, know where to go and when. I want to be like them, going from seasonal home to seasonal home, assured of heading in the right direction, following my nature, care-lessly.

A Sunbright Day Inside

On this day of splendid sunlight, with even a breeze to keep the midges away, I find myself at the computer printing small rectangles of captured light. I look up from time to time, out the window to the dappled hillsides, but really all my attention is on the small machine printing out images of other weathers: autumn blue sky and clouds reflected in a window; sunlight and shadow curled amidst eggs; a mossy post in shade. Caught in the past, I barely step outside.

28 Wind

All day long I'm aware of wind. Not big wind, but persistent, determined wind, very warm, a true southerly. At noon, the water in the cuaisín was churned up on the incoming tide, almost wild, but Adrienne and I swam anyway, exhilarated in the rough, warm water, topping up our courage for journeys to be undertaken far from here. Later, when I went down to Ventry to get butter, a slate-grey mist had descended, shrouding Sliabh an Iolair to within a hair's breath of Sandra's orange house. No wind up there?

On Freeing a Tortoiseshell Butterfly

When I walked into the living room this morning, looking out at a grey day laced with mist, I saw the tortoiseshell butterfly that had entered the house through the open doors yesterday perched on the edge of the glass door, looking out longingly it seemed. I did as I always do with small creatures indoors, went for a glass and paper, gently slipped the glass over the butterfly and then the paper under the glass, making a small and very temporary cage. I opened the door, went outside with the glass, and removed the paper. The butterfly perched in the glass for a moment, as if astonished to feel the fresh air, and then took off into the day heading east, a bright spot in all the grey. It is not much later now. I have since read an American friend's article on elm trees and the war in Iraq, and forwarded it to two other friends; phoned a friend who was not feeling well. But I wondered just for a moment if the simple act of releasing a butterfly could not be considered sufficient work in a day. We drive ourselves with meaning, with wondering and probing our worth in the world, our accomplishments. Perhaps we could rest a bit if we could allow that one act of kindness makes it a day with work well done.

29 Firmament

The firmament is twinkling above us tonight, my friend Cassiopeia a large W in the sky over Brandon, to the north. Out at Dún an Óir, we watched as the mist rose from the warm sea in an exhalation over Clogher, as the sky became streaked with threads of rose pink cloud, auguring well for tomorrow's weather. Seán, Jules, Eoin and Zak the dog are here for the week. May the sun shine on them! In the cuaisín at Ballymore, the water was warm in the later afternoon after a golden day. I stayed in for a full ten minutes and then for an hour on the rocks, basking in warm sunlight, listening to the ocean's song, connecting with the real world before heading to the west to visit the family.

Bumblebee on Orange House

As I come in from sweeping the grass clippings, I notice that beside the door clinging to the house as if it might be a huge orange flower, a bumblebee is resting. I've often thought the house might be a bit less bright a colour, but more and more, I think the orange suits it. It glows on the mountainside on a bright day and in the fog. Even driving I can spot it from almost everywhere around the harbour, and from the top of Sliabh an Iolair. When I give directions, I say 'the orange house in Ballintlea', and everyone seems to find it. But best of all is to think of it as a huge orange flower, soaking up the sun, calling and warming bees.

30 Beach

It was an inside day, all day, damp and overcast outside, generally uninviting. All day long I looked at days and dates, not actually picking up the phone to book a flight to Dakar, which would end the damned debate. Oh well, I guess it is fair enough to be fussing about small stuff when one is poised on the edge of a major life change.

At half past five, I managed to get myself to Ventry Beach. I'm sure the water was warm there but it was choppy so I didn't swim, just walked the beach. Back at the bridge, I met Britta and Heli and repeated the walk with them, glad to be out and in motion. In the distance, the mountains of the Iveragh were dappled in sunlight, the light defining rocks and valleys so sharply, it was as if one were looking through a telescopic lens from one little world into another.

I Wake Astonished

I wake astonished to a grey day and the sound of water falling down the rainspout outside the bedroom window. How could this be, even in Ireland? When I went to bed at after two in the morning, the sky was brilliant with stars, a perfect August night. As I looked out then, I saw an unfamiliar light on one of the mountaintops to the east. Wondering if it might be a bonfire, I went through the darkened house for the binoculars, only to discover it was the moon. But such a moon it took my breath away. Orange-gold, in its waning crescent, yet with the entire globe washed with light. And huge! Looming, it seemed just behind the mountain, come so close, as if it had rolled across the land and was not in the sky at all. Huge looming sphere

about to come over the mountain! I blessed my nocturnal habits for allowing
me moments like this, these glories while others are sleeping.

31 Light on Rock

At six in the evening, I get back to Ballymore, dazed after
a day spent between emails and phone calls at work. I HAVE TO
GET IN THE WATER! Adrienne's car is in the field, so I wander
over and lure her down to the rocks for a swim. It's our thing
together, our connection. We spend a little while in the sunlight on
the rocks but it doesn't last long between rushing clouds overhead.
The water is fresh and clear, like velvet on our skin. The lads are
out in the *naomhóg*, checking their lobster pots around the harbour.
It's a beautiful canoe, that particular *naomhóg*; it's always moored in
the cuaisín so it probably belongs to our neighbours, the Clearys.
We hang out in the water, relieved. We are two people who depend
on access to the ocean for survival, for our well-being, for the
sound of its ebb and flow and its salty vitality. As we towel ourselves
dry, an outlying strand of rock, the one with the great rock pool, is
sharply lit by the evening sun so that it seems unreal, too sharply
defined, as it were, like a graphic image that never existed in nature.
But it is nature, it is weather, it is actual light on rock at six in the
evening on the last day of August. We watch in silence until the
light shifts under heavy rain clouds. Then, rather blue, we go our
separate ways, content.

A Day Too Wet

I wake again to the sound of water in the rainspout, and know it will be a day too wet to mow the lawn, pull the ragwort, take a long walk, paint outside, or even to nap or read in the sun. The day is uniformly grey, soggy, not cold but yet somehow chilly. Clammy. I think back longingly to my first days here in Ballintlea, when I woke held in rectangles of sunlight, waking slowly, stretching, feeling warm to my bones.

September

1 Motion

Light, air, water, rock, clouds and sunshine: all in motion this first day of September. I swim with Adrienne again at high tide, then sit for an hour in golden sunshine, listening to wind and ocean. Like the rocks in the cuaisín, I am weathered, jagged sometimes, but also polished and refined like everything else in nature, in motion.

Bathing Weather

As I sit with my morning coffee, gazing out the living room glass doors, I realize a great splashing is going on in the pond. Three young thrushes are bathing there, fluffing their feathers, sending delicate sprays of water into the air to catch today's bright sun. They patter and preen, shiver off droplets, use their feet to make lightning quick scratches to their necks. I can hardly think of a better start to a day than sitting in this sunlit room, watching.

2 Coumeenoole

Eoin is ecstatic in the waves at Coumeenoole. They look enormous as we stand in the shore water but this twelve-year old nephew duck dives under the waves in glee. The ocean is turquoise today, the waves thunder into the cove, there's a lively southerly wind and the sun beams down out of an azure sky. What fun! Half an hour later I'm getting cold and retreat to base camp near the rocks where I have a good giggle reading Eoin's book *Horrible History*. When I was a kid I was just like him: my nose always stuck in a book, surrounded by adults. But here at Coumeenoole, he's an elemental boy and I think to myself how lucky I am, this year, to spend time in the great outdoors with two lovely nephews – Patrick last month and now Eoin. What sweethearts! Lucky me.

Suddenly

Yesterday afternoon in the midst of the bright day, it suddenly rained. The sun shone still, silvering the rain, a rain so dense and drenching, I didn't even look up to see its source as I dashed out to rescue the blue-striped cotton cushion on the white wicker chair. Then suddenly the air was filled with swallows dipping over the pond, at least a dozen of them dropping from the sky from all directions. What were they doing? Where did they come from? I realized I had no idea where they were when out of my sight. Clearly somewhere near. Just as suddenly the rain stopped, and the swallows disappeared. The day went on just as it had been before, warm and full of sun. Except for the raindrops glistening on the lawn, I might have imagined it all.

3 Where Did the Wind Go?

The night is absolutely still, the warmest night so far. Where did the wind go? In the morning, I went out on the bike around Slea Head and was almost swept over the side in strong gusts of amazingly warm air. I wonder if it is residue from Hurricane Katrina that has devastated New Orleans? On the way back, over Mám na Gaoithe, I didn't even have to use the brakes coming down the hill, the wind, acting as a brake, was pushing me back. Mám na Gaoithe, The Windy Pass, is well named. Tonight, in the backwater behind Burnham, we have come to witness Caoimhghín's Lughnasa fires. The three open-framed constructions – hung with white prayer flags – house the ritual fires which will burn into the night or until high tide washes them away at dawn. They are placed on the old Cemetery Road, in remembrance of the souls of the dead whose bodies were brought for burial along that route to the little graveyard nearby until a certain Lady Ventry had the bridge dismantled, thus ending the shortcut, for she couldn't tolerate the sound of the keening women on funeral days passing through her estate. Gathered here in ambient darkness, I imagine them all there with us, glad that Caoimhghín has called them back, interested in all the young people who are interested in them, listening, with us, to Duigo's tunes and slow airs drifting off into the night, resting in peace.

Burning

Today's large soft wind and threat of rain cease near dusk in time for Caoimhghín's event. We emerge from Burnham Wood to see three skeleton houses with fires burning in them. Made of slender wood painted pale blue, each house has five sections and thick rafts of white prayer flags tied to its roof beams. The structures are placed along a pathway clear at this low tide, the site of a former road leading to an old cemetery. The Monsignor, who used the road as a boy, speaks and remembers. People gather in a circle around him to listen as darkness falls. Each house has a slightly different arrangement. In the house nearest shore, the prayer flags are tied to the near half of the beams, the fire situated in the far side. The rafters of the second house are all covered, the fire centred under them. The third and farthest house has a fire, whether by chance or design the largest, in the near half of the structure, with the far half of this roof densely covered with the prayers, a thick sheaf of them hanging down from the central beam. Beyond it, the sound of water moving over the rocks and into the bay makes a shirring sound not unlike the sound of the burning. As the night progresses, people wander here and there, close to the fires, then far away. Silhouettes move, shimmering in the flames. Kathrin discovers phosphorescence at the edge of the water, and we press gently on the kelp, releasing a small barrage of twinkling light. Children's voices ring out from the woods. As if at a signal, people move away from the structures toward a bonfire on the shore. Conversations float through the darkness which, on this still, dark-of-the-moon night is not really dark at all. Off and on, people turn back to the structures to watch. For one breathless moment, wind catches the third fire, and it seems as if the flames are reaching the wood, licking up toward the flags. But the wind stills again, the fire calms to glowing. As we leave up the candlelit path, flutes begin to play. Their sound follows us through the night and back to the car.

4 Evening Glory

All day, the overcast sky sat on our heads, the muggy, soporific air like a heavy weight which eventually fell as a torrential downpour that seemed to go on for hours. But eventually the sky opened up, sunshine poured through and the mantle lifted, dissipating quickly so that when Angelika arrived, we went down to sit on Ballymore rocks watching an interesting shadow and light show between sky and ocean. Somewhere high over the Scelligs drifted a brilliant white cloud, the thermal rising high into the atmosphere, reflected just as brightly in the ocean below. In the cuaisín, the tide was thundering in, too rough for swimming off the rocks. This warm, damp atmosphere is perfect for midges.

Fire and Water

The day's fog and rain suddenly lift in the late afternoon, in time for me to return to the cove at Burnham Wood to see the Caoimhghín's shelters at high tide. Last night, Trish made the passing remark that the third house is nearly covered at high water, and I want to see this. When I emerge from the woods this time, only the roofs of the structures are visible, with the prayer flags fluttering in the slight wind. The water reaches the eaves, the frames rising from the water, a clearer, brighter blue than they had seemed in last night's dusk. The flags catch the sunlight and gleam white. On the far shore, the wood is a deep green background, the first faint tinge of autumn's gold beginning to dust the leaves. I stay for a while, watching the briskly moving water, remembering last night's fires. To have seen both the night fire and the day water feels like a completion, a knowing I cannot name.

5 Reminiscence

In the warm velvety evening, Angelika, Britta and I sit outside Quinn's in Ventry drinking and reminiscing about the years when there were three choices in Dingle for the winter: the dole, the fish factory or Éirí na Gréine, Duigo's wholefood café. A whole tribe of us virtually lived in that shop, an otherwise homeless crowd who landed up in Dingle, as far west as you could reasonably get from Berlin, Hamburg, Dublin or wherever. The calm evening is filled with laughter as we exchange memories, tell Connie and Paul about all the mad things that happened, all the curious people who passed through. People like us.

Cloud Fire

At 8 p.m., I am hunched over the computer in the back room, checking email. The nearby cows begin to call out loudly, and I suddenly realize they sound too nearby, and that the gate is still open. Abandoning the internet, I race outside and stand stunned at what I see. The cows are still in the field where they should be, but the clouds above Sliabh an Iolair seem aflame. A thick bank of fog is curling over the ridge, sending tendrils down to fall towards the lake. The upper edge of the cloud is catching the last bright flame of sunset, a blazing apricot gold. The fog indeed looks like smoke rising from the lake with flame at its tip, the reverse of what is actually happening. I stand leaning on the now-closed gate enraptured, watching the cloud twist and move and glow, watching another illumined cottony bank embrace Cruach Mhárthain. The cows are hungry and continue to bawl. They face me, a human with possible food, calling out. I face them, looking up toward the mountains. When I speak to them, they are silent, hopeful. To end their hope of me, I turn and walk back to the house. The utterly still harbour glows silver lavender. Shortly, I hear a car in the lane, and the cows are silent, fed. Night descends in a sapphire dusk.

6 Water Babes

The first swim of the day was at nine o'clock, the morning ablution in the cuaisín. The next swim was at noon, even though the tide was out. We clambered over the rocks and slipped into the water in the seaweed beds, lolling for ages in clear, velvety water, not cold at all, emerging salted, scrubbed and laughing. Then I cycled to Coumeenoole in a strong warm wind to meet the others who had gone ahead by car with the wetsuits. I had to push hard, the wind blowing against me all the way to Slea Head. Down in the cove, it didn't look like much was happening but we donned the wetsuits nonetheless and caught a few small waves, Britta and Ange gliding in on their boogie boards like a pair of seals, yelling with glee. I didn't last long in the water this time out, despite the wetsuit. My hands went blue and wouldn't warm up, so I quit and watched from the shore. The next stop was Quinn's where we ate huge plates of fish and chips, watching the overcast dissolve into a misty rain over the harbour, tired and content, ready now to slip into the waters of the great dream ocean of sleep.

Promise

> *Far out in the bay*
> *golden coins of light*
> *hold promise of good weather.*

7 Beating the Weather

Ange is a wild thing. I love this about her. With her as an accomplice, I easily do things I normally wouldn't consider. This morning, we were playing in the waves at Coumeenoole in a warm, wet wind even before I had brewed the morning coffee. It tasted all the sweeter on the return along with a huge brunch to warm us up and the sense of satisfaction of having beaten the weather at its own game.

Clouds

I am reading a friend's manuscript this chilly foggy afternoon, and find there a mention of a poem by Bashō:

> *Clouds come from time to time –*
> *and bring to men a chance to rest*
> *from looking at the moon.*

That kind of day.

8 Luncheon

Sandra and I lunch *en plein air* in a secluded corner of Tralee while misty rain falls gently on the huge white umbrella over our table. It's warm yet fresh outside, pleasant on the skin. We've both been to visit friends in the airless local hospital and are now partial to the outdoors again where we can breathe easily, enjoying this social day of visiting and good cheer, the perfect antidote to damp, enervating weather. By the time we're leaving, it's teeming down. Later, back at Sandra's ranch, we watch the rain falling on the pond. Anyone who ever hated rain should sit in Sandra's front room and immerse themselves in this tranquil moment when rain meeting pond water is the essence of welcome, of embrace, of unity.

The Pond of Great Pleasure

Trish visits in the afternoon, when the rain has been falling for a while. She sits in the white chair looking out at the pond, praising it. A gentle rain patterns the surface, mesmerizing, calming. She speaks of the way in which

314

the pond is an extension of the living room, the way in which it makes the room special. I know my own pleasure in the pond, in the swoop and dive of the swallows, the reflection of the moon in its surface. Trish says it gives the room, the house, a Zen feel, and she names it now The Pond of Great Pleasure.

9 Exhibit

We wander around temperature-controlled rooms in Cork's Crawford Gallery experiencing Heli's work: large, vaguely disturbing photographic images with themes of lost innocence; textural landscapes; a little girl's worldview captured on video in a city street; the flight of distant seabirds drawing us irresistibly towards the absolute stillness of Tiaracht, a nineteen–minute meditation soundscaped by the distant rumble of an eternally moving ocean. Later, from an upstairs window seat in the Ivory Tower, I watch torrential rain bucket down in pink neon.

Damp and Done

I wake to the predicted rain falling densely through the morning. I have asked that greens be reserved for me at a booth at the market, and feel an obligation to go in, despite the weather. And the shopping must be done for my mother and sister's arrival on Monday. I get to the market just as the rain becomes even thicker and the wind picks up. I sit in the car for a bit, hoping this is a passing squall, but it looks to have settled in. With a sigh, I zip up my jacket, collect my bags and head in. Once inside the gate, I see that almost no one has come today. Only six booths occupy the space, each person huddled in the chill, often clutching whatever shelter they have contrived, as the wind rattles the umbrellas. I am seized by gratitude at their coming out at all, and I walk immediately to a far vegetable booth, isolated from the others, where I buy a courgette and a cucumber, peas and a beetroot and some basil from a man with pale blue eyes. I move on to the next booth for some cheese, then to the next, Rosemarie's, for a bag of arugula sporting an orange nasturtium, and a bouquet of hydrangeas and calendulas for the guest room. At the next booth, where the woman is huddling behind a small umbrella sheltering her samosas, I add some curried potatoes. Moving on, I buy brown bread and scones, a porter cake, and chat with Derrick who is just visiting today. Finally, a batch of carrots from the Maharees vegetable man, and I'm damp and done. In one movement, without thinking, I've bought something from every booth, even booths I don't regularly visit. It is the only gesture of thanks I can think to make. The rain and wind still persist as I go sodden to the car, leaving the market people to sit out the rest of the afternoon as best they can.

10 Sultry

Downtown Cork on a Saturday afternoon in September is strangely quiet, hushed almost, under a thunderous sky, the air thick like syrup, breathless, sultry as a *femme fatale*.

Napping Weather

As I tend to be nocturnal, I often find myself napping during the day, short naps rather like a dive into deep water: the plunge, the tap of a touch on the bottom, the rise to the surface. If then I stay at the surface, the nap is refreshing, a brief interlude of rest. During the rise, the movement from sleep to not-sleep, I sometimes wonder where I will wake up. As napping often involves couches, it takes a moment before I realize which one I'm on, and then another to imagine the room around me. Will it be the deep blue couch in the river house, the firs and cedars filtering the light? Will it be the wide sage green city couch with the roses climbing past the windows? Or will it be my white couch here in Baile an tSléibhe, with the mountain and the sky, the pond and the harbour and the bay all possible when I open my eyes? Today was a napping day, grey with the sun trying to break through the haze. I knew I was on the white couch when I woke, that I'd slept with my head toward the outside wall, so my eyes would open to the fireplace and the window looking out onto Sliabh an Iolair. Just as I opened my eyes, the sun broke through.

11 Sundown

At half past eight, the turquoise sky is streaked with wispy, rosy clouds and the half moon hangs luminously, casting a long reflection across the ocean right into the cuaisín. The sky behind Parkmore is turning crimson as I bid Moussa *bonne nuit* on the phone and by the time I wander out the field, the sky behind Marhin burns orange gold, the same colour as the rock rose that went into the posy I collected for Sandra's mother. Over on Valentia, the lighthouse sends its signal into the blue, winking at the moon. The last band of colour has faded into twilight before I walk back across the field, hugging my fleece around me now for the temperature has dropped sharply after the very warm day. The sky will surely be star-studded tonight.

Night Driving Under a Quarter Moon

All day I'm distracted. Friends stop by, but start to speak of departure almost as soon as they arrive. I have announced I'm preparing the house for tomorrow's arrival of my mother and sister, but I think it is something deeper than that, some inability in me to focus. Or perhaps it is what Trish, one of the visitors, says, that I'm looking for distraction myself. If so, I'm scattered and in some real way not at home. The day is hot and near perfect, the sun blazing down, but with a breeze. Linda has gone walking up Sliabh an Iolair and Trish has cycled in from Ballymore. I am outside from time to time, but might as well not be for all the connection I make to the day. When everyone has gone and I am moving through the house in the final preparations, I'm aware of a brilliant sunset taking place outside, a festival of pink and lavender, deepest rose flushing the sky behind Cruach Mhárthain. The quarter moon catches the sun's light resting amidst skeins of delicate yet vibrant pink. I finally stop, and see. I set off for Shannon under this moon, my companion along the way. As I drive, I spot it from time to time, huge in the sky. My last sighting of it is in the car's mirror, a glowing deep orange tip above a mountain ridge. Somehow the moon has grounded me, reconnected me again.

12 Gratitude

Indigo-laden sky, low slung over headlands, coming to twilight as I walk with Kathrin down to the beach at Kinard, warm wind winding up to bluster, salt and seaweed smells filling our senses, invigorating, refreshing. We love this place, this ocean and one another. What a wonderful life.

Almost Sunny

The day dawns bright at Shannon, and I have the highest hopes for a splendid vista to greet Mother and Karen when they arrive in Ballintlea. As we come in sight of the peninsula though, clouds hover low at the far end, clinging to Binn os Gaoith, obscuring the ridges of Mt Brandon. By the time we begin the climb for Connor Pass, we are in the mist of low clouds veiling the view, and in Dingle it is raining. I suggest we stop in Dingle for lunch, still hoping for the day to clear. It doesn't do precisely that, although the rain stops and the clouds lift a bit. There is a vista in Ballintlea, but a muted one. As we sit in the living room talking, the sun begins to play on the Iveragh Peninsula. A sunny day across the bay. The line of mountains appears and recedes. My mother − or was it my sister? − comments on the amazing fluidity of the light.

13 Bluster

The wind is all a bluster today. Willows dance madly and birds ride the airwaves as if on a rollercoaster. I clung to a ladder this morning, silicone gun in hand, determined to check the seams of the caravan before the rain came. I've never quite got the hang of ladders; I always seem to need more than two hands to deal with the various bits and pieces needed to get the job done: knife, gun, cloth, whatever. Hey look! Kali on the roof, batons in various hands, conducting a storm. Watch out!

Almost Sunny Two

I wake in a pool of sunlight, hopeful again for the day, yet before I rise, a mist has descended and the day gone grey. High clouds race across the sky. Streaks of silver slash the bay, galloping as fast as the clouds. It is a beautiful day, with the dancing light, and Mom, Karen and I set off on a scenic tour around Slea Head. No Iveragh. No Scelligs. The Blaskets veiled, but visible. Stopping here and there, dawdling, we reach Ballyferriter too late for any lunch and set out for Dingle and the Goat Street Café. While we eat, the day dissolves into rain. No beach walk. No mountain ramble. Back home to the fire and conversation. Just before bed, I step outside and see stars. When Karen comes into the room a few minutes later, I tell her this. In her robe, she opens the door and looks out, says, 'It's raining'. I go to look, and indeed it is. Who knows what tomorrow's weather might be, what sort of a shape the day will take in it?

14 Strange Sights

The further peaks of the Macgillicuddy's Reeks seemed covered in snow, white and shining in evening light like small Alps as I cycled west towards Slea Head, pushing against the warm south wind. It was dense cloud descending, of course, spewing down mountainsides, pushed down by the weight of heavy air above. Further along the way, a brown donkey foal chased a woolly sheep round and round in a roadside field, very strange behaviour for a donkey. Such are the strange sights to be seen while cycling west.

Clearing

I've supplied a menu of possible activities for Mom and Karen's visit, most of them weather dependent, and today as we look at the calm sea and the emerging sun, we decide it's an island day. Karen and I leave Mother, who cannot make the climbs involved, at the house while we rush off to

Dunquin. We make an easy crossing, and on the island stop first at Sue's for tea. Seals float lazily off An Trá Bhán as we watch from the cliff top. The sun shines brightly enough that we can ignore the grey weather front moving in from the southwest. We cross to the west, peer down into coves, gaze toward the back of the island and out to the triangle of Tiaracht, climb up to the high road and cross back above the village. Rabbits race before us, and two young donkeys chase each other braying through the fields. We sit a while with the Scelligs in sight, then drop down again to the pier for the return. On the boat, Mick says the weather might be bad tomorrow, and I give him news of the fin whales and minkes spotted in the Sound. Wendela and her elegant mother are on board, having gone in for a short visit. When we return home, Mother says the sun has been shining, the air has been clear, and she could see forever.

15 Veiled

The veiled moon is suggestive, ominous behind stormy, indigo clouds. The night is warm despite predictions of a cold spell approaching.

Moving Through Weathers

I wake early and go off to town to meet with Dominique in Dingle where a dense mist is falling. I return home for Mom and Karen to find the sun shining. Back to town, and the rain has stopped. All along the bay on the way to Inch, I keep gesturing toward the right, saying there's water there, and mountains beyond. On to Killorglin where blue sky is beginning to show through the clouds. We look back to the Dingle Peninsula to see sheets of rain veiling the mountainsides. Even so, we risk Caherconree on the way *home, rising through the blooming heather and fields beginning to show the russets of fall. We descend into Camp in full sunlight, cross Connor Pass into fog. We eat dinner in Dingle, staying until dark. When we arrive finally back home, the moon is full out, shining serene in the sky.*

16 Within Hand's Reach

Ballymore rocks are bathed in warm light at half past four in the afternoon although the day dawned quite cold, announcing a definite seasonal weather change. I stripped down on the rocks, sat in a crevice to trap the warming sun on my skin, closed my eyes, listening to the music of ocean on rock. When cloud eventually obscured the sunlight, I swam in the cold dark water, the next peninsula – twelve sea miles hence – seeming within hand's reach at every stroke. An hour later, I was pulling on woollen socks, woollen sweater, woollen shawl over that and still feeling cold, so that by the time I got to the door of St James' for the last concert of the summer, I was still shivering and had to go off to Benner's for a shot of brandy to warm things up.

Still Night

After a bright day of sun and dazzling displays of light, the moon-filled night is utterly still. The water of the bay shimmers silver, but the moon is not in sight. Hidden behind a bank of clouds, it casts its light down through some distant opening. Not a breath of wind. Nothing stirs but the light spilling down into the night.

17 Shadows and Light

For six hours, I wander the complete round of Sliabh an Iolair with my brother, watching a magical show of shadows and light on ocean, rocks, islands, headlands, peninsulas and in the sky itself on this perfect autumn day. I had woken up cold this morning, shivering for want of another blanket, for the temperature had dropped dramatically during the night but as the day went on, warm sun graced our walking bodies on the mountain so that we, too, were dappled in the great show of shadows and light. Sometimes, I think that me and Peadar could walk off into another world together, a long ramble outside of space-time. Kindred souls going walkabout.

Moon Night

It is the night of the September full moon, a night of celebration in Japan. On this night, people gather to honour the moon, to watch it rise, to sip miso soup and sake. Perhaps someone will play a flute, or someone write a haiku in praise and attach it to a tree branch. At least that is what is done in the Japanese Garden in Portland, Oregon. Here in Ireland, the moon is elusive behind clouds. Its presence is felt in the pull of the tides, and the brightness of the night. Hints of moon everywhere, but the moon itself not seen.

18 Full Moon, Low Tide

It's the lowest tide of the whole year, this day of the full moon of September. And it's a day full of communion, thanksgiving and celebration. For breakfast, sitting meditation at Inch; for lunch, a birthday party for Mags, doubling as a housewarming at Ballywiheen; for supper, an exhibition of painting and ceramics in Dingle. The wind is warm again, blustery, the ocean rough and dappled with changing light. Ursula and David's ceramics, Liam's paintings too, are elemental, weathered, made by people who know and appreciate that flavour of life. The house at Ballywiheen is also weathered and elemental, like Mags, full of is-ness, honesty and humour. I am awed at the richness of the day, of my life here. Three Sundays from now, I'll be on my way to Senegal again. These riches shape, colour and refine my being, and are then part of an offering from one community to another, like food or water. I pray that I will merit the honour and be entrusted with an equivalent offering when I return at midsummer.

Moon Haiku

> *Above Ballintlea*
> *the so-full September moon*
> *slips out of the clouds.*

19 Ups and Downs

I woke this morning to strong wind and pelting rain, the kind of day you want to ignore completely, preferably by staying in bed reading a good book. But the day had to be entered into and it improved considerably after the first cup of coffee, mood and weather-wise, and by afternoon, things had settled down again into another pleasant autumn day. The temperature seemed to drop considerably in the evening but now, just before midnight, the sky is heavily clouded over, no sign of the moon, and the air no longer has that sharp nip that I felt earlier on.

No Laundry on the Line

In what is no doubt an act of hubris in the midst of the moon-bright blowing night, I put a load of wash in to be ready for the morning. Before I open my eyes, I can hear the rainwater coursing down the spout beside the bedroom window. No laundry on the line this day, but draped all over the house. Damp outside. Damp in.

20 No Hint of Wind

Driving home over Mám na Gaoithe from Riasc, I hear the midnight weather forecast of strong winds and rain before dawn. But there's not even a light breeze, no hint of wind in hedgerows as I drive along, no movement at all in the moonlit sky. It is warm again and quite still. Nevertheless, I take the clothes off the line – they are dry enough, not damp, despite the late hour – and hang them up inside the caravan. I've lived here long enough now to comprehend the vagaries of the weather, its turbulent moods, so I won't hedge my bets on what my senses are telling me about momentary conditions. As I write the Weather Watch, Sooki is insinuating herself around my knees, smelling of bonfire, so I know she's been lurking up the backyard while I've been out, the lingering bonfire smell on her coat another indication of windless weather.

Elemental Rock

It is the lowest tide of the year today, and I am fortunate to be at Coumeenoole, to walk to the far secret coves with their still pools of pale green water, the surrounding rock dense with mussels of every size, even to the tiniest not much larger than a pinhead. I have the sense some are smaller still, extending into a universe too minute to see. The tide returns quickly, and soon the coves are sealed off again, receiving the water that protects them. I walk, skirts raised high, sea rushing around my legs, around the last jetty, and back into the ordinary world.

21 Autumn Equinox

Stormy, warm wind, mist creeping down the hill, rough ocean: weather appropriate to the autumn equinox. It's the time of turning, the time when the light is receding, the time to think about lighting fires again, about long evenings over meals with friends, inside, cosying down, slowing down, changing gear. Sandra came for supper and we had an evening of much longed-for hanging-out together. It was ages since we did this. I could easily imagine the dark side of the year visiting with Sandra, sharing books and ideas, inspiring one another as we did last winter, long evenings with long suppers and ruby wine, walks around the hill, watching the weather. But I'm heading off to Casamance instead, into the unknown, to see if I could make a life there with Moussa. I will know more by the time of the vernal equinox, and more still this time next year when the earth has turned another full circle of our lives.

Beading

I wake to a calm County Clare morning, see my mother and sister off at Shannon, then travel into a West Kerry storm. Trees along Brandon Bay bend in the wind. The falls above Loch an Dúin are lost in the mist. Connor Pass is dense with fog. At home, the air is warm, but the wind fierce, rain flung against the door. As I go in and out unloading the car, I take great pleasure in the newly painted door. Rain beads on the blue, showing the world my care for this little orange house.

22 Photographs

At day's end, I'm sitting with Sandra in her house on the hill. We watch as a strong air current comes in from the southwest over Dingle, a long, thick roll of cloud moving rapidly towards Brandon, a separate entity in the greater overcast. I don't notice when rain moves in for I'm looking through Sandra's childhood family photos, absorbed, trying to find the face and expressions I know quite well, now, in these images from the past: toddler Sandra in the snow, bigger in the paddling pool on a summer's day. I wonder if she's gone skinny-dipping yet in the pond with the garden rat and the swallows, under the warm September overcast, kicking up the spray as she did in that childhood photograph? I asked her where she'd go in Europe for a snow thrill, now that she lives this side of the Atlantic. 'Up Mount Brandon,' says she without batting an eyelid. You know what? I wouldn't be surprised if she saw a snow leopard up there, so great was her delight.

Undecided

It is an undecided day, the weather going this way and that. One moment the grey seems settled in, the next the sun is out and gleaming. As I drive into town I note that while it is grey in Ballintlea, Dingle seems to be enjoying a summer day, Italian clouds floating above the town. Yet when I leave, after only the shortest errand, the afternoon has turned wintry and dull. This is the day of the equinox, balance, but today seems more tottering, one side and then the other.

23 Dark Horse

Somewhere on the road between Ennis and Galway, as the lovely autumn day descends towards sunset, a strawberry-roan horse rests in the lee of an apricot-coloured wall, its shadow a darker, mysterious other horse as the golden aureole dips lower and lower in the west. As I drive north on this lovely autumn day of blue skies and subtle light, I've been listening to news reports about the hurricane that is threatening parts of Texas and Louisiana, Hurricane Rita, following close on the heels of the devastating Katrina that recently wrecked the city of New Orleans, another dark horse on a far horizon. They are hoping it will change course overnight and bypass the Houston environs where a large proportion of the city's five million inhabitants are now stuck on highways out of town. By the time I arrive at Monica's home, way to the north past Bundoran in a village called Kinlough, the temperature has dropped considerably and there's a wintry chill in the gathering wind.

Rain in All Directions, Even Up

It is the first of the winter storms, the willows and even the sturdier bushes tossing in the wind. Clouds race across the sky, the light shifting from dull to bright, sometimes dim, sometimes sepia, sometimes gold. As I watch, a patch of blue laced with gold-tinged clouds opens in the grey, and at the same time a torrent of rain falls. A curtain swept by the wind, it falls down, dashes right, dashes left, clatters against the windows. Over the pond, it sweeps up, and then down. All this is over in seconds, the distant blue still in the sky. The day calms, brightens, then dulls, but oh! here comes the rain again!

24 Dreary Outside, Busy Within

Monica is home-making. We head off to Ballyshannon to hardware and furniture shops, seeking shower curtains, a bed, lightbulbs and whatnot. It's a really dreary Saturday of grey skies, cold wind and lashing rain. I feel like I've arrived in the far north, into another season for which I'm not sufficiently insulated. But when we've done the shopping tasks, it's back to the house to straighten things out and put some semblance of home on the place. Michael arrives with muscle and power tools and hey presto! we are busy within, indifferent to outer drear, helping Mon to feather her nest.

Faint Rainbow and Quarter Moon

Although yesterday's storm abated, the day turning bright with sunlight, this morning brought storms again, more fierce than the day before. Huge winds, hard rain falling, alternate spells of dry and wet. Yet in the evening, an abatement, the bushes stilled, the light lifting. In the sky a faint rainbow pulsed amidst glowing amber clouds. Now, at midnight, a bright quarter moon glows in the east, visible one moment, gone the next, giving no clue to the morning's weather still hours away. I think of Trish in her northern journey, hope her sheltered, encountering rainbows and moonlight too.

25 Autumn Sunday

There's a friary on the Ards Peninsula in Donegal with beautiful woodland walks and secreted coves with orange-coloured sand. It's a lovely day with occasional, misty showers – nothing to dress up for though – as I tread leafy trails bordered by saltwater inlets with Maureen, my eldest sister, who has recently come to live in this northerly place. A flock of black shags busily pluck and preen themselves on a submerged tree while a group of Poor Clares, brown-habited and veiled, with sunny expressions, chat animatedly with all and sundry on this exceptional outing from their enclosed convent in Galway. Maureen is a convent dweller too, but not enclosed. Over supper, the Donegal nuns enjoy having a Kerry person to taunt on this day of Kerry's defeat to Tyrone in the All Ireland Gaelic Football Final, but I've just heard the weather forecast and think to myself that the Tyrone crowd won't have much fun on Monday waiting for the team to parade through Omagh, for the forecast is for heavy rain and high winds.

Laundry and Silver Rain

I wake in a pool of warm sunlight, anticipating the day. I hear the wind at the small window. Laundry, I think. Yet I know enough to rise and check the wider weather, not just the southeast aspect of my bedroom, but all the sky around. Even when I step out the glass doors, what I see is blue sky, but a turn toward the mountain shows a fast advancing grey, a mass of soft cloud heading my way with moisture so dense I can see the patterns of the wind in it. The air goes dark. A bright band of light gleams on the bay, perhaps the opening to the sun that was here as I woke. The pond quivers in anticipation of the rain, wind shivering over it. I watch for the first drops to be recorded on its surface. None come. I look up to see the mountain ridge clear, no longer obscured by the cloud that has passed just beside my field and gone out to sea. Blue sky appears. I turn to gather the laundry. The light stays steady as I do, but when I look out again, the house is enveloped in a shimmer of silver rain. Holding the laundry, the shirts and the jumpers, the socks and the tights, I watch sun and rain together, enchanted. As I write now, the sun reaches into the living room and warms my toes, the grass glitters in the drying wind, the laundry revolves in the washing machine. I'll take my chances with this day.

26 Better Outside

Grey from early morning. Oppressive. I walk downtown in Letterkenny with Maureen in warm, blustery rain. As usual, it is better to be out in the elements than sitting inside whinging about how rotten the weather is! In the afternoon, I walk along a headland in Bundoran with Monica – where it's not raining – revelling in the strong wind and the force of the ocean below us.

Warm Storm

Yesterday's wash did get done, three loads including the kitchen curtains which will be packed away, allowing so much more light into that part of the house. Only a few things are still damp, draped here and there around the house. Although I sometimes wish for the convenience of a dryer, I like the necessity of work tuned to the weather, to the rhythms of here. No laundry today, as a storm brewed in the night. I heard the wind come up in the dark, and woke to find a fog descended, firmly in place and unperturbed by the gale. A day with sheets of rain, not bedsheets, tossed by the wind. The house holds the night's chill still, and I was astonished when I opened the front door to find it warm. Winter to the eyes, soft summer to the skin.

27 Homeward Bound

After Castleisland, on the long decline into Tralee, Macgillicuddy's Reeks are veiled in evanescence, filigree showers lit from below by a reclining sun.

Amazing Haze, Fierce Squalls, Waves Breaking White on Distant Shores, and a Rainbow

Yesterday's grey shifted ever ever so imperceptibly to become pale sun, stretching its bars into the living room. By evening, a golden haze hung suspended everywhere, over the harbour, across the water in Ventry, far beyond above Dingle, all the world held in its calm. Today's weather was pure shifting drama. Sun in the morning, shrieking winds and sudden fierce downpours, just as suddenly past. I did have laundry out, dried in no time by the wind, the squalls so rapid, hurried through by the wind, it seemed the rain didn't have time to light on the curtains twisting in their own dance on the line. In constantly shifting light, I could see waves breaking far off on Parkmore Point, exuberant bursts of brilliant white. Picking the sweet

SEPTEMBER

ripe blackberries in the lane, I was sent racing to the house by an onslaught of rain that wasn't hail, but felt as if it might be. Inside, I looked out to see a brilliant rainbow arced across the east, its faint shadow beside it. Gift of light. Then I watched as a single rose cloud crossed over the mountain, a messenger from the sunset. I wouldn't be anyplace but here.

28 Rainbow

Around six o'clock, after a day of stormy wind and heavy downpours, a rainbow appeared genie-like in the grey sky over Tralee, a perfect arc in glowing bands of colour, radiant, radiating, reminding me of 'The Showre', a poem by the Renaissance poet George Herbert: 'I would, I said, my God would give a sunshine after raine.'

Winter Green

Last evening's rainbow was a mere respite before today's fierce storms. As I drove into town through Ventry this morning, I was startled to see the harbour a winter green, the first of that colour I've seen in months. I wonder what it is that makes it. It cannot be the grey sky, as the sky has often been grey these last weeks. It is chilly, but not particularly cold. Perhaps it is the churning of the water by wind and squall, or perhaps, like swallows knowing when to go south, the water knows when to be green again, that milky winter jade.

29 Peculiarities

Fog on the road from Ventry to Ballymore was so thick and white that I had to drive in third gear, crawling along to find the gateway into the campsite. When I left Sandra's, she was enthusing about rain that wasn't wet. Such are the peculiarities of the weather in this peninsula. It's like a very eccentric elderly individual who enjoys scandalising those who think they know her well. You can easily imagine a smug toss of the wet-hair-clouds as the weather derisively sniggers at our innocent surprise. Rain that isn't wet, though? I think Sandra's been reading Myles na Gopaleen again. Or maybe she's been feasting on magic mushrooms up there on the hill?

Raining But Not Wet

Trish has returned from the north and come for dinner. We sit warm by the fire, eating roasted vegetables – potato, beetroot, pumpkin, aubergine, onion and sweet peppers red and yellow, all rich with olive oil and rosemary. Harvest food, Trish calls it. We catch up on the days past, the internal and the external weather, the aftermath of my mother and sister's visit, and Trish's departure for Senegal next week. As Trish goes to leave, the outside light illuminates a fine dense mist being blown about by the wind. I reach my hand up to it, into the glowing moisture, but my hand stays dry. I reach this way and that. Trish does too. Our hands are dry. I walk up to close the gate after Trish, saying it's not wet out at all despite the signs of storm. 'It's relative,' Trish says, and I think of this afternoon's drenching rains which would indeed make anything seem dry. I don't notice if Trish has the wipers on as she passes, as we bid each other good night, good sleep, warmed by friendship, by food, by fire. So warmed perhaps the rain evaporates around us, doesn't touch us, and we stay sheltered from the damp in a version of West Kerry virga.

30 Passing Through Weather

Driving, there's a sense of passing through weather, like passing through a landscape. Britta and I passed through different weathers on the journey to and from Tralee: gusting winds buffeting the car, intense but fleeting showers, occasional rainbows. Inside, I felt storm-bound, insecurity raging through me. We were at the hospital saying goodbye to Susan who is passing through another weather system, now, at the end of her life. A feisty, humorous soul, she has been a very generous landlady to all of us who have lived at the campsite.

Interval Between Storms

Just for a while this afternoon, blessed sunlight. Suddenly everyone is outside again. The wholefood store is full. The streets of Dingle are full. It seems as if the sun has released people from their indoor storm huddles. I go to the market, possibly the last of the year, and leave with cheeses and fish, olive oil and nuts, parsnips and carrots and beets, and a bright red ristra of peppers for the kitchen. I go up to the high street and down along to the fish stall. I drop quickly into Dominique's and eat lunch in Finbarr and Sophia's sunbright kitchen. No dashing from place to place, head down, shoulders hunched against the rain. I stroll. I look about. I stop to pick up the beautiful bird-shell pitcher to bring home. As I drive west, the sun dazzles my eyes. Leisurely, I open the gate, bring in the bags from the car. Even as I take some things out to the shed, the wind picks up, and I see a dark cloud coming in over Sliabh an Iolair. Almost before I shut the door, the sunlight fades. All night now, the wind has buffeted the house, and rain pelted it. The afternoon's breath of sun was enough respite, allowing me to deeply enjoy the storm as it rages through the night.

October

1 **Apprentice Weather Watcher**
Thomas sits in his chair gazing at the sea and sky. For a few moments he seems spellbound, his grey eyes the colour of the squally shower that is passing in front of us out in the harbour. He reminds me of monks who practice long-focus, open-eyed meditation. I wonder what he perceives with his four-month-old vision, if he is already a weather watcher by nature? Sylvia loves nature and has grown exotic plants outside her caravan despite salt and storms but Thomas is her most recent crop. We sip tea and talk about Susan who is dying in Tralee hospital. We hope she will slip across swiftly – like these autumn showers – to her destination, as serene as Thomas's limpid gaze. God bless her on her way.

Skip Rope
All last night a storm howled outside, the wind whistling through the vents, the rain pelting against the windows, yet when I turned the lights out for sleep, I looked out to a sky brilliant with stars, Orion floating serene above me. All day that pattern has continued, the north wind rushing weathers through. Sun, rain, obscuring fog, even a faint rainbow just now. I can see Ventry now in sunlight, but imminent rain approaches from Mt Brandon, no doubt soon to be drenching the field again. I've yet to go out for the paper, and may chance a run now, to do the few outside tasks still needed in this day. Trying to go out between squalls reminds me of the childhood game of skip rope, standing to the side, watching the spin of the rope, choosing the right moment to jump in.

2 New Perspectives

The fields and slopes rising from Ballyferriter up the sides of Cruach Mhárthain have always seemed uninviting – somehow cold and grim – but this summer I've found a different perspective on the place by walking a trail that rises above Dún Chaoin and then in a line across the skirt of the mountain, high up on the hill looking out over the valley to Clogher, nestling in a corner at the left of one's vision, Ferriter's Cove straight ahead, the Three Sisters further on, then Béal Bán and Brandon to the right. It's a beautiful, peaty trail, with no end of fabulous plant life despite the desperate winds and pelting rain that whip up the hillside. That weather cuts a lasting impression on the summer grasses, still tall now and burnished bronze and red, complementing the jewel-like clusters of moss nestling in between, ruby red and emerald green soft sponges. I point out a caterpillar, a 'hairy molly', to Kathrin and Peadar, she reaching to stroke and admire the pretty creature's jet-black and amber coat. The bright sunshine of early morning vanished quickly to complete overcast, a sort of grainy texture underlined by the quiet brown hill underfoot and the blue-grey ocean. Every so often, huge spumes of surf break high on cliffs in the distance, everything seeming to happen in slow-motion from this height and distance. There's a sting in the wind but overall, this is a benign day blessed with new perspectives.

Under a Star-Filled Sky

I began this day long ago at 2.30 a.m., rising at the time I usually go to sleep in order to drive to Shannon. As I left, the sky was brilliant with

337

stars, the veil and scatter of the Milky Way, the bright points of the planets, familiar Orion once again floating high. Even as I was rushing, I stopped for a moment to admire, to breathe in starlight, then turned and headed north.

3 Weather Talk

It's an interesting thing to sit back and listen to weather talk from other people's perspectives. Around Caroline's table at Cathair Ard tonight, Dave talked about listening to the sea area report to find out the whereabouts of weather as he sailed from Clifden to Dingle during the week. Where is the weather? Well, I thought it was everywhere, all the time, had no idea that it might be elsewhere. Speaking for surfers, Glen described weather in terms of motion and wind speed; gardeners like Caroline think about wind direction, salinity and where to put a polytunnel while Britta, who is watching her new home going up, is thinking about angles and guttering, hoping she'll get a heating system sorted out sooner rather than later.

Outside, meanwhile, it's been another overcast day. At this hour next week, I'll be sweating in Senegal, Dave will be enjoying the pleasant warmth of springtime in Sydney and Caroline, who is off to Venice with Paul and the children, will probably partake of supper alfresco.

Watching the Weather Watch

The day unfolds under high grey clouds, with a faint chill wind. Blair and Katie, visiting on break from their university in Virginia, decide to go in to the island, an unlooked for pleasure this late in the year. I stay home to *field a phone call about their lost luggage, and to work on the manuscript of* Weather Watch. *It's grown mightily since it was begun last November. I work to edit for consistency amidst all the variant spellings of this place, and then print it out for the first time. Trish is coming up tomorrow for a final edit before she leaves for Senegal later in the week. As it prints, I watch the pages scroll out, seeing the titles and the paragraphs flash by, remembering the days they record. They are full of dailiness, these pages, laundry and walks, birds and tides, but they also record a story of changes we had no way of knowing when we began. I bought the orange house in Baile an tSléibhe, moved from my Portland house to here. Changed home and country, and even name, retuning to my birth name of Landers. Trish has decided to move to Senegal for the better part of next year, to see what the shape of a life there might bring, leaving her home here – and Sooki the cat – in the care of friends. Large steps for both of us, but steps unfolded day by day. When it is printed, the manuscript – with still six weeks to go – is 333 pages. I look with wonder at the stack as it sits on my desk, amazed at what can be done one day at a time.*

4 Inside Weather

We've no time for the weather today, it'll have to take a run and jump, amuse itself elsewhere. We're too busy, chez Sandra, editing *Weather Watch*.

Weather Watchers Working

Trish comes up in the afternoon and we work together on this manuscript. The visiting young women are chilled by the Irish weather, so the house is spectacularly warm to make them comfortable. As Trish and I shed layers,

Blair and Katie bundle themselves under the duvet in their room to read. I suspect they have the heating pad on too, but don't ask. After good work and dinner, conversation and laughter and concentration, we finish today's task, 333 pages proofed and corrected. Trish heads home, away to Senegal day after tomorrow. After the warmth of the house, the night air feels soft, soothing. We say goodbye and I walk up to open the gate, watch my dear friend as she starts on her brave journey. 'Go in beauty,' I say after her as I watch her lights go down the lane. Go in beauty.

5 No Weather Report Today

Clouds Trying to Let In the Sun

All day the cloud cover stays high and grey above the land. Here and there, faint glimpses of blue appear, the beginning of a promise for clear skies to come. The clouds close together again though, and the grey holds sway. It has been grey for days, hazy, the temperature varying from cold to warm. I am yearning for clarity, the blue blessing of the sky.

6 Au Revoir

My friend the Lighting-Techie is saying *au revoir* as we cross the peninsula, the first leg of the journey back to Senegal, and Moussa. Kathrin is driving, so I get the full benefit of this daring, yet subtle, sky-lighting show. Finally, the complete orb of the setting sun, surrounded by darkening heavy clouds, is reflected in the side mirrors as we head due east leaving it behind us in the western world. It has been a lovely mild day although the wind was choppy enough down on Ventry Beach where Britta and I walked earlier today, admiring jade green water. Now, driving towards Tralee, the mountains are an intense dark blue, ridges etched vividly against the skyline. Immanent.

A Day to Open the Heart

The clouds finally open and sun spills over the mountainsides, dappling them with light. After the greyness of the past week, it feels like a blessing. Light. Warmth. Vivid colour again. I think of Trish departing today, of the wrench to her heart at leaving all this beauty. Of all the hearts wrenched, my own included, at departures over the years from this landscape that speaks so deeply to the soul.

7 Chiaroscuro

Golden sunlight filters through dense overcast this Tralee morning. It has turned warm overnight, Kathrin and myself t-shirt-clad in the garden admiring the second flush of blue campanula. The mimulus still thrives too, its velvety tiger-face reflecting the autumnal sun. Later, walking down a Dublin street to Seán's home, roses are incense in the evening air, the sky a whirl of smoky blues, apricot and grey. My senses are sharp, responsive to the world's beauty, as I set out on my journey. A favourable sign.

Romantic

Blair, Katie and I have been to Killarney to see the new film of Pride and Prejudice. *In it, there is a scene where the actress playing Elizabeth Bennet stands picturesquely on the edge of a high cliff, the winds blowing her skirt romantically about her. Katie and Blair decide that today's walk should include cliffs and if possible wind, so we head for Dunquin. The weather could not be more obliging. The stillness of the past days is gone, the wind everywhere. When we leave the house, we are buffeted almost sideways. As we get out of the car, the wind tugs at the doors. We start out above the cuaisín, and meet the full punch of the wind, nearly a gale. My hair is almost instantly torn loose from its clip. Wind-lover that I am, even I wonder if this might not be too much. I turn to the young women following to say we needn't do this. I see them struggling with their coats, eyes squinched, trying to find their balance as we walk. They say they want to go on, and we do. We stay well back from any edges, the wind a force to be respected. Had we worn skirts to be closer to the film image, we would no doubt have been turned into kites to sail high above the fields. As often happens with romance, the reality is far more vivid than what is imaged. More invigorating, more demanding, and far more full of the unexpected.*

8 Dublin Between Sun and Moon

Tramlines shine golden as the orb of the sinking sun is framed in a city street, passers-by intermittently gilded, highlighted by the Lighting-Techie who is working in close-up today. A red-headed woman dressed in bright green cycles down the line into the sunlight: Athena, city goddess. Across the line, an African man pushes a twin buggy, the light a halo around his children's heads, his own scarlet bomber jacket a moving exclamation mark. When the Luas pulls up at the Four Courts I notice the quarter moon, pale in an eggshell blue sky high above the city.

Splendour

The sun returns in all its splendour, showering light throughout the day. Beams rise and drop from passing clouds, rain shivers silver through sunlight. In warm sun we walk to Fionn Trá and wander the shell-cast beach. As the sky colours pale rose at sunset, the new moon sits a delicate sickle in the sky above the crest of Sliabh an Iolair. Later, when I cross the Clasach to Dunquin, a golden moon broods behind night clouds. By the time I return, the moon has set and the sky is a brilliant shawl of stars.

9 Looking Down on Weather

The funny thing about flying is that one is often looking down on weather from above. That's how it seemed today, flying high in celestial blue, looking down on cloud formations, choppy seas and snowy Alps below. It's hard to focus on weather watching because Eoin, a Carlow man, is regaling me with stories about life and business in Romania. He talks non-stop all the way to Milan but he's funny, completely at home in the material world. Someone has given him a copy of John McGahern's novel *That They May Face the Rising Sun*, a perfect story for this young property dealer abroad in a land like the Ireland of the 1960s. He'll surely find himself in one of the characters of the book. From my window seat, I can see the Cliffs of Dover shining in evening light like a long wall of salt. The English Channel is choppy, full of white horses, as was the Irish Sea when we left Dublin on a mild, fair day. By the time we cross over the continent, the atmosphere below is brownish-overcast and it's not easy to pick out where we are again until a huge lake, like a little sea, appears, followed immediately by the first snowy mountains, just as twilight begins, probably Lake Geneva. The glistening Alps rise into advancing darkness, town lights twinkling in valleys below.

In Milan, the air is warm and the half moon is hanging low and ripe in the sky. This little hostel is less than exciting but the Japanese girls on the desk are friendly, so who cares? I'm tired, neither excited nor perturbed, just sitting here on the bed writing the Weather Watch, sipping a glass of red wine, the window open wide to the warm night. Normal stuff!

Wind Up

The wind has come up mightily in the night, making the journey to Shannon a bit of an adventure. Just as we were buffeted on our cliff walk, the little blue car is pushed by the wind as we drive, nudged sideways by the occasional blast. When I call Blair's father, my friend Dave, to tell him Blair and Katie are safely off, he wonders how the weather will be on their landing in Boston. Dave, a nurseryman, is a serious weather watcher. Hardly a day goes by that he doesn't check the satellite images of the earth and its various weathers. He knows the view from above, holds the images of the earth as globe in his mind, not just his own California weather, but the weathers of all his far-flung friends too. It seems today both sides of the Atlantic are experiencing storms, working up to winter.

10 Milano

It's hard to know if the overcast here is weather or city smog, probably a combination of both. Anyway, the atmosphere seems a bit grubby and slightly damp as well. I'll be wearing my fleece when I head out to find the internet café. I'm sitting in the tiny lobby of this third floor tiny hotel. It's a Japanese outfit, maybe that's why everything is so compact, even the bonsai trees. The long window is open to the Viale Tunisia below and I'm sipping coffee as I write. The flight to Dakar boards at 19.55, so I'll be getting the airport bus around five o'clock. Just heard someone remarking how cool the weather is here today...I don't expect to hear that weather prognosis for quite a long time to come. *Avanti!*

Glowing Pewter Day

The wind is stilled. Fog descends and lifts throughout the day. The sun illuminates the fog, encasing the garden in glowing pewter light. Gentle birdsong laces the air. I walk up to close last night's forgotten gate, suffused with peace, held in the light.

11 Yoff

It has been a cloudy, slightly clammy day here in Yoff, the airport district of Dakar. The sun was obscured all day long by overcast and smog, like Milan was, but here it's at least 28 degrees, maybe more. Middle of the night arrivals are a dog. The flight was an hour late and I ended up paying a taxi driver a small fortune to get me to Le Toucan. I really thought I'd manage the taxi thing better this time round but facing down the touts at two in the morning is no joke. I have a hell of a lot to learn.

Later in the afternoon, I walked back to the airport to post a few cards in tawny light. I can't get a clear weather story from people here; they don't expect any more rain in Dakar, it seems, despite the humidity, but they say that the roads further south could be slow. Walking around Yoff, I'm aware of my feet directing me, unflustered, while my thinking mind is wondering what the hell I'm doing here. I'm here to learn something totally new, something essential, a revolution in awareness, whatever the weather. I feel amazingly calm and unflustered, despite the taxi business at the airport.

Floating Mountain

This morning, just to the left of Mt Brandon, a cloud Brandon floated, its ridge mimicking the shape of the mountain itself. Often, I've seen the clouds covering the mountain re-create its shape, but never before a cloud separate from it, an entity of its own. Was it some result of currents running across the mountain? Or simply cloud play for the pleasure of it?

12 La Route

The journey took too long. I woke up at 3 a.m. for a 4 a.m. start: first you take a taxi to the *Gare Routières*, the central transport depot, and hope to get a place in the first *sept-place* Peugot car going south. The cars were only going to the border with Gambia this time – which means several changes of transport and hauling of luggage – but at least nobody was talking about taking the long route around by Tambacounda, avoiding Gambia completely. Half an hour out of the *Gare* our car broke down so we sat in the dark on the side of the road for a long time waiting for a replacement vehicle. It was a long day of high humidity, no coffee stops and no sign of bottled water. It was absolutely blistering when we reached the border with Gambia. The immigration officer told me it would be cooler down in Casamance and he was right. The really long haul was between Sonoma and Ziguinchor because the old tin bus had a leaky radiator and the guys kept having to stop to top her up, so we didn't get into Ziguinchor until after 7 p.m. I could have gone on to Cap Skiring but opted instead to stay the night for I was dog tired. The *campement* where I lodged was pretty rough although at least it had an intact mosquito net. As for the toilet...well, I've seen worse but let's say it wasn't a pretty sight. I felt nervous about the place but I was just too bloody tired to find anywhere else; in fact, I felt like bursting into tears like an exhausted child.

Lucent

The sun shone all the day except for a brief fierce shower in the morning, and even then it was visible in the distance beyond the edges of the rainfall. Warm rectangles of light stretched across the living room so that I stretched my feet to reach them, napped a bit inside them. The clouds served to give great depth to the sky, and at sunset, colour, so absent these past days, glowed peach, glowed rose, glowed gold in a field of tender blue. Before night fell, the just-past-quarter moon caught the sun's light, adding glowing abalone to the scene.

13 Arrival

I woke sometime around 8 a.m. to rain pounding on the roof. It poured down for two hours non-stop but surprisingly, this didn't affect the transport going to Cap Skiring and it was a fairly swift trip down there. I got off at the crossroads and headed for Le Falafu, pulling my big bag behind me and was lucky to meet

Baba, who remembered me from last time, and he gave me a hand. Moussa was waiting for me along with Marie-Thérèse and several other folks, all of whom gave me a heart-warming welcome. Erika is still in Switzerland and won't return for another three weeks or so.

There are a number of people living here now, *les permenants*, long-term tenants who weren't here last spring when I first arrived: Papisse and Aisha, Tamsir, Lamine, Diamma, who is Moussa's cousin, and Jamilah. Maimi left during the summer after a row with Erika, I'm told. Marie-T used to work for an Italian woman who kept a room here, minding the woman's disabled child, but now she's taken over Maimi's job. Jano, the artist who lives at Bakine, also arrived to say 'welcome back'. Thio, who used to sell stuff on the beach, is now the night watchman. He lived in Gambia for a few years so he speaks a sort of pidgin English and not very much French, his own language being Mandinka, the same as Moussa's. Marie-T's language is Diola, the Diola being the native people of Casamance and she has the typical appearance of her tribe, being long and athletically lean, with a broad forehead and a gap between her front teeth.

Later on, walking in the shady gardens of the Hôtel la Paillote watching the sun go down behind an overcast, rain-laden sky, I told Moussa about my friend, the Lighting-Techie, and he agreed that the guy puts on a pretty good show.

Sunbeam

Just as I stepped out of the shower this morning, I noticed a small coin of sunlight on the radiator opposite the door. This was odd, as I had noted when I entered the room that, with the door closed, it was cut off from the bright sunlight of the day. I idly imagined that it must be somehow a reflection from the mirror, but was puzzled. As I looked around, I suddenly saw a narrow pure beam of sunlight dancing with dust motes arrowed straight across the room. It was entering through the keyhole, in the tiny available space around the key that was in it! As I watched, it began to fade, the sun moving on. It cannot have been in the room more than a minute or two. Had I slept later or showered longer, I would not have seen it at all. I went through the day lifted by this moment, feeling all the while a sense of wonders happening everywhere, even if no one is there to see.

14 Facts

By eight in the evening, I am completely exhausted in this climate. Today, I didn't venture outside until nearly four o'clock and then walked the beach down to the Royal Cap Hotel. It takes a lot of mental juice to communicate in another language, in this case French, which I only have at an elementary level. Added to that, the folks here are talking among themselves in Wolof, the principal national language of Senegal – there are at least six totally different languages spoken here and most people manage at least a smattering of the lot – but they tell me it is more useful to focus on French, first. The other source of exhaustion is, of course, the heat.

The ocean was like bath water, as the sun evaporated and as I came out of the water the moon was already hanging brightly over the beach. Apart from learning how to cook *tiéboudienne* – fish stew involving tamarind pods and a chunk of foul-smelling dried whelk

– I've done virtually nothing today, yet I'm completely washed out to the point that it is difficult to write the Weather Watch. Such is the effort in this climate.

My feet and legs are destroyed by ants. More than once today I've asked myself what the hell am I doing here? Stupid question, for I know the answer: I came back to know Moussa Kamara, to see if we can make a life together. He is brimming over with joy that I have returned, I with the joy of seeing him again. But how the hell shall I work in this heat? This time round it's not a holiday; I've taken up Erika's offer to join the team at Le Falafu in return for my keep. Here I am, it's as simple as that, an indisputable fact, just like the weather.

Splendid

Weather? Splendid! Days, sun-filled, crisp, wind picking up. Nights, moon transit followed by scintillating stars, Orion vivid in the sky. I am emanating gratitude.

15 Deliciously Warm Wind

Rice fields surround the villages in the district. Moussa borrowed his cousin's motorbike and we made our way along the tracks though the rice fields until it became too muddy for the bike to negotiate. It didn't rain this morning but yesterday's groundwater still hadn't drained away in some places. By the time we got back in the early afternoon, the yard thermometer was reading 41 degrees. The hottest hours seem to be between three and five in the afternoon, not midday as one might expect, and the heat has a draining effect on the brain like a battery going down. The temperature is daunting, but the tourist season apparently opens on the twenty-third of the month regardless of the weather, and we have plenty to do here at the *campement* to get things cleaned up. Before sundown, we go for a long beach walk and return in bright moonlight, caressed by a deliciously warm wind.

Narrative

I wake in the morning with a southeastern view, my window full of sky before I lift my head to look across Dingle Bay to the Iveragh Peninsula. It is not until I enter the living room or kitchen that I can see the weather to the west above Sliabh an Iolair. I must go into the bathroom or the guest room to know the skies to the north toward Mt Brandon. One of the pleasures of the morning is the different weathers the windows hold. This morning I woke to haze and a silver slice of far water lit through an opening in the clouds. It seemed a tranquil day, and still. But in the windows to the west and north, dark ominous clouds loomed, threatening rain and storm. It is often this way, the windows of the house giving on to what almost seem to be different days. I have seen rain on one side and sun on the other at the same time. As I wander through each morning, I gather the narrative of the day, and must look out each window to read the full story of the weather. Then I must open the door to taste the wind.

16 Sweeping

Sweeping house, yard and the area outside the gate is a thorough task resulting in deep sweat. It pours out of me, into my eyes, down my body, sticking the clothes to the skin but still we sweep until the job is properly done. Today I can only listen, not speak. After we finish the job, I stand under the shower and thank God there's no shortage of water in this place. It's good, potable water coming from a well below the *campement*, so we can drink from the tap without hesitation.

At seven in the evening, the sun seems pale in a hazy, silvered sky over the vigorous ocean. The current is really strong today; paddling in the foreshore, it pulled me way down the beach. I am not a strong enough swimmer to get out past the breakers, but to bathe in warm water is pleasant enough. Sea mist thrown up by the turbulent tide obscures the coastline. As I write, the warm wind dries my skin at least for a little while, for when I go back inside the *campement*, the heat of the day – trapped inside despite open windows and doors – will surely squeeze further moisture out of my body.

Captive

I am a captive of my belongings. The weather continues splendid, perfect days for walking. Bright with no rain. Warm with a slight wind. I drink coffee outside on the blue bench, lean against the sun-warmed wall, then reluctantly drag myself back indoors to confront all my belongings that arrived from America last Thursday. Laura comes for a visit tomorrow, so I must make the house habitable, sort as much as possible into pleasing chaos, if not order. I am surrounded by my history crowded into this small house, out on counters and piled on floors until I can make a space for it. This involves removing many of the things that came with this house, deciding what to keep and what to pass on, weeding out duplications with my own things. I have overcome the panic of the arrival day, when I was near sick with the sheer amount of things, and questioning my decision to integrate past and present rather than start anew here. As order slowly appears, I find myself pleased to be surrounded by the beauty I have known before, happy to hold loved books again in my hands. A rug I bought five years ago fits into the living room as if it had been made for it, its size and colour perfect in the room. I imagine some strand from now intertwining with then, and the sigh of rightness as the rug meets the room. Before bed tonight, I'll find a stopping point, order enough for the moment to greet an old friend. And while she's here – oh joy! – time for walks and a blessed respite from sorting.

17 Busy

Today we were too busy to pay attention to the weather. It was a late morning start but between the three of us – Moussa, Marie-Thérèse and myself – we made a good assault on Erika's apartment in preparation for her return later this week. The plan was to start on the rest of the house and scrub it down before painting it afresh but three clients showed up, all of a sudden, so we had to look after them. The painting can't happen until the rain ceases, otherwise it just won't stick to the walls.

In the middle of the night, the heavens opened and rain thundered down for hours, so hard I thought the tin roof above us would collapse. Thunder and lightning continued for ages, or so it seemed, and it felt mysterious to be curled up in the mosquito net with Moussa watching the room become illuminated in strangely blue light, listening to thunder and rain. It is full moon time again, a white night with Mars glowing brightly a few million miles out in the firmament. The ocean rumbles below, a continuous soundtrack.

Fall

Early in the morning in the still dark my headlights illuminate leaves falling as I pass through Burnham Wood. All the way to Shannon it's the same, a swirl of leaves in the headlights as the car passes by. True autumn. Then, by evening, rainfall, hard, steady, drenching, the clouds so thick any chance of seeing tonight's eclipse is lost in the sursurration of the rain. Fall.

18 Weather, Cooking and Language

At noon, the thermometer is reading 40.5 degrees. Various people are hanging round the house complaining about the heat, just like how we whinge about the rain in Ireland. Erika's immanent return will mark the end of the open house situation; at the moment, it's rather like a club. This morning, Marie-Thérèse and Badou gave me my first lesson in Wolof; trying to sort out what's a verb, what's a noun and so on, is tricky enough. Denis – a retired Parisian fish dealer who has fond memories of Irish fishing towns like Dingle, and who also happens to be Erika's bad-tempered bookkeeper – went off without giving Moussa the money for the paint, so the lads are clearing the ground outside the gate instead so that Thio can do some gardening there. It's too hot, now, for me to work outside, so I'll help Marie-T in the kitchen and learn how to prepare *colda*, another fish stew, with lemon juice added; yesterday it was *mafé*, a sauce made with peanuts. All the sauces have a base of onions, tomatoes, red chillis and salt and Marie-T is a great believer in the power of stock cubes, lots of them!

It's full moon tonight, so bright one could almost read by it.

Moon Sail

The morning rain passes inland leaving the skies clear and piled high with amber then peach-tinted clouds. By night the moon sails full across the sky. Shy during last night's eclipse, hidden above a cloud blanket, tonight the moon turns the darkness a lucent blue, boldly crossing the sky in company with a bright planet.

19 Perfect Day

Moussa and I sit on the beach watching the waves break blue-white in the veiled moonlight. It was full last night. There's a lot of lightning out at sea and occasional thunderclaps suggesting heavy rain to come. It's been cloudy all day. We worked flat-out preparing Erika's apartment, painting and cleaning like busy bees then, and later, Moussa and I went down to the ocean to scrub the paint off our skin and bathed in the warm water for an hour watching the dissolution of the sun. What a perfect day! *Alhamdu'lil'ah.*

Beyond Dún Chaoin

Laura and I are visiting the ancient sites: Riasc, Gallarus, Gallarus Castle, Brandon Cove. The peninsula spreads before us as we move along it, passing the Three Sisters, skirting the side of Smerwick Harbour, approaching Brandon. Slight rain falls, a mist, as we watch the sunset developing beyond Dún Chaoin. We race for the Clasach as clouds pile golden in the sky, broad rays of sun shooting upward. When we finally reach Dún Chaoin, only a patch of sun shines, a throbbing orange eye in the offshore clouds. Gradually, the light fades. Bands of blood orange streak the sky which remains a tender blue. Dusk descends and night falls, bringing with it rain.

20 Deluge

The rain finally showed up at lunchtime, just after Marie-Thérèse and I had finished cleaning up after yesterday's paint job in the apartment. It came hard and heavy and continued for over an hour. You could hear the garden slugging it down. The problem now is that nothing will dry properly, everything is breathlessly clammy. At half past four, the thermometer is reading 40 degrees yet again. Late afternoon sunlight slants into the yard, dappling the trees and the huge fronds, spilling into the dining area where I write. The guest rooms, arranged around the yard, continue to sweat even as sundown bleeds swiftly into twilight, a brief, subtle prelude to the vastness of the tropical night. As day falls away, the *wu-hu, hu-hu hu-hu, wu-hu, hu-hu hu-hu* of doves echoes in deepening shadow.

Shift

It is a day for weeding, as the former owners of my orange house are visiting tomorrow, and the garden is all ahoo. Sun wakes me. I put in laundry and hang it on the line, thinking of all the outside work to be done. Before noon, dark grey clouds appear above Brandon. At the first rainfall, I don't panic by bringing in the clothes, still hopeful that it's a passing storm. Half an hour later, the mountains of the Iveragh disappear, then the bay itself, and the rain sets in with an undeniable steadiness. I admit defeat and take

down the clothes. No weeding and tidying outside today. The garden will
have to be greeted as it is. All afternoon, I watch from inside, wrapped in the
warmth of the house, in the pleasure of being sheltered from the rain.

21 Internet Café Hour

When 5 p.m. arrives, I'm showering off the day's sweat,
for the moment at least, before walking into Cap Skiring to check
out the local internet café. The twenty-minute walk to the village
is pleasant; it's the first time today I'm not pouring sweat. Dry skin,
even for a few minutes, is such a relief. We've been working since
ten this morning, more cleaning and painting, trying to get the
place in shape before Monday, the official beginning of the season.
At a constant 40 degrees with high humidity, the best I can muster
is four hours' work until the afternoon meal, but after that I'm not
worth a curse workwise. It's better, though, to do physical work
while one's energy is up because the mental fatigue that sets in
makes it just about impossible to concentrate on reading, writing
or studying anything. The internal weather is okay, though. I'm not
sorry to be here despite the rigours of the weather and the endless
insect bites that make my legs feel as if they were on fire, especially
during the sweaty night. Everyone is very kind to me, very patient
with my lack of language and eager to include me at every moment.
Moussa is so happy I'm here again. He sweetly places tasty morsels
on my end of the common platter at lunchtime. Everyone in the
house refers to him as my husband, *ton mari*. The weather between
us is tranquil.

Ten minutes after I get to the internet café, the system goes down, just after I've dumped most of the fifty messages waiting for me but before I get to read the ones I've saved! The technicians spend an hour trying to get the lines cranked up again, but no luck. I walk back to Le Falafu in the dark, glad I've got my Maglight torch, otherwise I could see nothing at all on this totally broken road, more dust than asphalt, full of craters.

An hour later, it's truly dark; there's lots of stars and Mars is clearly visible, all suggesting a clear sky but I don't think the rains are finished yet.

Attractive

Danny and Máire come to dinner, and of course the subject of weather arises. The story they have is that the TV weather was for a long time presented by trained meteorologists who actually understood what they were reporting. Then recently the stations decided the weather news should be delivered instead by attractive young women, usually in short skirts and low necklines. Apparently viewers protested this flippant treatment of an important subject, and demanded back the meteorologists, who duly returned to their posts, with not a short skirt in sight on the horizon.

22 Maritime Climate

The thermometer sits at 40 degrees and doesn't budge. Surprisingly, it didn't rain last night or this morning, so we were able to get on with the painting and cleaning up. At least there was a breeze down on the beach when we were washing the clothes so by noon the laundry is dry as a bone. Because of the maritime climate, there's no point in doing the laundry later than ten in the morning – things just don't dry; in fact, dampness is just as much of a problem here as it is at home! The house is badly constructed; the three best rooms have balconies above the beach and, as a result, any drying wind is blocked off from entering the rest of the domain. Today we scrubbed thick green algae off the walls, then we scrubbed the concrete floor of the dining area getting rid of the whitewash residue after yesterday's paint job. Marie-Thérèse and Moussa are indefatigable, or to be more precise they work like racehorses, determined to get the place sorted out. How they work so long and so fast in this heat baffles me entirely. It's half past five now and the *mange mil*, a bird like a woodcock, is singing. I'd better head into Cap Skiring before it gets too late to try the internet café.

Weatherless

After yesterday's drenching rain and wind, today's rain seems almost nondescript. I hang laundry on the line. We take the beautiful drive from Baile an tSléibhe to Kenmare along Dingle Bay, then rise beside the lakes in Killarney National Park. The sun shines. Cloud shadow dapples the hills. Fields glow vivid green edged by russet grasses. Even so, the weather in its mildness recedes. An ordinary sunny day.

23 What to Wear?

Moussa and I head down to Ziguinchor to meet Erika in the early afternoon. We are lucky, no hanging around waiting for the *sept-place* taxi to fill up. It's hard to know what one should wear going outside before five in the evening, so I bring a wide shawl to cover my upper body, for even a ten minute exposure to the sun at this hour is likely to result in a bad burn and it's just not practical to smother myself in sunscreen all the time for I just sweat it off. We arrive in Ziguinchor in time for sundowners at Erika's hotel. We sit and chat, pleased to see one another. The sky turns a delicate shade of rose before darkness falls, then we walk down the street to have supper at Le Perroquet. Later, at Moussa's family home – the house of Madame Kamara, his father's second wife – the rain comes, but not for long. Everyone is talking about the heat. As I write the Weather Watch, the family is watching an action movie while the crickets sing in the background, a counterpoint to the electric fan. They take no notice of me, which is restful, so I kick back and write these notes, at ease.

Gurgle

The rain has come on with a vengeance, strong winds hurling water onto the house. The front walk is a lake, the clay poem tablet and the curved clay fish underwater at the base of the Japanese water jar, which can only be rapidly filling. Water is running down the compacted driveway onto the cement entranceway, pouring across the foundation, and gathering into an ever-larger pool at the side of the house. After midnight, we begin to hear a rhythmic gurgling, and, torch in hand, I go outside while Laura looks anxiously on. Two of the overflow drains are underwater, the third the source of the gurgle. Not really understanding this system, I can do little but stand in the wet identifying the source of the sound. It is far too late to ring anyone. The house has stood as it is for seven years. I turn off the torch and go inside, spangled with water. For the night: hope. In the morning: a plumber for advice.

24 Shopping

Today we have to do the shopping for the *campement*, stock up on food and utilities for the house now that the season is officially open. At about six this morning it started to rain and then it poured down steadily for two hours so that the town was a muddy wash afterwards. We plodded from one store to the next looking for kitchenware and whatnot, then on to the grocery store for products that are imported from France for foreigners and middle-class people here. I watch Moussa doing the business and reckon it takes at least twice the energy to get things done here than it does back home; everything has to be gone into and over several times before things are concluded. When we've finally finished the tasks it's late in the day and the car that Moussa had organized has turned up already half full, so he's had to go off and find another car, a pain in the neck task at this late hour but, finally, we're on the road. The going is slow in the dark, very slow, and the road is really a mess after torrential rains. Back at the ranch our room is horribly damp after the long night of rain. Erika doesn't seem very impressed by our efforts with her apartment. I guess she's exhausted after the journey.

Drenched

In a break in these wet days, we try to walk on Béal Bán. Enchanted by the storm-arranged beach, the configurations of stones, we don't notice the rain coming fast from the southwest. One drop catches our attention, then a few, followed by a downpour. We are at the farthest end of the beach, away from the car. Returning rapidly into the wind, we are soon hopelessly drenched. Driving home through slanted silver rain, we steam up the car. At the house, first water for tea, then the fire, dripping coats hung to dry. Almost as soon as we're inside, quiet descends. Before bed, the moon, accompanied by a few stars, glows in the sky, and the lights of Ventry shine clear across the harbour.

25 Soirée

Today was overcast and it seems to me that the temperature has decreased somewhat in the past two days. I realize that I've been reading the thermometer in the yard imprecisely, so perhaps it hasn't been a constant 40 degrees after all, making nonsense of my Weather Watch! In fact, it may have been higher because the thermometer hangs in the shade.

Sometime after six o'clock I went down to the beach to wash off the day's sweat and grime. The sky was clustered with dense, rain-laden clouds in a texturally varied sky, one could almost say a mackerel sky, in various matt shades of indigo and grey. In such light the ocean has a silvered appearance. Moussa showed up and we played in the waves until it was dark. Then we joined Erika, Tamsir and his two friends and Marie-Thérèse in the garden for a pleasant few hours of conversation and supper under the mango tree in a still, but not suffocating, atmosphere. Marie-T has made her lovely concoction of millet and slightly fermented milk sweetened with sugar, laced with limes. Yum!

Rising

I wake in a warm pool of sunlight only to find when I leave the bedroom, the rain lashing against the other side of the house. This Janus weather

continues all day, fierce squalls interspersed with sun. As I go outside in the
morning, I check the Japanese water jar that stands high as my waist. It
arrived a dozen days ago, and is two-thirds full, winter not yet come.

26 Weather and House Design

Today we started the physical work too late: it was already
noon when we started scrubbing the wall outside the main gate.
That's tough enough work to be doing anyway but, even in the
shade, tackling it in the middle of the day is just too much. I find
it hard to sleep here so it's often several hours before I actually nod
off, compounding the situation. The thermometer reads the same as
yesterday, 35 degrees, but today is full-on sunshine, airless, and I can
feel the whole house sweating. The walls are full of moisture after
the prolonged rains. This house has a closed-in design, the seaside
rooms blocking off the natural ventilation from the ocean directly
below. This is a miserable structural error that causes the house to
retain humidity, reflecting it back at itself, more or less. It feels like
I'm going to suffocate.

Warm

A wretched day by most accounts, but made enchanting by the wind.
Outside, rain fell, gales blew. It looked like winter. One step out the door
though, and the warm wind wrapped round me, soft as summer. Redeeming
the day.

27 Brewing

The sunny morning enabled us to get quite a lot of work

done on the walls and stairs leading down to the beach. There's plenty of shade there thanks to the bougainvillea, so I was able to work without fear of being burnt. Today I took things more gently; I stopped trying to compete with my own idea of how much work I should be able to do, so now, at the end of the day, I'm not wrecked and miserable like I was yesterday.

By mid-afternoon, we could feel a storm brewing. Everything became very still and airless and all hell broke loose around five o'clock just as I was about to go for a beach walk. Instead, I ran down to the line to grab my clothes but no luck: the rain comes straight down here with no preamble and I got soaked to the skin, literally, in a few seconds. Thunder and lightning followed for about an hour and a half and the whole show was so loud it completely screened out the music Moussa was listening to. I have to admit I was glad. Moussa is a music freak; he recites his prayers with music on in the background, for heaven's sake! This challenges me considerably, for my habits of silence and living alone are deeply ingrained. As a result, a big-bang thunderstorm is my current idea of enviable silence. Laughing as I write the Weather Watch, I tell Moussa why he features in this episode.

Inside
The wind howls through the vents, the rain lashing against the house. All day I am inside, warm and dry and home.

28 Walk
All is quiet today in the ocean, in the sky, in the house. We

didn't do any hard work because Moussa spends the middle of the day at the mosque for Friday prayers. Earlier in the morning, while I was washing my clothes under the trees alongside Marie-T, there was no wind, the horizon seemed to be closing in, the sky clouding up rapidly and it looked like there would be no chance of drying anything. I was sure it would pour again in the afternoon but my forecast was way off. In fact, the sky cleared completely giving way to hot sun and when Moussa returned from the mosque he was seriously sweating. At five o'clock I set off down the beach for a decent walk and, as usual, was assailed by a young fellow who took it upon himself to accompany me, uninvited. So it goes here. I've decided that it's easier to accept this than try to resist it: one expends less energy in the long run. My policy is to walk long and fast, ration my conversational input and let them do most of the talking. This time I walked all the way down to Cap Roxo and back – a fourteen kilometre walk according to Moussa, although my feet don't believe that – and it was already quite dark when I arrived back at Le Falafu. My accompanist was pretty surprised at how fast I walked but my strategy didn't work: he just marched along, undaunted! Now the sky is star-laden in the Milky Way and pitch black everywhere else. The lights of the Club Med village illuminate the far end of the beach, otherwise only the glow of Thio's cigarette lights the beach.

Lawn Gleams

Lawn gleams in sunlight,
blades of grass stroked by the wind:
calm before winter.

29 Overcast

A totally overcast day. I took advantage of this and walked to town in the early afternoon, glad to be out without sunscreen or long sleeves. I met Fernando, a young fellow from Guinea Bisseau who remembered me from last April, and he invited me into his house to meet his sisters. Maimi is a trainee nurse at the medical centre in Kabrousse run by the Italian nuns. She showed me all her personal photographs, a considerable pile! It turns out that Fernando lives with this family but isn't actually related; this is the African way: people make all kinds of domicile arrangements that are hard to figure out. People are introduced as *ma grande soeur* or *mon grand frère* but this only signifies that there's a mutually acknowledged relationship that may, or may not, be consanguinous. I had hoped to poke around town by myself but no chance: Fernando insisted on walking with me. In the late afternoon, Marie-T joined me for a walk along the beach; the young lads leave me alone if she's with me. We came back just as darkness fell to find that guests had arrived, so we ended up scrubbing floors and whatnot post haste, for these rooms had yet to be painted and we didn't expect guests. That's how it goes here. It's impossible to organize things properly; no advance system seems to work out which is pretty crazy-making.

Unfolding

Last night's bright stars gave way to morning rain. I putter in the house, showering, straightening, making tea. The rain stops, and I take ashes down to the compost, crossing the sodden lawn. I drive out to Ventry for the

Saturday paper, then on into Dingle for a box of chocolates from Murphys, as Orna has rung in the morning with an invitation to Sunday dinner this bank holiday weekend. Once in town and it still dry, I remember I should take wine as well, and stop at the wholefood store, and then again at the Spar for eggs forgotten in Ventry. Passing the garden store, I inquire about paperwhite narcissus, only to find the last already sold. This reminds me of Orna's birthday next week, and I determine to visit Louis Mulcahy's on the way home, for a blue pot in which to plant some small yellow daffodils for her. Looping around toward Ballyferriter past Rahinanne Castle in the still dry day, I think to walk on Béal Bán, and do, in a wind that skims back the crests of the waves forming in the jade green water. The beach stones have been scoured by a north wind, leaving each now standing on its individual bluff. White quartz gleams on the beach, and red jasper. I admire the scrolls of the intricate worm casings, and think of the Book of Kells. At the pottery, I choose a container, blue, banded with warm brown with a trace of green. I wander back home by way of Slea Head, where the sun breaks through and lights the churned water to a metallic gleaming somewhere between pewter and bronze. At Baile an tSléibhe I unload my scattered parcels from the car, then walk up to close my pink gate. Just as I light the fire and settle to read the paper, rain falls heavily outside, lashing against the windows. I read quietly on, in for the night.

30 How the Sun Vanishes

Today was my first day to get up early to do the breakfast shift. I felt refreshed and really awake at 7 a.m., the first time since I arrived here. Also, I really appreciated an hour alone before anyone else appeared in the kitchen area, an hour of silence without interaction or music, an hour to drink a complete cup of coffee for a change.

It has been sunny all day so maybe the walls will dry at long last. My clothes and books smell rotten with dampness and any fruit we keep goes off faster than we can eat it.

What looked like a tranquil Sunday proved to be utterly exhausting and I was on my feet in the kitchen until late afternoon without a break. Erika, having declared that she didn't want to be seen all day, suddenly took a notion to rearrange the kitchen completely. I'm finding out that this is her style and wonder how to install sensible boundaries for myself.

Later on I spent an hour on the beach, immobile, trying to revive my energy. The sun was a huge orange orb hanging over a metallic sea, the surf strong again after a few windless days. Sea mist gathers quickly at this hour of the day, erasing all detail at either end of the visual field. Wispy clouds briefly turn rosy as the sun changes from deep orange to translucent cherry-red then melts, like an ice-pop, without even falling into the ocean.

Fall Back

The clocks were turned back last night, and I watched with some amazement as the sun went behind Sliabh an Iolair just before four in the afternoon. I arrived to this house in March near the time of equinox, and now contemplate the seven weeks to solstice, and the light they might contain. Even with the sun's early departure, the dusk was long and luminous. I watched the gold slowly depart from the fields below me, and then the clouds light with the sunset I could not see. Clouds glowed amber, pulsed peach. The sky turned rose, then as the warm colour faded, the clouds gleamed silver against a background of tender blue.

31 Sitting and Watching

I went to the village with Moussa before noon, a trip that provided ample opportunity to sit and watch the action without interacting myself. He was trying to arrange transport for some of the clients at the house but hardly any cars were coming and going today from Ziguinchor and at least twenty people had been waiting all morning already, so we ended up spending nearly three hours there in the heat of the day. I sat under a tree and covered myself up in my long shawl, determined not to be sunburned, and just watched life going on around me: two boys playing together, creating a fortress out of the dust and dried mud outside their house; men sitting on mats with their wares spread out at their feet, doing as little as possible because they are practicing *sawm*, the sunrise to sunset fast for the holy month of *Ramadan*; other people reclining in shops, avoiding the heat; the comings and goings at the taxi rank, the ritual greetings, arrangements being made etcetera, the only visible action being negotiations via mobile phone.

A second trip to the village came about later on in the afternoon because newly arrived clients wanted a fish dinner in the evening, so Moussa had to go back to town to look for fish. This time round it seemed so much cooler: a light breeze was circulating and the slanting golden light cast beautiful contrasts of shadow and light on the women sitting under the *neem* trees, their trays of peanuts and snacks laid out around them.

Samhain Swim

As a girl I was raised among lakes. For some reason each spring, the level of the lakes was lowered, leaving behind mud and pools of tadpole-filled water which my friends and I loved to walk in. We would capture tadpoles to be brought home and placed in bowls of water so that their transformations into frogs could be witnessed. Rarely though did they make it much beyond the appearance of the smallest of legs, as our dog would drink from their bowls and the water become unhealthily stagnant. Still, we loved to wade out into the mud, to see the lakes without their water. I thought of this yesterday as I decided to weed the pond in an interval of sunshine. A serious weeding, not just the breaking off of some branches of the growth, it involved pulling up masses of green and many mud-filled roots, a mud that was slimy and black and reminiscent of childhood. Then today Orna came over to collect the weedings for her ducks, and we decided to try for cuttings for her of the water lilies. We completed one in shallow water easily, but when we went to try another, found ourselves unable to return it to the platform it seemed to have been placed on. Despite all out manoeuverings, we could not get the heavy pot back into place, and resorted to leaving it exposed in the shallows. Back in the house, I knew that the only resolution would be to enter the pond and place it properly. The day was brisk, the pond water cold, but the sun was out and as warm as it was likely to be for the next six months. I put on my bathing suit with a long-sleeved t-shirt over it, and went out to the pond, where I tried again to place the heavy pot. No luck. I faced the inevitable and went in, quickly found the right position, and was soon out again, arms and legs bright pink from the cold. I gathered the greenery that had come loose in the pond, taking it behind the house for the next delivery to the ducks, then returned the shovel I'd been using to gauge the depth of the water to the shed. After that it was into the house for a long hot shower, concluding what I hope is the last swim of the season conducted on this day before tomorrow's first of winter.

Samhain
Winter

November

1 Heat Rash and Prickly Issues

The first day of the month looks like a day to create a few personal boundaries. I was up before 7 a.m. and found the kitchen full of leftovers and unwashed ware although I had done all the washing up after Moussa had cooked the meals for the guests last night; the sink was clogged, there was no sign of the washing-up stuff and the three tea cloths were filthy. Then Erika showed up and wanted to know who was partaking of the evening meals, virtually asking me to list the comings and goings of the locals who show up for the communal platter twice a day. I told her it is not my place to watch this, that she must ask Moussa, not me, because I'm not willing to be the watchdog on her behalf. On the other hand, I see clearly where she's coming from on this issue: it's a typical clash of cultural interests. She's willing to feed those of us who work here but not *les permanents*, the rent-a-room folk and their hangers-on. But everything here is communal, especially meals, and whoever happens to be around shares the meal. This is a tricky issue for me because I'm living with Moussa, therefore I'm falling between two opposing systems, so I must set clear boundaries with Erika and with the locals around the house, otherwise I'll spend my time here being either a watchdog for her or a kitchen slave for my colleagues and their associates.

At mid-morning, I exited the work area and am now working on this Weather Watch in our room, making my own boundary about what work I'm willing to do. I can tell the temperature has declined because, while I'm sweating under the tin roof of this humid room, the sweat isn't actually running down my body in rivulets any more. My torso, however, resembles a pincushion, prickly red with constant heat rash.

Winter

This first day of winter dawns bright and mild as a spring day. Birdsong laces the air, and the wind is gentle. Long bands of sunlight lie across the rooms. Before I can take my coffee outside, it is raining, a delicate silver rain backlit by the sun. It is quickly over and I sit outside on the blue bench admiring the day. All the ridge of Brandon is clear, a sharp line etched against the sky. Slight furls of white break on the far cliffs near Ballymore, and I wonder how Trish is in the heat of Senegal. Each field and wall is distinct in this clear light, each house, and almost each bush. I suddenly yearn for some of the blackberries still clinging to the hedge, but know it too late past last night. My mind wanders on down the lane to Bob and Orna's, the feast of pond pullings their ducks must be enjoying. I wonder if I will ever have one of their eggs, tasting in it The Pond of Great Pleasure, a cycling round of effort and offering and conversion. One cycling amidst all the cycles, a thought on this day as autumn turns to winter.

2 Full Moon

The thermometer is reading 32 degrees but it feels a hell of a lot hotter. Maybe it's because I've been in the kitchen for the past hour or so preparing the mid-afternoon meal — it is *caldo* today — which everyone gobbled up very quickly.

It's full moon today and I have a lot of energy although I didn't sleep last night; something was biting, so I got up every half hour or so to check the mosquito net which looked perfectly tucked in. My legs were on fire, covered in huge red welts. All through the night it sounded as if the ocean would come right up to the level of the house yet there wasn't a breath of air in these horribly humid rooms. I thought about going down to the beach and trying to sleep there instead but there are so many creepy crawlies everywhere, day and night!

I attacked the bed at noon, threw the mattress up on the tin roof in the sunshine and then scrubbed a field of mold off the plank underneath. The walls are still incredibly damp and it's a real pain in the arse that one can't just leave the door open to help air the room: doors have to be locked all the time or everything vanishes. I'll go into town in a while to pick up my stuff from the tailor – alterations, mostly. If he's any good, maybe I'll buy some nice material and get something made.

Unassuming

A day of delicate and unassuming weather. Morning rain. Various afternoon showers. Moderate temperatures. Air with an invigorating freshness. The sea this morning one of its deeper winter greens, veering toward blue. A haze in the air as much salt from wind-churned water as any moisture. A background, holding kind of day.

3 Korité

Today was the feast of Korité – generally known as *Eid al-*

Fitr throughout the Muslim world – a day of prayer and asking forgiveness of one's neighbours, *kareem*, for any transgressions against them during the year past, the holy day that marks the end of *Ramadan*. Moussa presented me with a set of clothes for the occasion – a *grand boubou* – for people wear their best new clothes today. I appreciate the gift and will wear it on such occasions in acknowledgement. Moussa visited his neighbours here in the morning because he couldn't take time to go down to Ziguinchor to be with the family. I helped Marie-T in the kitchen; a communal meal had to be available today. Actually, it was an enervating day, airless and mosquito-ridden throughout. Around sunset, Moussa borrowed Tamsir's scooter and we went over to the little airport to visit cousins – Moussa's uncle is a technician there in the control tower and the family lives on site. Before darkness fell, we saw the new crescent moon, wafer-thin and platinum-coloured, in a rosy-blue sky. The next holy day is *Tabaski*, two lunar months hence, a day of sacrifice symbolized by the ritual killing of a lamb and the sharing of the meat with the poor.

North Wind

A fierce north wind blows this midday. The pond shivers continually under its onslaught. A white frill laces the entire edge of Ventry Harbour, and the water is churned to a sepia green. The light itself is cold, metallic, the far hills indistinct in the mist. The wind grumbles in the vents of the house. When I go out, I find the two empty plastic bins tumbled past the corner of the house, rolling about beside a small lake of water formed along the front of the house, stretching back the side, a gathering of mountain waters.

I collect the bins, return them to their places, feeling the cold in the wind on my still-damp hair. Time, past time, to batten down for winter.

4 Humidity

The humidity today is incredible although the sky is only partially clouded. It's very unlikely now that the rains will resume; the precipitation is more likely to just evaporate. Everyone is still complaining about the heat. This morning, we opened all the stinking, feather-down pillows. Erika wanted the feathers washed and aired but I persuaded her that they were a serious health hazard in a damp climate like this and that the only thing to do was burn them and buy foam instead. I'm finding out quickly that she's doing things on the cheap here, that this is only her second year running this *campement*. Marie-T earns 30,000 CFAs/West African cents per month (€46.15) and Moussa 40,000 (€61.53). Moussa buys and sells stuff on as a sideline income. They get full board but they live on the job non-stop and have to find solutions to all the logistical problems in the house.

The house itself is pretty rotten, badly constructed and poorly ventilated and the wiring is a mess although Moussa has done what he can to repair it. Erika is never happy with the results. She wants rid of the place but still doesn't have all the legal papers; at the same time, she insists on micromanagement because she's sure that everyone is stealing from her all the time. Why on earth am I here, I wonder? What is motivating me to have this experience?

In the late afternoon I walked into the village with Moussa. I tried to send the Weather Watch to Sandra but the system in the internet café wouldn't accept the files from my memory stick today. So it goes. Maybe tomorrow. Maybe next week. Before going back, we stopped for a glass of café Touba, sitting on benches around the coffee vendor's charcoal stove as evening crept in, quietly chatting with the regulars there, enjoying a break from the *campement*.

Clatter

For the past few days the clatter of the palm tree fronds has been the dominant sound in the garden. Surely it must always be present when there is wind, but perhaps the absence of leaves in the willows now gives it free rein in the chorus, offering no competition as there is in summer. Bare as the willows are, small buds line the branches, a possible response to the recent warm weather. I like the clatter of the palms, a friendly sound accompanied as it sometimes is by birdsong. The magpies so present for a few weeks seem to have moved elsewhere, and the small brown birds to reappear. Just this afternoon two robins danced above the olearia. As it is the wrong season for imposing mating intentions on them, I am free to say it seemed to be they danced just for joy.

5 Dispirited

The thermometer read 36 degrees in the shade this morning. Even in the open dining area the sweat poured down my face and my hair was soaked but it was far too hot for me to venture out for a walk although there was nothing concrete to do.

In the afternoon we went down the road to La Résidence, a *campement* owned by Moussa's uncle where he used to work. Moussa's friends were hanging out there for the afternoon because it is still the holiday and nothing is happening. Luna talks to me in English, a relief today because I'm really tense and finding it difficult to communicate with Moussa. It's a real effort to stay awake. My mind just wants to blank out, unable or unwilling to process what's going on. Then we went up to Bakine to call on Jano but he wasn't home. Later on I managed to connect with Sandra via the mobile phone but the battery, and then the credit, ran out and she got cut off when she tried to phone me back.

Feeling really frustrated and very close to tears, I told Moussa that I was going down to the beach for a while. The tears came as I was trying to express why I find things difficult here but couldn't explain to him why I need to be alone to deal with internal stuff. He doesn't relate to tears at all. Only children cry here. I feel dispirited, as if I'm failing at this endeavour. I wish I were at home but at the same time, I'm aware that I need to overcome this feeling sooner rather than later if I'm to have any peace of mind or quality of life here.

Relationship

Last night's drenching rain gives way to mild morning. I take my coffee and go outside to sit on the blue bench. The only sound in the garden is the trickle of water into the pond from the still-sodden mountain, and the occasional mutter of a hooded crow passing overhead. The variability, the unpredictability in the weather utterly delights me. The conditions at night do not presage the day's, nor the morning's the afternoon's. I think of relationship. I would not find this pleasant as a constant condition in a human companion, wishing for more steadiness and grounding, even rest.

Yet in my relationship with this place, with the weather, it only fascinates and exhilarates. It must be love.

6 A Breath of Air

Thank God there's some air today. It's Sunday, there are no guests and Erika is down in Ziguinchor, so I'm trying to make some space for myself by hiding out on the balcony of one of the seafront rooms, which is presently unoccupied, to write this Weather Watch and do some reading. The yard thermometer is still reading 36 degrees. This morning I covered myself in sunscreen and went into the water for half an hour between 10.30 and 11 a.m. I'd hoped to walk the beach as well but it was already too hot for me, yet every day I see French people spending the hottest hours outside, unabashed. Instead I came back up to the house and cleaned our room, trying to be useful, while Moussa swept the yard. The walls are still wet and sweating. The mosquitos just love it. In the early afternoon, I managed to connect with Kathrin via the mobile phone, at long last. She was on her way to Minard to walk in the wind. In the evening, Moussa and I went to town for our weekly feast at the *dibieterie*, a type of chophouse that specialises in charcoal-grilled meat. The town seemed really quiet and the atmosphere was full of dust.

Thunder

Early evening, thunder rolls across the land. I've never heard thunder quite like this, shaped as it is to the curve of the hills, to the stretch of the water between peninsulas. My father used to say they were bowling in heaven, and as I listen tonight, I feel the boulders rolling down the mountainsides, gliding along the water, rumbling across the floor of the clouds.

7 Too Much

It was a very long, intensely hot day. We left the house before 7 a.m. but it was two hours before we could get any transport down to Ziguinchor and when we got there Erika had no money because the banking systems were down, so we went to visit Moussa's mother, Khadi, to see her new baby. She and her husband, Tiam, have two other daughters as well as Fatou, Moussa's girl. The naming day is tomorrow so we'll stay overnight and do the errands for Erika as well, if she sends money. To get anything done here takes lots of patience and lots of time. This bad cold doesn't help the intensity of spending all day visiting with people who are speaking Mandinka. Everything here is communal and the small concrete bedroom (no door, just a curtain), is suffocating. But that's life here and the sooner I get used to it, the better. In this part of the world, people don't dish out sympathy: life is hard and one is expected to get on with it without whinging. Crying is totally unacceptable except at funerals.

Bones

Despite the clearing after last night's storm and the tranquil star-filled sky I saw before bed, a fierce gale rages today. Any last leaves are being driven from the garden, and its bones are beginning to show again. The red branches of the dogwood flare here and there. The willows reveal their shades from tender green through ochre to bright yellow. The young hazels, the ashes, the oaks, and the hawthorns become sculptural. The evergreens, shrubs and trees, take on a different prominence. The blocked views re-emerge, the beautiful curve of Marhin seen from the back rooms, a patch of harbour from the front. The lawn barely grows, is just raggedy. The thick grasses of the field are flattened, with only a few firm stalks resisting the wind. Larger segments of the stone wall that surrounds me emerge. Much is still green. None of the starkness of a New England winter will appear here, no landscape gone to brown and grey, black branches etched against snowfields. Today's storm is a different winter, harsh in its blowing, its force. The house drums with it. Under its onslaught the garden outside clears itself, prepares to open the way for the daffodils of spring.

8 Too Hot to Sleep

During the night I had to go outside to sleep in the yard, for the tiny concrete cubicle was suffocating and the mosquito net was full of holes. So Moussa threw the sheet on the ground in the yard, without mattress or mosquito net, and I lay there for an hour or two under a star-studded sky. It began to feel almost cold but I guess that was the result of the rather rheumy cold I've developed. The call to prayer began at 4 a.m., after which time the yard was busy with people praying, talking, coming and going to the latrine, pulling water from the well in the yard, getting ready for the day.

The naming ceremony was due to happen at half past eight but the *Imam* was an hour or so late and we sat in Khadi's airless, dark room, waiting. The naming ceremony is a brief affair; the *Imam* and the menfolk sit on a prayer mat in the yard and the child is presented not by the mother but by an aunt. She holds the child while the

Imam whispers the name, Rabiatou, into each ear three times and then quietly recites the collective prayers. Then packets of biscuits are handed out to whoever is present and afterwards, the *Imam* ritually slaughters a sheep which is carved up and shared between the neighbours. There's no fuss or bother; the mother doesn't attend the ceremony; the other family that shares the house and yard just get on with washing the children and doing the laundry as the ceremony is taking place.

Because of the intense heat and the now late hour, we decided to do the shopping in the later afternoon and take a room in a hotel for the night to get a proper rest. Moussa slept in the afternoon while I sat in the bank for two hours, waiting in line. Luckily, the system was up and running. *Dieu merci!* the bank is air-conditioned. We walked back to the market when the day began to cool down and managed to find most of the items on our list. The walk itself lifted our energy and we enjoyed a glass of Touba coffee on a street corner before heading back to the town centre. This hotel is owned by some cousins of Moussa and it's clean, pleasant and friendly. This room has an air-conditioner that actually works! And as I write this report, Moussa is reading the football news and I'm beginning to feel like a human being again, not a walking zombie.

Hail

A day so bright, light etching the details of the mountainsides, I cancel the plan for Tralee and race home from Irish class in Dingle, wanting to be out walking. Before I can finish lunch, I see the surface of the pond gently pock-marked with rain. A passing shower, I think, but begin to re-contemplate

Tralee. A half an hour later hailstones are bouncing off the car, the fall so dense a few even find their way down the chimney. I cannot even see the hills of Dingle for the rain. The storm clouds give rise to a rich golden light. The surface of the harbour turns an ethereal silver green. Dark grey clouds shift, moving like gossamer curtains, veiling then revealing the mountains of the Iveragh Peninsula. As the hailstones rocket against the windows, I'm indoors for the day. I'll watch this show from beside the fire, maybe study some Irish, perhaps to the accompaniment of Mozart.

9 Cool Room, Hot Body

Thank God for a decent night's sleep in a cool room! Before heading back to Cap Skiring, I bought an electric fan for our room which I hope will make things a little more bearable. Moussa says the month after the rains finish is always very hot before the real winter arrives suddenly. All this is news to me; I thought the season was October to March but I'm finding out that many *campements* don't do any significant business until December.

We waited nearly two hours at the transport depot – there really seems to be a dearth of cars at the moment for whatever reason – but finally got going at half past noon. I wrapped myself in a sarong because I was sitting on the sun side for the journey and it's so easy to burn, even sitting in a car. I was coughing a lot and my sinuses were streaming and by nightfall, I was very hot indeed but I'm pretty sure it's a chesty cold like I often get at home and not malaria; I don't have a chronic headache, although I'm quite febrile.

Pockets of Rain

All day as I travel from Baile an tSléibhe to Dingle, Dingle to Ballyferriter, Ballyferriter to Tralee, around Tralee, and then back home again, I travel rapidly through different weathers. As I move in the car, I go from faint mist to hard rain in a matter of feet. I'm constantly re-adjusting the wipers, and never seem to have them quite right. Friday night as I left for a lecture, I was drenched, rain pouring off my hair and into my eyes in the few minutes it took to walk to the car, then open and close the gate for the car to pass through. Yet before I left my lane, the rain had stopped entirely, not even a drop on the windshield. The same thing today. Even the temperature seemed to go up and down, warm one moment, cold wind blasting the next. Never boring, the weather of this place.

10 Change

The latest weather news I hear is that it will be cold after the fifteenth of November ...

Wet

That was it today: wet. In the morning, the sun tried faintly to break through the fog, but by midday it was misting, then raining, a constant steady drenching rain, giving rise to the first true sense of winter dusk. In town, hoods were up, the streets were running with water. Everyone's hair was wet, hoods or no. The whole peninsula feels sodden, squishy. How the mountain absorbs all this water, I don't know. The odd thing of it is, it's still warm, but it feels chilly because of the damp. This night, I start the fire and read. Nothing else to be done.

11 Fever

Cloud Definition

I think here not of the great rolling names of clouds, cirrus, cumulonimbus, altostratus, but of the way pale clouds can be seen against a pale sky. This morning, I woke to a white sky, or rather one so pale a grey as to be called white, yet I could see, barely marked, clouds of the same colour against it. Defined by a faint line of darker grey, they floated here and there on the canvas of sky, deftly sketched on in their passing.

12 Flattened

Moussa brought breakfast to our room this morning but when I got up to sit in the chair, I fainted. Sweat was flowing off me like a river. I went out to the yard just now – it's 6 p.m. – to check the thermometer and it's reading only 32 degrees. The sky has been completely clouded over since early morning and I have spent the entire day lying down, as I did yesterday, letting this thing pour out of me.

The fever went on all day yesterday and last night, although neither the headache nor the body temperature merited a trip down to clinic at Kabrousse for a malaria test. Moussa rubbed me all over with something like wintergreen, stuff for treating muscle damage, then wrapped me up tight in a sheet for half an hour to sweat it out. He's been coming and going during the day with various offerings but I only want fruit and water; the most helpful tonic of all is to spend the day alone, without having to do the communal thing, in silence, for once. Moussa says it is fatigue as well as *le rhume* and he's quite right. I realised today that things had been going reasonably okay until Erika arrived but that since then the atmosphere has been very stressful here, aside from the climate and the endlessly biting insects, not just for me but for Moussa and Marie-T as well.

Tá Sé Fuar

Some years ago my Irish teacher in Portland, Ger Killeen, reported a moment when one of his students told him she knew she was making progress in the Irish when a thought came to mind in Irish, not English, which was her native language. In her case, she had pulled out to overtake a car, saw an oncoming truck, and thought 'Ní féidir liom'. The change in the weather to cold yesterday, and its continuation today brought my first thought formulated in Irish: 'Tá sé fuar.' And indeed it is.

13 Enervating Atmosphere

The sky is a nicotine-yellow blur, completely overcast and airless. These clouds won't fall as rain any more but will just evaporate into the higher atmosphere. When I went down to look at the ocean, the visibility was about fifty metres and it was muggy and unpleasant even there. Invisible biting insects are everywhere. The whole show is enervating but let's see what happens when the weather changes…maybe this is just the doldrums, on land.

Cuaisín

After the Christmas fair at the Blasket Centre today, I traded my town shoes for hiking boots and headed down to the cuaisín, one of my favourite places to walk when I lived in Dún Chaoin. I have a very vivid memory of having stood there even before that, when I first travelled to the Dingle Peninsula in 1996. It is the place I went for solace in the weeks after my father's death in 2000. The Blasket Islands offshore seem near from the cove, whose name on the map is Béal Átha. In winter, the water gives the illusion of somehow being well above anyone standing there, and in summer the entering river offers a ford to the high cliffs along the way to Dún Chaoin pier. The stones of that place are distinctive, a mottled purple on grey, a pale jade green, smooth stones. This evening's visit yielded a handful of quill feathers, an apt gift after yesterday's calligraphy class. The sun set as I sat there, the sky suffused with a hot pink that faded to rose with a hint of palest lavender, all of it held in tender blue. When I left, the moon shone bright and near full, glowing in the sky over Sliabh an Iolair.

14 Day of Changes

The morning brought plenty of wind and a clear sky, a great relief. I thought that perhaps the weather reflected the definitive change of season but this wasn't the case. I thought, too, that I was better, that my energy was returning, and I cleaned the room and threw the mattress up on the roof. But the wind fell and by afternoon the sky was clouding up again quickly. My energy fell too and I had to retrieve the mattress and lie down. At six o'clock, I went down to the beach for the sunset. It was an interesting sky, the clouds mottled and dense, the obscured sun finally slipping out of its cloud bag, pumpkin orange and over-ripe, hanging over a metallic ocean at high tide. My eyes hurt even in the fading light, for I have been inside nearly all the time for the past four days and despite feeling utterly drained I needed to go for a walk, to be outside, out of the room, out of the house, to move this poor bodymind that is so under-the-weather.

Ribbon Mirror

This afternoon, I walked up the mountain to the lake, crossing Cúl Iarhaigh as I went. When I had climbed a while, admiring the intricacies of russet in the grasses, I turned to look back at the bay. The overcast clouds had shifted themselves into soft curves of light and dark, like a cloth gently folded, or like ribbons across the sky. Grey tinged with a dense blue green, they stretched diagonally across the bay. Below them, the surface of the water reflected them exactly, the blurred shades folding into each other, the mountains of the Iveragh a solid line connecting the two, sky and water.

15 The Magic Date

Morning sunshine gave way again to overcast humidity. Today was the magic date, November fifteenth, when winter is supposed to begin according to the local knowledge. We aren't quite there yet although the yard thermometer read only 34 degrees in the afternoon and it was reasonably cool last night under the almost full moon. I slept for nearly twelve hours, didn't hear Moussa at all, and woke feeling quite a lot better than before. Erika was in Ziguinchor so the house was peaceful, a boon to overall wellbeing after the endless tension that has been going on all through the weekend.

As the sunset spread its colours over sky and ocean, I bathed in the warm water and wondered what I should do next, what choices I need to make now. Things here seem just too complicated. I feel stuck in a dynamic, a strange weather system that really has nothing to do with me, so I should probably just close this chapter and move on. Meanwhile, the full moon is bathing the world in clear, white light and the ocean is quiet again.

A November Moon

> A November moon,
> ripe and full, scarved by swift clouds,
> floats over Ventry.

16 Weather Change

The weather has changed. Definitely. It's a day late but who's counting? Today the sky is clear and the ocean is calm after the full moon. I went down to the beach at four o'clock, swam, lay in the sun, talked to the occasional person and it wasn't too hot. In the house it's still very humid but that's due to the airless construction and the fact that the walls are still drying out. Moussa is still painting and there's nothing for me to do, so I used the time today to write.

The emotional storms are by no means over, unfortunately. There was a huge brouhaha this morning between Erika and Diamma that left a distinctly bad taste; in fact, Papisse and Aisha intend to bail out and take a room in another *campement* this week because they find the atmosphere so unpleasant.

Aisha's real name is Yvonne. She's French and very laid-back. A grandmother, she affectionately calls Moussa her son; he, too, is very fond of her. She advised me to stay calm and wait a while longer to see if this energy would pass. I suppose it's like waiting for wind when one is stuck in the doldrums, motionless. She also proposed the possibility that people here actually enjoy this dramatic kind of behaviour, certainly everyone pitches in as loudly as possible, even people who have nothing at all to do with the action. Then they all talk about it endlessly afterwards. There seems to be endless interest in the goings-on of the household, endless questions about where people are and what they are doing. *Ana Erika? Ana Moussa?* Where's Erika? Where's Moussa? All the time. And then it is extended to all the other goings-on as well.

Abed

I like to lie awake in the morning, watching the weather out the window across from the foot of my bed. In the half hour or so I indulge in this, I can see any number of conditions passing. My day can start in warm sunlight or a glimpse of silver water far out in the bay. Moments later, fog might descend, blotting out all the view but the near garden inside the stone wall. And then it might lift, the sky opening to blue, with white clouds moving stately across it. Or it might as easily turn to lashing rain. With all this to see, it's a wonder I ever get out of bed at all.

17 Rose-Tinted

Some time before seven in the evening, the sky all of a sudden turned a deep rosy hue, as if in a dream or a film and then, just as quickly, vanished.

Quarter Turn

In these days moving toward solstice, the sun rises above the mountains of the Iveragh Peninsula, visible out the window at the foot of my bed. I think back to summer when the early sun entered through the small high window in the wall to my left as it began its arc across the sky. Now it rises almost a quarter turn around the horizon as it slinks low and quickly through the day. Yet it is deeper in the house, the sun. In summer it marks neat intense rectangles about a human tall in the living room, rectangles that in the bedroom enclose the bed completely, but barely reach my head. Now it fingers far into the rooms, touching the far wall of the hall, shining into my eyes in the morning. I noticed this long caress toward winter beginning when the sun reached far enough across the rug to warm my toes as I sit in the chair by the hearth.

18 Low Weather System

The day was a mental blur that didn't clear until late afternoon. On days like this, when my mind is turning itself inside-out, I feel trapped in an internal low weather system. Deepak Choprah talks about the difference between change and transformation: transformation is permanent, change just keeps changing. I have created a dramatic change in my life yet I seem to be repeating old material in a new context. How can I get through this weather low and emerge intact, laughing at my boring distresses?

Eyebrow of Light

When I reach outside for a bundle of peat tonight, I see an eyebrow of light above the hills behind Ventry, and know that the moon is rising. I gather

*the green shawl around me and lean out the door to watch. It takes hardly
any time at all, this just-past-full moon being born into the night, floating
luminous egg entering the star-pierced winter sky. The lower rim clears the
ridge, and I, replete, go inside to feed the fire. Rising moon, rising joy.*

19 Early Morning Weather

It's beginning to feel quite cool now in the hours
before the dawn and I find myself regularly reaching for a sheet.
The morning is full of birdsong: the *mange mil* that sounds like
a woodcock, pigeons cooing, songbirds calling back and forth,
another hoarse-sounding bird like a raven and below this canopy of
twittering voices, the eternal rumble of the Atlantic.

Testament to Dailiness

*The Pond of Great Pleasure is a mirror today, reflecting the blue dome of
sky. A faint north wind blows, glimmering the grass. The sun-warmed house
rests, full of peace. Sliabh an Iolair rises behind me while the fields in front
slope down to the harbour, today a deep marine blue. Behind a faint haze,
the mountains of the Iveragh stretch almost indigo in the distance across
the bay. Everywhere I look, the view is clear, all my world around me this
November day. Cruach Mhárthain and Brandon, Cnoc na dTobar, hills and
townlands I don't know the names for yet. A year of watching weather ends
on this pacific day. No storm, no drama, but the exquisite beauty of this
place in calm, and me at rest amidst it. All the past year, each unfolding day,
my eye and heart have been tuned to the weather. Now, in my study a stack
of paper inches thick holds our observations, Trish's and mine, a testament to
dailiness, to friendship, and to love of place, place being here in this cupped*

harbour, or out in the wide world of all the earth. A year of reports from whatever here we inhabited. Whichever place. Whichever now. I am changed by it, these daily watchings, these daily communications. The formal writing may cease, but the watching will not. No eye so opened to this world could ever turn away, ever take its beauties for granted, ever not watch the weather all the days of a life.

Glossary of Place Names and Irish

Irish spelling can be, particularly with regard to place names, as variable as the weather. Perhaps this is because the complex sounds do not lend themselves to capture in letters. Perhaps it is because things are pronounced differently in different places, even from one side of the mountain to the other. We've tried to be consistent, using the Ordnance Survey maps as reference, even though they sometimes don't spell things as we would locally. For townlands and features not on these maps, the 1939 *Tríocha-Céad Chorca Dhuibhne* by An Seabhac (Pádraig Ó Siochrú) has been our reference. This is a brief guide to the place names we mention and to any Irish phrases we use in the text.

General terms
Many places are mentioned only in passing. These general Irish terms will give a sense of what they are.

Irish	English
baile	place, townland
binn	peak
carraig	rock
cill	church
cnoc, cruach, sliabh	mountain
com	mountain recess
cuaisín	small cove
cuan	harbour
dún	fort
gleann	glen
inis	island
loch	lake
mám	mountain pass
tigh	house
trá	beach

Place names
Some places are known only by their Irish names. In those cases, no English is
supplied. In others, we use only the English name, so we have given no Irish entry.

Irish and/or English name	Location
An Cheathrú, Ceathru	townland of Dunquin
An Chonair, Connor Pass	pass north of Dingle
An Daingean, Dingle	town on Dingle Harbour
An Ghráig, Graig	townland of Ballyferriter
Baile an Trasna	townland of Ventry
Baile an tSléibhe, Ballintlea	townland of Ventry
Baile Ícín	townland of Dunquin
Baile Móir, Ballymore	townland of Ventry
Baile na Rátha	townland of Dunquin
Ballaghbeama	pass on Iveragh Peninsula
Béal Bán	beach on Smerwick Harbour
Beginish	a Blasket island
Blasket Islands	off the coast of Dunquin
Burnham Wood	near Ballymore
Carrauntoohil	highest peak in Ireland, in the MacGillicuddy's Reeks
Cathair Ard	townland of Ventry
Ceann Trá, Ventry	village on Ventry Harbour
Cill Uru/Cill Dhorcha/Kildurrihy	townland of Ventry
Clasach	pass leading to Dunquin
Clogher	headland and beach near Dunquin
Cluas	inlet of Dingle Harbour at Burnham
Cnoc Bréanainn, Mt Brandon	sacred mountain
Corca Dhuibhne	Dingle Peninsula
Coumeenoole	beach in Dunquin
Cruach Mhárthain, Marhin	mountain above Dunquin
cuaisín, small cove	in Ballymore and Dunquin
Cuan	headland of Ventry Harbour
Cúilín	townland in Dingle
Cúl Iarthaigh	area on Mt Eagle

Irish and/or English name	Location
Dún an Óir	townland of Ballyferriter
Dún Chaoin, Dunquin	townland at western end of Dingle Peninsula
(An) Dún Mór, Dunmore	westernmost headland in Dunquin
Fán, Fahan	townland of Ventry
(An) Fear Marbh, The Dead Man / Inishtooskert	northernmost Blasket island
Fionn Trá	Ventry Beach
Great Blasket/the Blasket	largest Blasket island
Inishtooskert	a Blasket Island
Iveragh Peninsula	south of Dingle Peninsula
Macgillicuddy's Reeks	highest mountains in Ireland, on Iveragh Peninsula
Maharees	area on northern coast of Dingle Peninsula
Mám na Gaoithe	pass between Ventry and Ballyferriter
Masatiompan	peak near Mt Brandon
Parkmore Point	headland of Ventry Harbour
Scelligs, Skellig Rocks	two islands off the Iveragh Peninsula
Slea Head	headland at western tip of Dingle Peninsula
Sliabh an Iolair, Mt Eagle	westernmost mountain
(An) Tiaracht	farthest Blasket island
Tír na nÓg	mythical land of eternal youth
(An) Trá Bhán	the beach on the Great Blasket
Valentia Island	at end of Iveragh Peninsula

Irish references and phrases

Irish	English
ag bothántaíocht	visiting
amuigh faoin spéir	outside under the sky
Bealtaine	feast beginning summer, 1 May
buíochas	thanks
Codladh sámh	Sleep well.
Dia dhuit.	God be with you.
Dia 's Muire dhuit.	God and Mary be with you.
Conas tánn tú?	How are you?
Ana-mhaith.	Very well.
Tá sé fuar inniu.	It's cold today.
Ach tá sé tirim, buíochas le Dia.	But it's dry, thank God.
fanaile	vanilla
fear an tí	man of the house/master of ceremonies
houseen	small house
gaofar	windy
Garda, Gardaí	policeman, police
Imbolc	feast beginning spring, 1 February
Is maith an scéalaí an aimsir.	Time (or the weather) is a good storyteller.
Lá 'le Bríde	Brigid's Day, 1 February
Lughnasa	feast beginning autumn, 1 August
meitheal	work party
naomhóg (naomhóga, pl)	sea going canoe, currach
Niamh	lover of Oisín
Ní féidir liom.	I'm not able
Níl sé tirim inniu. Tá sé fliuch.	It's not dry today. It's wet
Nollaig na mBan	Women's Christmas, 6 January
Oisín	warrior and poet of the Fianna; sojourner in Tír na nÓg with Niamh
Samhain	feast beginning winter, 1 November
Scairbhín (na gCuach)	windy April days borrowed by March
sean-nós	the traditional manner

402

Tá sé fuar.	It's cold.
Tír na nÓg	Land of the Ever Young
tonnta móra agus sneachta	large waves and snow
trína chéile	all ahoo

Calendar

NOVEMBER

20. Amaryllis, *Moon*
21. Dusk, *Darkness*
22. Castlemaine Harbour, *Blood Orange*
23. Tunnels of Gold, *Wind*
24. Sci-Fi Weather, *Misery*
25. Night Colour, *Stillness*
26. Weather and Society, *Curtains Drawn*
27. Tiaracht, *Persimmon*
28. Confusion, *Phases*
29. Cock Crow, *Sapphire*
30. NWRT, *Roil*

DECEMBER

1. Robins, *Robin*
2. Smoke Rising Straight Up, *No Smoke Rising*
3. Cloud Cocktail, *Tír na nÓg*
4. Sound, *Grey*
5. 2 p.m. Sunday, *Pathetic Fallacy*
6. Zen, *The Solace of the Colour of Water*
7. Hey Presto, *The Brightness of a Morning without Visible Sun*
8. Hey Ho, the Wind and the Rain, *Drum*
9. Wind from Below, *Rocked*
10. Rising Mist, *Gift*
11. Grey Day, *Clarity*
12. Blue-Grey World, *Intense*
13. Stormlet, *Windows and Weather*
14. Bonsai Waves, *Every Which Way*
15. Cúl Iarthaigh, *Sun*
16. Etiquette, *Squalls*
17. First Quarter, *Wild Sea and Slanted Winter Light*
18. Downtown Tralee, *Jade*
19. Loo Light, *Silver Lake Far at Sea*
20. Under a Sistine Sky, *Sound and Fury*

21. Solstice, *Sky Like a Painting*
22. Solstice, Part Two, *Exuberance*
23. Dark, *Ventry Green*
24. Hail, *Forecast*
25. White Christmas, *Hail Cocktail*
26. World Weather, *Freesias Against a Changing Sky*
27. Wet Wren, *Auditory Hallucination*
28. Power, *Axis*
29. Inward, *Fog*
30. Mud, *Night Walking*
31. Last Light, *Revision*

JANUARY
1. Stormy Weather, *Azure*
2. Energy, *No Weather*
3. Blowing Hard, *Bled*
4. Inside Looking Out, *Dome*
5. Still Storming, *NWRT*
6. NOLLAIG na mBAN
7. Wind, *Back*
8. Desire, *Spring Sills*
9. Frayed, *Captive*
10. Apprehension, *Walking*
11. WIND
12. Return, *Rose*
13. Drop, *Jade Again*
14. Torrential Rain, *Pelting*
15. Pause, *Dunquin Tsunami*
16. Reflection, *Clear Mornings and Afternoon Rain*
17. Listening to the Wind, *Sun Stretches*
18. Bluster, *Tonnta Móra agus Sneachta*
19. Turnabout, *A White Accumulation*
20. NWRT, *Trína Chéile*
21. Silence, *Breathe*
22. Blue Green Scene, *Reading*
23. Sun Day, *Moonrise to Glowing*

27. Holy Smoke!, *Ramble*
28. El Greco Sky, *Repeating Epiphanies*

MARCH

1. Theatre Weather, *Dazzle*
2. We Are Stardust, *Tiaracht in a Copper Sea*
3. NWRT, *Snow on Mountains*
4. NWRT, *All Weather Day*
5. NWRT, *Custom*
6. Starry Starry Night, *Guests*
7. Exhaustion, *Driving*
8. Post-Show Clean-Up, *Still, So Still*
9. Last Minute, *Flat Grey*
10. Setting Out, *A Sunset the Colour of My House*
11. Tale of Two Cities, *Time and the Weather*
12. Breakfast in Dakar, *Nondescript*
13. Down in the City, *Moving Weather*
14. Acclimatizing, *Return*
15. Joal-Fadiout, *Wind Again*
16. Pirogue, *Luminous*
17. St Patrick's Day, *Walk*
18. Toward the Delta, *Home*
19. The Relief of a Strong Wind, *A Day So Gentle*
20. Baobab-sur-Mer, *Heat*
21. White Heat, *A Day of Quiet Rain*
22. Killer Heat, *Long Weather*
23. Mind, *Grey Blanket*
24. Going with the Flow, *Coin*
25. Birthday in the Bush, *Sail*
26. In Search of Cooler Weather, *Moonrise Over Cuan*
27. Mopping the Brow of Christ, *Easter*
28. Transit, *Translucence*
29. Fleuve de Casamance, *Breath*
30. Ziguinchor, *Still*
31. Overcast, *Curl*

APRIL
1. Sundown, *Moon-Inhabited*
2. La Lutte, *Summer Skin*
3. Dance, *Distant Blue Vista*
4. Cooling Wind, Warm Embrace, *Slashing Silver Rain*
5. Decision, *Sweaters Back On*
6. Here and Now, *Fierce Squalls and News of Snow*
7. Market, *North Wind*
8. Afternoon, *April Snow and Seagulls*
9. Flight, *Quiet Weather*
10. Lost, *Now*
11. The Rain That's Not Falling, *Trimming*
12. Cold, *Inside Gardening*
13. Weather Change, *How Many Weathers Can a Day Have?*
14. Changing Trains at Mallow, *Driving into Elusive Rainbows*
15. Oblivious, *Sunlight Wakes Me*
16. Picnic, *Red Tulips*
17. The View from Sandra's Loo, *Computer Weather*
18. Dawn to Dusk, *Eating Murphys Ice Cream Outdoors*
19. Garden, *Glenbeigh Glowing*
20. Between Two Mountains, *Crossing Mountains and Many Sunsets*
21. Tropical Sunset, *Teaching Me the Morning*
22. Revelation, *Sea Indigo*
23. Photosynthesis, *Distractions*
24. Atmospheric Pressure, *Two*
25. The Values of Grey, *Milky Day*
26. Turn and Turnabout, *The Glories of the Night*
27. The Possibility of a Jungle, *Hardly Looking Up*
28. Storm and Bluster, *April, Baile an tSléibhe*
29. Luscious Still Dreaming, *Janus Sunset*
30. Soundscape Saturday, *No Mountain Day*

MAY
1. Stormy May Day, *The Kindness of Damp Weather...*
2. Sky Sisters, *Warm*
3. To Everything a Season, *Sunlight Floods*

4. Dinner Alfresco, *Is Maith*
5. Unravelling, *Floating*
6. Clarity, *Mist and Marble*
7. Light, *Long Light*
8. Skylarks, *Bees Knocking*
9. Weather and Home, *Bright Blue Weather*
10. Wind Shadow, *Oh So Still*
11. Absorbing Blue, *Rain Again*
12. Low Pressure, *Jubilant Haze*
13. March in May, *A Wintry Day in May*
14. Skirmishing with the Wind, *Lessons in Flirting*
15. Sociable Weather, *The Absence of the Green Flash*
16. Concert, *This Mildness*
17. Cotton Wool Sky, *Sunburned*
18. Release, *Beaded*
19. Wind and Silence, *Shushing*
20. Wind in the Willows, *Moonbright*
21. A Moment in the Here and Now, *Blue-Laced*
22. Changeable, *Shimmering*
23. Writing the Weather, *Ripple*
24. Listening to the Weather, *Ahead*
25. A Delicate Pink Suggestion, *Drenched*
26. Calm, *Aflame*
27. NWRT, *Dreary*
28. No Need to Water, *Breathing*
29. End of an Era, *Ventry Blues*
30. Flirting, *An Island Day*
31. Sensory Perception, *Velvet Sky and Metal Sea*

JUNE
1. Crimson Dreaming, *White*
2. Special Effects, *Possible Wind*
3. Bank Holiday Blues, *The Incredible Length of June Dusk in West Kerry*
4. Slug, *Things to Do Inside*
5. Sunday Best, *Bank Holiday Weather*
6. Clearance, *Cloud Play*

7. Sandra's Cure, *Lily*
8. Transformation, *Sky Blanket and Full Sun*
9. Sickle Moon, *Bees Hum*
10. Light, *Summer Morning*
11. Invoking the Goddess, *Warmth*
12. Song, *Alphabet of Ballintlea*
13. Perspectives, *Maps*
14. The Sensual World, *Name*
15. Texture, *Goldfinches! In the Garden!*
16. Blur, *Internal Weather*
17. Grace, *Above the Clouds*
18. Sap, *Market Weather*
19. Headache, *Storm Light with Volcano*
20. Summer Solstice, *Sips*
21. Restlessness, *City Sky*
22. Dressing Up, *Storm Light*
23. Rites, *Weather*
24. Slumber, *Rustling*
25. Summer Breeze, *Who Can Say?*
26. Paradise, *An Irish Kind of Day*
27. Morning and Evening, *Pervasive*
28. Heavy Weather, *Some Possible Clouds*
29. Fragrance, *Summer in the City*
30. Night Lights, *Summer in the City Too*

JULY

1. Mí na Samhradh, *Summer Here*
2. Weather and the Warrior, *Weather in the City*
3. Still Blowing Hard, *Moonless*
4. The Colour Purple, *Pink Sky at Night*
5. Discomfort, *Promise of Rain*
6. Is the Sun Up in the Sky?, *Oh Dear! Oh Dear!*
7. Sweat, *City Summer Deep Translucent Blue*
8. Weather Here and There, *Rain*
9. The Water at Caherdaniel, *Featureless*
10. Ballymore Picnic, *Missing Weather*

11. Lost, *Distant Weather*
12. Hot Rocks, *Filter*
13. Weather Clues, *Moving Weather Again*
14. Edge, *The Second Sighting of the Moon*
15. Still Lake, *Traffic*
16. At the Top of the World, *Down in the Basement*
17. Ventry Regatta, *Is There Weather?*
18. Warm Wind, *Heat*
19. Forecast, *Outside*
20. Cloudscape, *Bearable*
21. Full Moon Weather, *Full Moon in Portland*
22. Fire and Rain, *Visiting Weather*
23. Relief, *Last Market*
24. Batik Sky, *Location, Location, Location*
25. Still, *Partings*
26. Swim and Shiver, *Hasty Weather*
27. Rain Coming, *All Weathers*
28. Indecisive, *Bruised*
29. Tinge, *Weather Perspectives*
30. Airing, *Balmy*
31. Sky Painter, *Burning*

AUGUST
1. Lá Lughnasa, *So Far from Lughnasa*
2. Starry Night, *A Day with Neutral Weather and Little Food of Note*
3. Changeable, *Indoors*
4. Closing In, *Heat Again*
5. Tingling, *Cool of the Night*
6. Diamanté, *Far Dawn*
7. Hum, *Basement Weather*
8. Signals, *NWRT*
9. Anticyclone, *It Takes a Meitheal*
10. Sure-Footed Weather, *Beyond*
11. Overview, *Dispersal*
12. Wind Rising, *Parting Weather*
13. Slumber, *NWRT*

411

17. Shadows and Light, *Moon Night*
18. Full Moon, Low Tide, *Moon Haiku*
19. Ups and Downs, *No Laundry on the Line*
20. No Hint of Wind, *Elemental Rock*
21. Autumn Equinox, *Beading*
22. Photographs, *Undecided*
23. Dark Horse, *Rain in All Directions, Even Up*
24. Dreary Outside, Busy Within, *Faint Rainbow and Quarter Moon*
25. Autumn Sunday, *Laundry and Silver Rain*
26. Better Outside, *Warm Storm*
27. Homeward Bound, *Amazing Haze, Fierce Squalls, Waves...*
28. Rainbow, *Winter Green*
29. Peculiarities, *Raining But Not Wet*
30. Passing Through Weather, *Interval Between Storms*

OCTOBER
1. Apprentice Weather Watcher, *Skip Rope*
2. New Perspectives, *Under a Star-Filled Sky*
3. Weather Talk, *Watching the Weather Watch*
4. Inside Weather, *Weather Watchers Working*
5. NWRT, *Clouds Trying to Let In the Sun*
6. Au Revoir, *A Day to Open the Heart*
7. Chiaroscuro, *Romantic*
8. Dublin Between Sun and Moon, *Splendour*
9. Looking Down on Weather, *Wind Up*
10. Milan, *Glowing Pewter Day*
11. Yoff, *Floating Mountain*
12. La Route, *Lucent*
13. Arrival, *Sunbeam*
14. Facts, *Splendid*
15. Deliciously Warm Wind, *Narrative*
16. Sweeping, *Captive*
17. Busy, *Fall*
18. Weather, Cooking and Language, *Moon Sail*
19. Perfect Day, *Beyond Dún Chaoin*
20. Deluge, *Shift*

A note on the typeface

Weather Watch is set in *Bembo* an old serif font revived by Stanley Morison for the Monotype Corporation in 1929. It was first used by Francesco Griffo in A.D. 1495 and was the inspiration for the typefaces of Claude Garamond. The text was set by Chris May.